Scotland's Referendum and the Media

Scotland's Referendum and the Media

National and International Perspectives

Edited by Neil Blain and David Hutchison with Gerry Hassan

EDINBURGH
University Press

Edinburgh University Press is one of the leading university presses in the UK. We publish academic books and journals in our selected subject areas across the humanities and social sciences, combining cutting-edge scholarship with high editorial and production values to produce academic works of lasting importance. For more information visit our website: www.edinburghuniversitypress.com

Edinburgh University Press Ltd
The Tun – Holyrood Road
12 (2f) Jackson's Entry
Edinburgh EH8 8PJ

Typeset in 10/12 Goudy Old Style by
Servis Filmsetting Ltd, Stockport, Cheshire,
and printed and bound in Great Britain by
CPI Group (UK) Ltd, Croydon CR0 4YY

A CIP record for this book is available from the British Library

ISBN 978 0 7486 9658 1 (hardback)
ISBN 978 0 7486 9659 8 (paperback)
ISBN 978 0 7486 9660 4 (webready PDF)
ISBN 978 0 7486 9661 1 (epub)

Contents

Preface   vii

Part One   The Referendum in Scotland

1   The Unexpected Campaign   3
    James Mitchell
2   The Media Landscape in Scotland   16
    Neil Blain and David Hutchison
3   Broadcasting and the Press: Some Key Moments   26
    David Hutchison
4   Scotland's Changing 'Community of the Communicators':
    The Political Commentariat and the Independence Referendum   33
    Gerry Hassan
5   The Scottish Press Account: Narratives of the Independence
    Referendum and its Aftermath   46
    Marina Dekavalla
6   Scottish TV Coverage of the Referendum Campaign from
    September 2012 to September 2014   59
    John Robertson
7   'Liked', 'Shared', Re-tweeted: The Referendum Campaign on Social
    Media   70
    Margot Buchanan
8   Sport, Gender and National Identities   83
    John Harris and Fiona Skillen

Part Two   Views from the UK

9   English Television News Coverage of the Scottish Referendum   97
    Andrew Tolson

10   The English Press and the Referendum   109
     Karen Williamson and Peter Golding
11   Wales, Devolution and the Scottish Independence Debate   121
     Sian Powell
12   Our Friends Across the Water: Northern Ireland Media Coverage of
     the Scottish Independence Referendum   132
     Anthea Irwin

Part Three   International Perspectives

13   'Knock-on Consequences': Irish Media Coverage of the Scottish
     Referendum   147
     Kevin Rafter
14   Spain, Catalonia and the Scottish Referendum: A Study in Multiple
     Realities   159
     Enric Castelló, Fernando León-Solís and Hugh O'Donnell
15   The French View   173
     Didier Revest
16   The Scottish Referendum in Austrian, German and Swiss Media   182
     Klaus Peter Müller
17   The Scottish Referendum: The View from Quebec   195
     Catherine Côté
18   The Scotland Referendum in the English-language Canadian Media   204
     Christopher Waddell
19   Australia and the Scottish Independence Referendum   217
     Brian McNair
20   Afterword: Reimagining Scotland in a New Political Landscape   228
     Neil Blain

Notes on the Contributors   242
Index   244

Preface

There can be no doubt that the Scottish referendum of 2014 was a unique event in the history of both Scotland and the United Kingdom. There have been referendums before in both polities but this was the first one which could have led to the dissolution of the UK. Furthermore, as we note in an Afterword which traces events until the UK general election in May 2015, the referendum result offered no resolution to the constitutional wrangling it was designed to end.

In any contemporary public debate the media are central in facilitating, and to a degree constructing, the discussion, although what was most striking in the run-up to September 2014 was the extent to which the citizens of the country were galvanised into participation through meetings, rallies and canvassing. The final turnout of 85 per cent is testimony to a level of involvement never seen in any of the previous referendums, or indeed elections, since 1945.

Inevitably the performance of the media themselves became a subject for debate in the media, particularly online, and that debate intensified after allegations were made that the Better Together campaign had privately re-christened itself 'Project Fear'.

The implications of the vote, whatever way it went, were bound to reverberate beyond Scotland, most obviously in the other nations which make up the United Kingdom, Wales, Northern Ireland and England. But there were also implications for the European Union, which could have found itself confronting a challenging situation as one of its member states ceased to exist. And in at least two constituent states of the EU, the Scottish result was watched with considerable interest by groups which seek increased autonomy or independence from their existing states. Likewise, there are several countries in the world where there are large Scottish diasporas with more than a passing interest in the future trajectory of their ancestral home.

In putting this collection of essays together we sought out contributors we believed would have insightful comment to offer not only on how the media in their own parts of the world represented what was happening in Scotland, but also on what that might tell us about both these media, and the polities of which they are a part. These international perspectives also give us an invaluable general sense of how Scotland as an idea may be received beyond British shores, as it partly re-emerges from a notion of the UK/Great Britain as synonymous with England.

Obviously we could not cover the globe, and indeed there will be aspects of the debate at home and abroad which some readers may feel are given less attention than they deserve. However, we do hope that the canvas we present here is a broad one and offers sufficient detail to illuminate and surprise.

The first section of the book is firmly located in Scotland, and, after introductory chapters on the campaign as a whole and the structure of the media industries, there are contributions which examine how key moments in the run-up to the vote were dealt with, the role of the commentariat, editorial positioning in the press, and the online campaigns. The performance of the broadcasters became a matter of some controversy as the campaign progressed, and one of our chapters derives from an intervention in what was at times a rather ferocious debate. Another chapter explores how major sporting events became entwined with the campaign.

In the second part of the book the focus shifts to the other parts of the UK, with two chapters on pan-British broadcasting and the press in England, followed by one from a Welsh perspective and one from a Northern Irish viewpoint.

The international section begins with an examination of how the referendum was reported and received in the Irish Republic, a country with a clear interest in the constitutional implications of any revision of the boundaries of the United Kingdom. Although Spain has no direct stake in the constitutional future of Scotland, it is a country where the assertion of regionality or nationhood within, or distinct from, the current state boundaries is very much a live issue. What was happening in Scotland was therefore perceived as having clear implications for its own domestic debates. As far as Germany and France, the two major founding states of the EU, were concerned, the possibility of the UK ceasing to exist was obviously a matter to be taken very seriously.

Australia and Canada are the largest remaining Commonwealth countries which share a monarch with Britain. Almost 9 per cent of the Australian population can claim Scottish ancestry, while the figure in Canada is almost double that. It is not therefore surprising that in both countries there was considerable interest in the outcome. In Canada an additional factor in play was the long-running campaign for a separate Quebec state, which in 1995 almost came into being after the federal side won the second referendum on the subject by a mere whisker.

It is clear that the tightening of the polls as the Scottish campaign drew to a close and a victory for the Yes side seemed a possible outcome acted as a fillip for coverage all over the world. That is very much reflected in what follows.

Our contributors are for the most part university teachers, though some of them have also worked as journalists. We asked them to write for an audience beyond the academy and they have done so without sacrificing scholarly rigour in the process.

As to who we are, we have made our living as full time academics, while the colleague who worked with us on the project has combined writing and academic work. It was a secret ballot, but we are happy to reveal that we did not all vote the same way, and we all had several reasons for making the choices which we finally made after considerable thought. In that regard we are probably representative of our fellow citizens north of the border. As to how those of our contributors who had a vote cast their ballots, we did not ask and we were not told.

We thank all our contributors for delivering such valuable and engaging studies of the topics we requested them to address, for their goodwill in making amendments as we sought to maximise coverage of the media account, and for much extra effort beyond the call of duty in helping us update events after the referendum. We are very grateful to our publisher, Edinburgh University Press, to our commissioning editor there, John Watson, likewise Ellie Bush and other colleagues at EUP, for their encouragement and support. Thanks too to Alan Stewart and Alison Preston at Ofcom for pointing us to some useful audience research. Our gratitude is due also to Gerry Hassan, who contributed much of value in some stimulating conversations during the initial stages of the project which led to this book.

It is clear that the 2014 referendum did not bring any kind of finality to the debate about the governance of either Scotland or the United Kingdom. The essays which follow in one sense are already about the past but it is our belief that they also illuminate in a variety of ways how the future might unfold. Conscious of how the referendum period became continuous with a new phase heralding a further momentous shift in Scottish politics, this volume's Afterword explores media accounts in the UK and internationally of developments around the 2015 UK general election. The May election results, in some part a consequence of realignments triggered by the referendum, seem set to further energise and extend the narrative of Scottish constitutional change.

Neil Blain, David Hutchison
May 2015

PART ONE

The Referendum in Scotland

I

The Unexpected Campaign

James Mitchell

Introduction: Campaigning and Governing in Difficult Times

The election of the Scottish National Party (SNP) majority government in May 2011 meant that a referendum was near certain, though there were some objections to holding a referendum on a retained matter. The British constitution remains a political constitution in the sense intended by Griffith,[1] despite trends towards a constitution founded on law[2] especially when it comes to such contested matters as Scotland's status in the union. In the event, the issue soon became less about whether there would be a referendum than about how it would be conducted.

The Scottish referendum campaign was long and intense. It was set against a difficult economic and fiscal backdrop that meant governing would be challenging enough without what some saw as the distraction of a referendum. In 2011, it was widely anticipated that the heat of the referendum would spill over into everyday Scotland and UK business, making government even more difficult. A number of commentators and opponents of the referendum warned that it would be divisive and vicious. What ensued was unexpected.

Asymmetrical Campaigns

Elections and referendums in the UK are now normally conducted under the terms of the Political Parties, Elections and Referendums Act 2000 (c. 41) (PPERA) passed by Parliament at Westminster. However, the Scottish independence referendum was conducted under ad hoc arrangements agreed between the UK and Scottish governments, since the Scottish Parliament has no equivalent legislation for the regulation of referendums. The Edinburgh Agreement, signed by the governments of both the UK and Scotland in October 2012, removed any legal dubiety and allowed for a single-question referendum, subject to review by the Electoral Commission, to be held before the end of 2014. The electorate would include all those eligible to vote in Scottish parliamentary and local government elections, with the prospect of also allowing sixteen- and seventeen-year-olds to participate, and with the Electoral Commission having responsibility for the referendum's conduct, including campaign regulation. It was also agreed that there would be a twenty-eight-day period during which government ministers would refrain from using their offices to campaign. A unique feature of this referendum was that two governments would be ranged against each other, one on either side of the debate.

In December 2013, the Electoral Commission started the process of registering campaign organisations. Any organisation that planned to spend more than £10,000 during the period between 30 May 2014 and referendum day was legally obliged to register. In April 2014, the Commission recognised Yes Scotland and Better Together as the lead campaign organisations. Yes Scotland and Better Together were umbrella organisations, each having a board consisting of politicians from different parties. The extent to which each would be the real 'lead organisation' was unclear. Yes Scotland's board chairman was Dennis Canavan, former Labour MP and MSP, and Better Together's head was Alistair Darling, former Labour Chancellor of the Exchequer. Labour voters would be the main target of each campaign organisation so it was important to emphasise connections to Labour. Messrs Canavan and Darling would play important parts, though the SNP leadership took on the dominant campaigning role on the Yes side whereas Prime Minister Cameron was largely kept out of the campaign. This may have been a campaign in which the two governments played key roles but each attempted, to differing degrees, to suggest otherwise.

The 'designated lead campaigners' were permitted to spend £1,500,000. In addition, each political party involved was set a spending limit related to electoral support at the 2011 Scottish elections. But these figures pale beside the unregulated resources that would be marshalled by campaigns. It is difficult to quantify press support, but although the press has declined in importance, both sides were keen to attract the support of newspapers. However, the response was overwhelmingly hostile to independence. With the exception of the *Sunday Herald*, the press was uniformly opposed or neutral, and official neutrality often meant subtle – and sometimes not so subtle – opposition. Many newspapers and journalists abandoned any pretence at impartiality.

In November 2013, the Scottish government published its White Paper *Scotland's Future*, the product of many hours of civil servants' time. There were complaints from opposition parties that the SNP was politicising the civil service. But the Scottish government's input was small by comparison to the efforts of Whitehall. The UK government's 'Scotland analysis' series of reports published across the referendum period included papers on fiscal policy and sustainability; work and pensions; energy; forecasts for the Scottish deficit; defence; sterling currency union; borders and citizenship; EU and international issues; science and research; security; macroeconomic and fiscal performance; business and microeconomic framework; financial services and banking; consumer protection in the UK; banks; currency and monetary policy; devolution and the implications of Scottish independence. The cost involved in the production of these alone would have well exceeded the total budget regulated by the Electoral Commission. UK civil servants were under much less pressure to remain neutral than their Scottish counterparts. Civil service impartiality is a keystone of the Civil Service Code, sustained more by the knowledge that partiality would make a civil servant's position untenable in the event of a change of government. However, while this discipline existed for Scottish civil servants, no such discipline existed across Whitehall, where civil servants knew that there was little prospect of a Westminster government that supported Scottish independence being elected.

From the outset, supporters of independence knew they would be easily outspent by their opponents and that press coverage would place YES at a considerable disadvantage. They also faced the prospect that the Yes campaign would be perceived to be an SNP campaign. In addressing the SNP conference in March 2013, Dennis Canavan summed up the attitude of many campaigning for independence: 'I'm often told we've got a mountain to climb – well I like climbing mountains.' Supporters of the union, on the other hand, were aware that the SNP had a slicker and more professional campaign organisation than the other parties, that they had many more activists on the ground, and that many Labour supporters would find campaigning alongside Tories extremely difficult.

Yes Scotland was launched in May 2012. It set out to be seen as positive and upbeat in contrast to Better Together. It also set out to appear to be more than just the SNP, which had sixty-nine members of the Scottish Parliament (MSPs), with involvement of the Greens (two MSPs) and the Scottish Socialist Party (no MSPs). There were tensions from the outset between the SNP and Yes Scotland and between Patrick Harvie, Green Party leader, and Yes Scotland. Harvie initially expressed concern that Yes Scotland was 'entirely an SNP vehicle' but the Greens came on board some months later. Yes Scotland's efforts focused on building up a network of local activists and niche campaign groups across the country. This decentralised approach had its risks and was different from the successful campaigns that brought the SNP victory in the 2007 and 2011 Scottish elections. It was a strategy by necessity as much as design but it would prove to be one of the most significant aspects of the campaign. The problem that Better Together faced was not so much that it engaged in negative campaigning but that it did little to counter the impression that it was negative. The strategy was even referred to as 'Project Fear' by one of its directors of communications, though this was denied at the time (*Herald*, 22 June 2013).

There is little agreement amongst academics on whether positive or negative campaigning is most effective. Some research suggests that negative campaigning can demobilise and demoralise supporters,[3] while other research suggests that it has the opposite effect.[4] The SNP's strategies in the 2007 and 2011 elections had been influenced more by the work of political psychologist Martin Seligman, especially his argument[5] that elections were won by parties projecting positive messages.[6] Public opinion research in Scotland had found that when a party's campaign was perceived to be negative then people were less likely to vote for it.

The extent to which each side balanced positive and negative campaigning was not the same as the public perception of this balance. Both sides engaged in both forms of campaigning, though Better Together was perceived as almost entirely negative.

Better Together was launched in June 2012 and, as noted earlier, was headed by Alistair Darling, former Labour Chancellor of the Exchequer and Edinburgh MP. There had been little doubt that the No campaign should be led by a prominent Labour politician but it proved difficult initially to get one to come forward. It has been suggested that Better Together consisted of 'Tory money and Labour foot soldiers' (*Telegraph*, 24 February 2013) but the situation was more complex. If Yes Scotland struggled to convince people that it was more than an SNP front, then Better Together had the opposite problem. It needed to provide coherence to a disparate group.

Opposition to independence was emphatically cross-party, with Labour, Conservatives and Liberal Democrats all strongly opposed. The rise of the SNP in a highly adversarial political environment meant that any pro-independence voices inside any of the other parties had been marginalised. Opposing independence had become a central tenet, if not *the* central tenet, for each of them. While the Liberal Democrats were closest to the SNP in policy terms, they had been in coalition with Labour in the Scottish Parliament between 1999 and 2007 and with the Conservatives at Westminster from 2010. Historic enmity and ideological differences would make for an uncomfortable pro-union coalition. While some Labour politicians, notably Gordon Brown, sought to distance themselves from the Conservatives, Alistair Darling was much more willing to engage with the Tories. Annabel Goldie, former Scottish Tory leader, remarked that 'Alistair is my Darling' when the former Chancellor addressed a fringe meeting at the Scottish Tory conference in June 2013.

Businesses, trade unions and other organised interests are usually significant forces in elections and referendums. Past experience suggested that business would be hostile to independence and trade unions would follow Labour's lead in opposing independence. In the event, many business leaders opposed independence while some prominent figures came out for it, but the vast majority of business people offered no opinion in public. There were suggestions from both sides that pressure was applied on business people to remain out of the debate or back one side or the other. Those involved on both sides had difficulty understanding that constitutional change was not perceived by everyone as quite so significant as they imagined.

The Confederation of British Industry (CBI) opposed independence and briefly registered as a campaign group while the Institute of Directors remained neutral. The CBI initially registered with the Electoral Commission as a campaign organisation only to change its mind when a number of affiliates withdrew from membership. It then claimed that the decision to register had been a mistake made by a junior member of staff. The CBI had flown into the core of the debate unprepared and looking amateurish, and thereby lost credibility and unintentionally drew attention to the limited number of members it had amongst Scottish businesses. The precise membership of CBI Scotland remained unclear. The Scottish Trades Union Congress (STUC) played a more sophisticated role. Its annual Congress in April 2014 made no recommendations to its fifty-two affiliated organisations and 640,000 members. In the past, the STUC would have enthusiastically supported the union, emphasising the unity of the working class across the UK. But support for the SNP and independence amongst trade union members made this difficult. The GMB, NUM, ASLEF, USDAW, CWU and Community came out for NO and the Prison Officers' Association and RMT came out for YES, while the overwhelming majority remained neutral or challenged both sides to state their cases.

Constitutional and Normal Politics

In their study of American politics, Gutmann and Thompson distinguish between two 'mindsets': a governing mindset that inclines decision makers to respect opponents and find common ground and a campaign mindset that precludes compromise and mutual respect.[7] American government, they maintain, has become increasingly difficult as a consequence of continuous campaigning. This phenomenon is familiar in most liberal democracies; it had particular resonance in the context of the Scottish independence referendum. There were two aspects to this: first, the need for agreement on the conduct of the referendum and second, the need for each government to continue with everyday business while engaged in a lengthy referendum campaign. Fears were expressed that the referendum would contribute to a febrile atmosphere and make government even more difficult. It was thought that difficult decisions would be avoided, that adversarial politics and populist measures would dominate. The length of the campaign and the backdrop of major public policy challenges resulting from the economic and fiscal crises added to concerns. However, there was a counterview: the referendum offered an opportunity for the electorate to become engaged in policy making debates. In practice the distinction between 'constitutional' and 'normal' politics broke down and Scotland witnessed an unanticipated democratic renewal.

At the heart of the referendum was a series of issues and debates that proved highly adversarial in which claim and counterclaim generated much heat. But while it could be heated, the referendum was a model of democratic conduct. In the final days of the referendum, the Scottish Police Federation issued a statement dismissing as 'preposterous' impressions of 'impending societal disintegration'. The debate had been 'robust but overwhelmingly good-natured'. Brian Docherty, Police Federation chairman, stated that 'One of the many joys of this campaign has been how it has awakened political awareness across almost every single section of society. The success enjoyed by the many should not be sullied by the actions of the few'.[8]

This reawakening was more evident in the grassroots campaign than in the media. Indeed, much of the media was slow to move out of the Holyrood and

Westminster bubbles. This was partly due to the decline of the Scottish press. The days when major newspapers employed municipal correspondents and journalists based across Scotland are over. Much coverage was viewed through the lens of the Holyrood media tower or the parliamentary press gallery in the Commons. Through this very narrow lens, journalists report politics as political theatre, taking their lead from the adversarial politics of the parliamentary chamber. It may be a fair representation of parliamentary behaviour but fails to acknowledge the much richer, more nuanced and sophisticated form politics takes in the world outside the chamber.

The BBC was unusually well resourced to cover the referendum and was thus able to cover it beyond the Westminster and Holyrood bubbles, though coverage by the BBC was dominated by high profile people and events. Both STV and the BBC broadcast debates between Alex Salmond and Alistair Darling. But these were only a tiny part of broadcast coverage of the referendum. As well as being dealt with intensively and extensively in daily news bulletins and on political programmes, the referendum seeped into many other programmes including talk shows, daytime television and comedy. It was difficult for viewers, even those who consciously sought to avoid politics, to escape the referendum.

However, in March 2014, Laura Bicker, one of the Corporation's journalists, noted the 'rise of the town hall meeting'.[9] There has been no systematic analysis of the debate and discussion that took place in communities across Scotland. The town hall meetings that were covered were only a tiny fraction of what was going on. Both sides engaged in this kind of activity but Yes Scotland was far more active at this level and employed more imaginative approaches. There is widespread agreement that these meetings attracted turnouts and engagement never before seen in Scottish politics but even accounting for this remarkable level of activity, the vast majority of the eligible electorate engaged mostly in informal settings, amongst friends, at work or with acquaintances. We have little sense of how deep and meaningful such discussions were. Engagement with the referendum operated along the spectrum from highly adversarial public differences through to informal, consensual deliberation. The balance was tipped more towards the participatory and deliberative end of this spectrum as compared with previous electoral contests and engagement was greater right across the span of different forms than ever before. The electorate would have had difficulty avoiding the referendum. Issues and information were abundant, however partial. In the closing stage opponents of independence urged those who might feel they did not have enough information to vote No, provoking the *Sun*'s inimitable Scottish political editor to comment, 'If you don't know vote no. Seriously? If you don't know after two years and nine months, stay home and do some colouring!'[10]

Few people will have engaged at only one point in this spectrum. Large numbers tuned in to the debates, and if not all, then very close to all will have engaged in informal discussions. Those who participated most in the referendum debates are most likely to have done so in a partisan manner, seeking out like-minded people who would reinforce attitudes. The more deliberative nature of informal discussion was most likely punctuated by observation of the highly adversarial debates. While a distinction can be drawn between deliberative and participatory forms of democracy,[11] in practice the electorate, including partisans, are likely to have encountered the full range of experiences in this long campaign.

Throughout the campaign, but especially in its early stages, opponents of independence had argued that the referendum was a distraction from the 'real issues' facing communities. This view might have gained wider currency had a sharp distinction been drawn between constitutional and normal politics but what became very clear was that the issues debated *were* meaningful and everyday. 'Should Scotland be an independent country?' provided the core to the referendum but also a stimulus to a much more extended debate. This unanticipated debate ranged wide and free. The future of Scotland, its relations with the rest of the UK, Europe and beyond, the type of society and economy it should have, its internal constitution, local democracy and much else besides were part of a democratic renewal. In large measure, this emanated from the grassroots campaign mainly, though not exclusively, forced on supporters of independence. The need to adopt a grassroots type of campaign had involved giving considerable autonomy to local campaign groups. These groups and individuals set agendas that did not fit with the more controlled form of politics familiar to students of modern elections.

Framing the Referendum

The classic account of issues that arise in elections distinguishes between position and valence issues.[12] Position issues are matters on which individual voters may disagree on policy prescriptions, for example along a continuum of state intervention through to the primacy of markets. Valence issues are those on which there is broad agreement on the prescription but differences on which party or conditions are deemed most likely to deliver, for example economic prosperity. Research on recent Scottish and UK elections suggests that valence issues have become more important in electoral contests as the policy differences between parties have declined.[13] The SNP's victories in 2007 and 2011 were a result of voters' belief in that party's ability to govern Scotland effectively, rather than its support for independence. The challenge for the SNP was to turn support for an SNP government into support for independence.

Scotland's constitutional status was one of the key issues dividing parties in recent elections. This was a matter of principle for some voters while for others it was viewed instrumentally, that is, whether constitutional change was considered likely to further or undermine other policy preferences. Both sides were clear that this was a debate about much more than flags and symbols of identity. If it was simply a matter of identity, then the referendum would have been comfortably won by supporters of independence given the long-standing strength of Scottish identity.[14] National identity was important but was refracted through everyday public policy concerns.

Given the breadth of ideological positions on both sides it was unlikely that major positional differences would emerge. Labour and Conservatives campaigning against independence disagreed on a range of matters. Labour and the SNP have long had more in common with each other than either party has with the Conservatives. Opponents of independence emphasised valence issues, stressing that the union was the best means of achieving commonly agreed objectives, especially economic prosperity. Advocates of independence emphasised valence issues too but also focused on position differences and the prospect that an independent Scotland would never be governed by a party or parties with little support in Scotland. These position differences were partly designed to highlight contrasts in preferences north and south of the border but also highlight divisions amongst supporters of the union. The future of welfare and the National Health Service and nuclear weapons were important themes for supporters of independence. The impression that was created was that pro-independence supporters were more progressive than opponents.

None of the main issues were new. Economic prosperity was at the heart of the debate. Membership of the European Union has been at the centre of this debate for quarter of a century. What was striking was that EU membership was assumed by both sides to be in Scotland's interests with contention only over whether that would be threatened more by independence or by remaining in the union. This contrasted with debates elsewhere in the UK where there is no agreement on EU membership. Opponents of independence argued that Scotland would find itself outside the EU but this was undermined in January 2013 when the Prime Minister announced that there would be a referendum on continued membership of the EU by the end of 2017.[15] This raised the prospect that by voting to stay inside the UK Scotland might find itself outside the EU.

The currency question has been a running issue in UK and Scottish politics for several years. Whether the UK should join the Euro had divided opinion inside UK Cabinets of both main parties in the past but there is now fairly universal support for the retention of sterling, at least in the foreseeable future, and few senior politicians venture to suggest that the UK might join the Euro even at some distant time. Supporters of independence faced similar problems, with the added dimension of having to decide whether a separate Scottish currency was desirable. The independence White Paper confirmed the SNP's position of retaining sterling, provoking the reaction from UK parties that they would block this if Scotland became independent. In a remarkable show of unity, Tory, Labour and LibDem front benches came together to insist that they would not permit Scotland to use sterling. This was the campaign mindset at work, for such an outcome might well have been damaging to an independent Scotland but it would also damage the economy of the rest of the UK. The Governor of the Bank of England adopted a more circumspect attitude. In a carefully worded speech in January 2014, Mark Carney set out the case for and against currency union in a balanced manner that allowed each side to focus on different parts of his speech.[16]

Purposeful Opportunism and the Referendum

While some organisations rushed into the heat of the battle and others kept their heads down, a number saw the referendum as an opportunity to pursue interests and agendas that were not directly related to the referendum question. As noted above, the CBI showed what could happen to an ill-prepared organisation that flew into the heat of debate. The Institute of Directors (IoD) maintained a position of studied neutrality, setting out a series of questions for both sides.[17] The IoD acknowledged that views on constitutional change were 'more varied than in previous times e.g. 70's 90's'.[18] The STUC took this approach a step further. While maintaining its neutrality, it aligned its long-term campaign for a 'Just Scotland' with the referendum debate. It was a classic example of 'purposeful opportunism'.[19] Instead of standing aloof or engaging in the core issues, the STUC sought to reframe the debate in terms that allowed it to pursue its 'Just Scotland' agenda. It avoided packaging proposals in an adversarial manner and mobilised support having prepared the ground well in advance.

There were other organisations that operated as purposeful opportunists. The Scottish Refugee Council (SRC) set out to consider the implications of constitutional change for refugees and asylum seekers in Scotland. It succeeded in challenging both sides and making proposals for a more just system for refugees under different constitutional scenarios.[20] The Scottish government adopted some of these recommendations into its White Paper on independence and the chief executive of the SRC was seconded to the Scottish government for four months to assist in two policy areas: helping design a new asylum system for an independent Scotland and developing policies to increase the proportion of women on public sector boards.

Other issues that were insinuated into the referendum focused on local democracy. The Convention of Scottish Local Authorities established a Commission on Local Democracy and the three Islands authorities, led by Orkney Islands Council, established a joint campaign, Our Islands Our Future. These initiatives were not centre stage but gave depth to the debate. They forced Scottish and UK governments to respond to demands for reforms and ensured that whatever the outcome of the referendum, there would be changes in how Scotland is governed. There is a long history of Shetland using debates on Scotland's constitutional status to win concessions. In the 1970s, Shetland Islands Council opposed devolution and threatened that Shetland would remain part of the UK if Scotland became independent. In the late 1990s, the Constitutional Convention recommended that Orkney and Shetland should each have one constituency in the proposed Scottish Parliament. In this referendum, Shetland Council established a campaign with the Western Isles and Orkney in which a series of demands were made. In July 2014, David Cameron became the first Prime Minister to visit Shetland in thirty-four years and announced a deal that involved subsidising the cost of electricity.

The referendum was an opportunity to place issues on the agenda but it needed to be done carefully. Shaping agendas in this way required packaging policies and interests without taking sides in the debate, mobilising support, preparing the ground well, and having the capacity to adapt to changing circumstances in the campaign. Some participants proved much more adept at this than others.

Polls and Promises

Support for independence rarely reached 35 per cent in polls in the years prior to the referendum. Polls continued to suggest trendless fluctuation in support for independence until towards the end of the campaign, when the gap started to close, though support for the union was almost always ahead. At various stages, polls suggested a closing of the gap were followed by the gap widening again. The variety of polling methods and findings created divisions among pollsters. What was clear was that opposition to independence had a significant advantage for most of the campaign but that supporters came much closer to victory than most commentators anticipated. Polls suggested a very tight contest in the closing weeks, with some implying that support for independence was ahead. It remains unclear whether these polls were aberrations or whether support for the union was pulled back in time. What was clear was that the polls elicited panic amongst supporters of the union.

The three party leaders at Westminster agreed to cancel Prime Minister's Questions (PMQs) in the Commons in the week before polling day to allow them to campaign in Scotland. They also agreed to a statement that appeared on the front page of the *Daily Record* as 'The Vow', undertaking that 'extensive new powers' would be granted to the Scottish Parliament according to an agreed timetable. They also stated that the Barnett formula, used to determine Scotland's share of public spending, would continue and that Holyrood would receive 'powers to raise revenue'. They acknowledged that people wanted to 'see change' and argued that 'A No vote will deliver faster safer and better change than separation' (*Daily Record*, 16 September 2014). Gordon Brown set out a timetable to furnish the Scottish Parliament with more powers.[21] The UK government had started the campaign resisting the call for a third option on more powers but had been forced to concede this in the final week.

Conclusion

The referendum on Scottish independence came about because the SNP had included a pledge to hold it in manifestos in elections for the Scottish Parliament, but it was never a central commitment, since the party sought support from voters who might disagree with independence. The Holyrood electoral system had been designed to ensure that no party was likely to win an overall majority but the 2011 election had seen the SNP win sixty-nine of Holyrood's 129 seats, and therefore it was now obliged to honour the referendum pledge. The SNP initially proposed that three options should be on offer in the referendum: independence, the status quo and more powers. The last was rejected by the UK government and was not formally on the ballot paper. Polls suggested, however, that, had that option been available, it would have commanded most support. Opponents of independence were divided on whether more powers should be granted but agreed that the referendum should focus on independence. But this line became difficult to sustain as referendum day approached. Scotland voted to remain in the union but the 55 per cent who voted against independence included a substantial element that wanted more powers for Holyrood. When combined with the 45 per cent who voted for independence, this confirmed what had been apparent at the outset. The majority of Scottish voters wanted more powers, however ill-defined. The campaign had forced this scenario on to the agenda.

But the most significant impact of the campaign was the revival of Scottish democracy. The 85 per cent turnout in the referendum broke records. Scotland witnessed a level of engagement never previously seen. The political parties and established media normally set the agenda and did so again, but to a far lesser extent. As a means of public engagement the referendum had been a spectacular success.

Notes

1. Griffith, 'The political constitution'.
2. Loughlin, *Sword and Scales*, 2003, p. 4.
3. Ansolabehere et al., 'Does attack advertsing demobilize the electorate'; Ansolabehere and Iyengar, *Going Negative*.
4. Freedman and Goldstein, 'Measuring media exposure and the effects of negative campaign ads'; Goldstein and Freedman, 'Campaign advertsising and voter turnout'; Seligman and Kugler, 'Why is research on the effects of negative campaign so inconclusive'; Lau and Pomper, *Negative Campaigning*.
5. Seligman, *Learned Optimism*.
6. Pattie et al. 'Raising the tone? The impact of "positive" and "negative" campaigning on voting in the 2007 Scottish Parliament election'; Carman et al., *More Scottish than British*.
7. Gutmann and Thompson *The Spirit of Compromise*.
8. STV, 'Police Federation dismiss reports of referendum campaign disorder'.
9. BBC, 'The rise of the town hall meeting'.
10. Nicoll, tweet, 2014.
11. Mutz, *Hearing the Other Side*.
12. Stokes, 'Spatial models of party competition'.
13. Clarke et al., *Political Choice in Britain*; Clarke et al., *Performance Politics and the British Voter*; Johns et al., *Voting for a Scottish Government*; Whiteley et al., *Affluence, Austerity and Electoral Change in Britain*; Carman et al., *More Scottish than British*.
14. Bechhofer and McCrone, 'Choosing national identity'.
15. Cameron, 'EU speech at Bloomberg', 23 January 2013.
16. Carney, 'The economics of currency unions', speech at Scottish Council for Development and Industry, 29 January 2014.
17. Institute of Directors, 'Independence referendum policy issue and questions'.
18. Ibid.
19. Cram, 'Calling the tune without paying the piper? Social policy regulation: the role of the Commission in European Union Social Policy'.
20. Scottish Refugee Council, *Improving the Lives of Refugees in Scotland after the Referendum*.
21. Brown, 'Full text of Gordon Brown's letter setting out new powers plan', 2014.

Bibliography

Ansolabehere, S. and S. Iyengar, *Going Negative: How Political Advertisements Shrink and Polarize the Electorate* (New York: Free Press, 1992).

Ansolabehere, S., S. Iyengar, A. Simon and N. Valentino, 'Does attack advertising demobilize the electorate?', *American Political Science Review*, 88 (1994), pp. 829–38.

BBC, 'The rise of the town hall meeting', 13 March 2014, <http://www.bbc.co.uk/news/uk-scotland-scotland-politics-26558087> (last accessed 16 September 2015).

Bechhofer, Frank and David McCrone, 'Choosing national identity', *Sociological Research Online*, 15(30) (2010), p. 3, <http://www.socresonline.org.uk/15/3/3.html> (last accessed 16 September 2015).

Brown, Gordon (2014), 'Full text of Gordon Brown's letter setting out new powers plan', <http://news.stv.tv/scotland-decides/294068-full-text-of-gordon-browns-letter-setting-out-new-powers-plan/> (last accessed 16 September 2015).

Cameron, David, 'EU speech at Bloomberg', 23 January 2013, <https://www.gov.uk/government/speeches/eu-speech-at-bloomberg> (last accessed 16 September 2015).

Carman C., R. Johns and J. Mitchell, *More Scottish than British: the 2001 Scottish Parliament Election* (London: Palgrave Macmillan, 2014).

Carney, Mark, 'The economics of currency unions', Speech at Scottish Council for Development and Industry, 29 January 2014, <http://www.bankofengland.co.uk/publications/Documents/speeches/2014/speech706.pdf> (last accessed 16 September 2015).

Clarke, H., D. Sanders, M. Stewart and P. Whiteley, *Political Choice in Britain* (Oxford: Oxford University Press, 2004).

Clarke, H., D. Sanders, M. Stewart and P. Whiteley, *Performance Politics and the British Voter* (Cambridge: Cambridge University Press, 2009).

Cram, Laura, 'Calling the tune without paying the piper? Social policy regulation: the role of the Commission in European Union Social Policy', *Policy and Politics*, 21 (1993), pp. 135–46.

Freedman, P. and K. Goldstein, 'Measuring media exposure and the effects of negative campaign ads', *American Journal of Political Science*, 43 (1999), pp. 1189–208.

Goldstein, K. and P. Freedman, 'Campaign advertising and voter turnout: new evidence for a stimulation effect', *Journal of Politics*, 64 (2002), pp. 721–40.

Griffith, J. A. G., 'The political constitution, *Modern Law Review*, 42 (1979), pp. 1–21.

Gutmann, Amy and Dennis Thompson, *The Spirit of Compromise: Why Governing Demands it and Campaigning Undermines It* (Princeton: Princeton University Press, 2012).

Institute of Directors, 'Independence referendum policy issue and questions', January 2013, <http://www.iodscotland.com/images/Referendum/referendum%20document.pdf> (last accessed 16 September 2015).

Johns, R., J. Mitchell, D. Denver and C. Pattie, *Voting for a Scottish Government: The Scottish Parliament Elections of 2007* (Manchester: Manchester University Press, 2010).

Lau, R. R. and G. M. Pomper, *Negative Campaigning: An Analysis of US Senate Elections* (Lanham, MD: Rowman and Littlefield Publishers, 2004).

Loughlin, Martin, *Sword and Scales: An Examination of the Relationship Between Law and Politics* (Oxford: Hart Publishing, 2003).

Macwhirter, Iain, *Democracy in the Dark: The Decline of the Scottish Press and How to Keep the Lights On* (Edinburgh: Saltire Society, 2014).

Mitchell, J. and L. Bennie, 'Thatcherism and the Scottish question', in *British Elections and Parties Yearbook, 1995* (Ilford: Frank Cass, 1996), pp. 90–104.

Mutz, Diane (2006), *Hearing the Other Side: Deliberative Versus Participatory Democracy* (Cambridge: Cambridge University Press, 2006).

Nicoll, Andrew, tweet, 17 September 2014, <https://twitter.com/andrewsnicoll/status/512278435155431424> (last accessed 16 September 2015).

Pattie, C., D. Denver, R. Johns and J. Mitchell, 'Raising the tone? The impact of "positive" and "negative" campaigning on voting in the 2007 Scottish Parliament election', *Electoral Studies*, 30 (2011), pp. 333–43.

Scottish Refugee Council, *Improving the Lives of Refugees in Scotland after the Referendum: An Appraisal of the Options*, January 2013, <http://www.google.co.uk/url?sa=t&rct=j&q=&esrc=s&source=web&cd=2&ved=0CCgQFjAB&url=http%3A%2F%2Fwww.scottishrefugeecouncil.org.uk%2Fassets%2F5495%2F4087_src_referendum_report_v3.pdf&ei=OLeeVMyFKNLnapG9gtgI&usg=AFQjCNGcx6ntFkqxS94vKwq-4t8coRvmRA&sig2=v_YZ7gXELyHDrWdsPXMM1w&bvm=bv.82001339,d.d2s> (last accessed 16 September 2015).

Seligman, Martin, *Learned Optimism* (New York: Simon and Schuster, 1998).

Seligman, J. and M. Kugler, 'Why is research on the effects of negative campaign so inconclusive? Understanding citizens' perceptions of negativity', *Journal of Politics*, 65 (2003), pp. 142–60.

Stokes, Donald, 'Spatial models of party competition', *American Political Science Review*, 57 (1963), pp. 368–77.

STV (2014), 'Police Federation dismiss reports of referendum campaign disorder', 17 September 2014, <http://news.stv.tv/scotland-decides/news/292447-police-federation-dismiss-reports-of-referendum-campaign-disorder/> (last accessed 16 September 2015).

Whiteley, P., H. Clarke, D. Sanders and M. Stewart, *Affluence, Austerity and Electoral Change in Britain* (Cambridge: Cambridge University Press, 2013).

2

The Media Landscape In Scotland

Neil Blain and David Hutchison

It should be acknowledged at the outset that, vitally important though they are, traditional communications media such as broadcasting and the press, and the online provision which has extended their range, offering alternative voices, collectively provide only a part of the information and opinion influencing citizens in their role as electors. Our perceptions are formed through many social and cultural processes with a much longer history than the relatively recent arrival that is the mass media, which all contribute to our sense of who we are and where we belong, locally, regionally and nationally. In the case of Scotland, the nation long pre-existed the modern world and has survived it, too, perhaps improbably. Preservation of Scotland's geographical and institutional boundaries, and the perception of Scottish society and its cultures as having distinctive characteristics and rights, have enabled a negotiated existence in the dual spaces of Scottish nationhood and British statehood since union with England in 1707.[1]

Limited elements of a Scottish infrastructure of state, which take us beyond the political apparatus associated with the Secretary of State for Scotland and the Scottish Office, have begun to develop internally since devolution. The outward relationships, meanwhile, of both Scotland and the UK have altered through globalising processes and the impact of supranational organisations, affecting how 'independence' can be conceptualised. This complex terrain can present anomalous forms. To take a key example, the Scottish Census of 2011 records that 62 per cent of the Scottish population defined themselves as 'Scottish only', whereas the second most common response, 'Scottish and British identities only' was registered by merely 18 per cent of respondents.[2] Yet a majority of Scots have so far, as of 2015, elected to stay within the British state.

Can we gauge the role of the media in the Scottish political sphere? One of the most contested fields in the social sciences is that of media influence, and the literatures it produces are vast, complex and disputatious. It is not the contention here that the media directly affect voting behaviour. There is no adequate calculus available for determining the influence of communications media besides other affective factors – education, alternative information sources, peer group, family – in the formation of awareness and opinion about the worlds we inhabit. We know that the media affect the picture of the world we have, and we know that they can direct our attention. If during 2015 we became much more conscious of the political presence of Nicola Sturgeon, the leader of the SNP, we were doing so to a significant degree through media influence.

But it is much less likely that the media were forming our attitudes to these matters. When polls signalled a possible Yes victory and again seven months later, in April 2015, when Nicola Sturgeon became a major feature of London media coverage, English media consumers became alert in much greater numbers to the Scottish dimensions of UK electoral politics. This was a clear example of media influence, actually a direct result of editorial choice; just as the more habitual invisibility of Scotland in London media is an editorial choice. However, taking Sturgeon's emergence beyond Scotland as example, reactions ranged from her being the UK's most popular politician (in polls, and in various London-based opinion pieces) to her characterisation, not least in the London editions of the *Daily Mail* and *Telegraph*, as dangerous and disruptive, and the SNP as 'racist'.

In other words, the switch of London media attention to the SNP First Minister certainly worked to direct media consumer attention, but evidently did not dictate attitudes, either among London editors and journalists themselves or, as was very evident on comment threads, among media consumers. Positive, if sometimes qualified, accounts of Sturgeon's emergence as a figure on the UK political stage came from many sources, but representations both of Sturgeon and of her party were highly variable.

It is an anomalous fact that as the self-affirmed Scottish element of the nation's identity was rapidly growing on either side of the millennium, much of the ownership of a vigorous and once indigenous press – a public forum formerly unrivalled in comparably sized societies – had passed out of Scottish hands. Many newspapers available nationally in Scotland are owned in England, or in the case of *The Herald*, indirectly in the USA. Johnston Press, owner of the *Scotsman* group, is registered and headquartered in Edinburgh but has an office in central London, also sometimes referred to as the group head office. The company has been listed on the stock exchange since 1988, and has many major shareholders outside Scotland. Only *The Courier* in Dundee and the *Press and Journal* in Aberdeen, defined as Scottish regional newspapers (there is some contention over the distinction), are owned in Scotland, by D. C. Thomson. Several 'national' newspapers, despite having Scottish titles, are 'editionised' Scottish versions of London-produced newspapers subject, to varying degrees, to external editorial policies, and are now read in substantial quantities in Scotland as well-resourced alternatives to 'indigenous' newspapers suffering from under-investment.

The indigenous dimension of Scotland's TV broadcast provision still remains relatively under-developed. Its critical mass in areas such as commissioning and overall resource has always been determined by policy elsewhere, generally in London. It was the arrival of online news and opinion sites, and social media, which first signalled the kind of challenges the traditional media might face in adapting to a changing political landscape in the approach to the independence referendum.

The existence of a Scottish nation with a strong sense of its identity has always been a fact to which those who own and control its media – wherever they might be based – have to respond, at least in the commercial sphere (in the broadcasting world, the BBC presents a distinct case). More recently, the adaptation of well-resourced London newspapers for the Scottish market has raised questions about the consequences of this shift for Scottish civil society. There are complex affiliations associated with the editorial voices speaking through 'Scottish' titles. Generalisations about any dominant position on the part of the media in Scotland on the subjects of devolution and independence would be unwise, but it is fair to say that a popular perception has existed since the late 1970s of a traditional media whose voice generally sounds resistant to constitutional change.

Yet there have been striking exceptions too, including during the devolution debate prior to the establishment of the Scottish Parliament under Tony Blair's Labour government, when much of the media became positive about devolution, and these exceptions multiplied in 2014/15 as two press titles, the *Sunday Herald*, and the newly arrived *National* took a pro-independence stance. They were followed in 2015 by the declaration of the *Scottish Sun* for the SNP in the approaching UK general election.

Individual columnists variously in the *Herald*, *Daily Record* and *Scotsman* voiced positive sentiments about independence in 2014 and also about the SNP in 2015, and the *Record* and its sister paper, the *Sunday Mail*, produced reports and opinion pieces at odds with their generally unionist, pro-Labour line. Several of the chapters which follow examine press coverage and behaviour. On the broadcasting front, the outputs of Scottish Television (STV) and BBC Scotland are also considered elsewhere in this volume: there was little or no popular sense that the former strayed far from impartiality, but some controversy about the performance of the latter.

The history of the press, radio, and TV in Scotland is replete with examples of economic challenge, typical of small nations under the influence of much larger nations speaking the same language. The economic life of the Scottish media has suffered many setbacks and often appears more restricted than enabled; as when, for example, some of its newspapers introduce successive waves of redundancies, or its independent TV sector serially finds commissions hard to come by. Prolonged debate over the adequacy of Scottish media provision, leading to inquiries such as the Scottish Broadcasting Commission,[3] or into the Scottish press at Westminster[4] and into the local press at Holyrood,[5] testifies to a widespread perception that the media spaces adequate for the democratic and cultural needs of Scottish civil society are cramped.

The first constitutional referendum on the future governance of Scotland took place in 1979, the second in 1997 and the third in 2014. Over that thirty-five-year period there have been very significant changes in the media landscape. There may be more indigenous newspapers, in the sense of being edited in Scotland, with *Scotland on Sunday* appearing in 1988, the *Sunday Herald* in 1999 and *The National* at the end of 2014, but the overall picture in the press is one of decline. Broadcasting, by contrast, has expanded, particularly in the commercial and community radio sectors; furthermore, there are now a digital Gaelic television channel and the beginnings of local television.

The press in Scotland comprises indigenous titles and others which, with or without Scottish editions, are London newspapers that circulate throughout the UK. Indigenous titles are also to be found in Wales but not on the Scottish scale (the Northern Irish situation is more comparable). There are a number of factors which explain the survival of the Scottish press. The inability of London-based titles to employ the railway system in the late nineteenth and early twentieth century to thoroughly penetrate the Scottish market as they were able to penetrate the English and Welsh markets, and to wipe out much regional competition in the process, is usually cited as the principal factor. But it is also the case that titles edited and written in England struggled to offer the kind of comprehensive coverage of events north of the border that an indigenous title could provide. Only the *Daily Express* had a major impact in Scotland, and it did so by establishing in 1928 an autonomous Scottish edition which dominated the market in the immediate post Second World War period but declined thereafter and effectively ceased to exist as a Scottish-based title in 1974.[6]

A further relevant factor is that most Scottish titles, even when they have sought to cover the entire country, have always had a regional orientation which has encouraged regional loyalty, a loyalty which historically has been a weapon against which the London based press – and newspapers based in other Scottish urban centres – had no entirely effective defence. However, the situation has been changing in recent times (Table 2.1).[7]

Newspapers throughout the Western world have been facing serious circulation falls, declines driven not only by the increasing power of the electronic and digital media but also by the apparent indifference of many younger people to the print medium.[8] The position of Scottish titles has been exacerbated by a serious loss of market share within Scotland, as Scottish versions of what are basically English titles have improved their relative position and pursued their Scottish competitors with remarkable determination. Since the 1990s, the number of London papers printing separate editions for the Scottish market has increased dramatically.

In the mid-1970s Scottish dailies took 64 per cent of sales and Sundays took 66 per cent.[9] Scottish Sundays still managed in 2014 to outsell their English rivals by a small margin but the dailies' share of the market was 43 per cent.[10] Obviously, better funded titles such as the *Telegraph* and *Daily Mail* can offer a wider range of news and features than their Scottish competitors. If they also provide a significant quantity of Scottish news – and Scottish sport, particularly football – they are an attractive buy.

Table 2.1 Daily newspaper circulations in Scotland, 2013/14.

Scottish titles	
Courier	50,539
Daily Record	216,029
Herald	38,939
Press and Journal	63,796
Scotsman	29,452
English titles	
Daily Express	51,496
Daily Mail	92,137
Daily Mirror	16,567
Daily Star	45,181
Daily Telegraph	17,820
Financial Times	2,360
Guardian	10,422
Independent/The i	2,622/19,320
Sun	248,035
Times	17,759

As Table 2.1 demonstrates, it is an English paper, *The Sun*, which sells the highest number of copies in the daily market north of the border and the *Daily Mail*, another English title, sells more copies than the combined circulations of the *Scotsman* and *Herald*, the two newspapers which aspire to be national Scottish upmarket titles. A similar situation is to be found in the Sunday market.

It is very strange that the once dominant *Daily Record* – which sold over three-quarters of a million copies in the 1980s – has been so vulnerable to the onslaught of the Scottish edition of *The Sun*, which now outsells it. What is even more remarkable is that the general loss of market share has accelerated since devolution. We have noted that census results reveal a sharp decline in British identity in Scotland. Does this aspect of consumer behaviour signal a contradiction? Or are many Scottish readers simply exercising consumer choice and opting for titles which, despite the limitations of their coverage of events north of the border, offer a more extensive bill of fare, and in several instances have a lower cover price than their Scottish rivals. In fairness, it should be noted that both *The Courier* in Dundee and the *Press and Journal* in Aberdeen have been much more resilient, probably because of the skill with which they blend local, Scottish and UK material (with a judicious but not over-generous smattering of international news).

All Scottish-based titles have an online presence but to date none has been any better than most newspapers elsewhere in the world at turning 'visitors' into revenue streams large enough to offset the precipitate loss of circulation and advertising revenue.

In this dispiriting context, the decision by the Herald Group to start a new title after the referendum vote is a remarkable one. *The National* is overtly committed to independence, though, like its stablemate the *Sunday Herald*, which, as noted earlier, was the only paper to come out in favour of a Yes vote, it claims to be a critical friend of the independence movement, not a slavish supporter. It remains to be seen whether there will be a big enough market to enable this rather brave venture to prosper.

Scottish papers have a variety of owners, and there is a clear east/west divide. The Dundee company D. C. Thomson, still a strong force in the magazine and children's sector in the UK as a whole, owns the morning and evening papers in that city and in Aberdeen, as well as the *Sunday Post*. The residually Scottish Johnston Press – largely a publisher of local papers, which was originally Falkirk-based but, as noted above, has a diluted Scottish identity, and does the bulk of its business south of the border – owns the corresponding Edinburgh titles and *Scotland on Sunday*. The Herald Group – a morning and evening title, as well as the *Sunday Herald* and now too *The National* – is owned by Newsquest, a subsidiary of the American Gannett Corporation; and London-based Trinity Mirror owns the *Daily Record* and the *Sunday Mail*.

Viewers and listeners north of the border have access to a range of UK-wide broadcasting services and some customised, in whole or in part, to Scotland. ITV, which is now a pan-UK service with some regional opt-outs, rather than the federation of regional companies it once was, is available via Scottish Television, which has been one of two independent commercial broadcasters not owned directly by ITV plc (the other was Ulster TV). However, most of STV's output is provided by ITV, including some network news and current affairs provision, that is, from London; and its own contributions in the form of opt-out programming are mainly in the areas of news, current affairs and sport. It is remarkable that STV, which took over the Aberdeen-based Grampian in 1997, remains stubbornly independent in ownership. It would be an even stronger company were there an end to the anomaly whereby Carlisle-based Border Television, which is part of ITV, continues to provide programming in the southern part of Scotland. In 2013, Ofcom, the UK regulator, awarded STV the licences for the first two local television services – in Glasgow and Edinburgh – in the country, and subsequently awarded it other local licences in Aberdeen, Dundee and Ayr.

The BBC's two main channels, BBC1 and BBC2, have the suffix 'Scotland' added north of the border. In practice this means that there is a significant amount of opt-out programming, mainly, though not exclusively, on BBC1. This takes the form of news, current affairs, documentaries, sport plus some light entertainment and drama, though as with STV, what are seen as 'main' news slots and current affairs programmes are shared with the rest of the UK, with additional Scottish opt-outs in these areas. (This raises a question, to which we return below, about the relative salience in Scotland of London-originated and Scotland-originated news.)

Both STV and BBC Scotland seek network commissions, particularly, though not exclusively, in the area of drama, and there are ongoing arguments about what the appropriate proportion of network output sourced in Scotland should be (arguments replicated elsewhere in the UK). STV's presence as part of ITV's network drama output ceased when the long running crime series *Taggart* ended in 2011, having begun in 1983. For many years the company produced soap operas, the most successful being *Take the High Road/High Road* (1980–2003), which was transmitted in a number of other ITV regions. BBC Scotland's soap, *River City* (2002–) has yet to be shown south of the border; however, *Shetland* (2013–), a police series set in the northern islands, has been networked. The establishment of the Broadcasting Commission referred to earlier stemmed in part from the general feeling that Scotland, whether in the shape of the broadcasting companies or the independent production sector, was inadequately represented at UK level onscreen and in terms of commissions.

BBC Alba is a Gaelic-medium television service financed jointly by the BBC and the Scottish government. It transmits a range of programmes, including news bulletins (which mix the regional, the national and the international), up to seven hours per day, and its establishment in 2008 marked the successful outcome of a long running campaign. The channel continues to attract audience numbers well in excess of the number of Scots who speak the language, helped by its sports coverage and by its judicious use of subtitles.[11] In the context of the referendum and the subsequent election, its influence in shaping awareness of the issues was inevitably not great in the overall Scottish voting context.

As in the rest of the UK, there is a plethora of other channels available via satellite, cable and digital terrestrial. The Broadcasting Commission proposed that a new pan-Scottish channel be established, with an emphasis on factual programming, but since neither the Holyrood Parliament nor any other body has offered to provide the necessary funds, to date it remains only an aspiration. At one point it was proposed by an Expert Group, established by the SNP government, that the estimated annual running cost of £70m might come from the UK television licence fee but this proposal, like those of the Broadcasting Commission, was superseded by a different and less specific set of proposals in the independence White Paper which preceded the referendum, making any further phase of development of Scottish broadcasting a matter merely for conjecture.

The specific relevance of the present state of provision for the referendum is that Scottish viewers who, as is common more widely, receive most of their news from TV, did so in the continuing absence of any channel (apart from BBC Alba) offering news output beyond the limitations of opt-out channels, much of whose news comes from London. Scottish listeners have access to all of the BBC's national services and two stand-alone services, BBC Radio Scotland (there are similar channels in Wales and Northern Ireland) and Radio nan Gaidheal, a Gaelic service. In addition, Scotland is covered by a range of commercial stations (mostly owned now by the Bauer Media Group of Germany), and a growing number of community stations.

The online world was more than a decade from its foundation in the run-up to the 1979 referendum, but by the time of the 1997 vote the World Wide Web was firmly established. During the recent campaign its presence has been especially obvious. Newspapers and broadcasters, in particular the BBC, have developed strong online presences and they function alongside Internet-only operations such as the *Scottish Review*, which began life in 1995 as a print magazine and abandoned print for online in 2008, and other sites such as *Wings Over Scotland* and *Newsnet Scotland* which have always been based online.

Despite the growth of non-traditional media, broadcasting and the press remain vitally important, not least when considering political news and opinion. Ofcom publishes a useful annual survey of the Communications Market, and reported in its 2014 edition that of those interviewed by its researchers 80 per cent said that their main source of Scottish news was television, with 2 per cent citing radio, 8 per cent newspapers and 6 per cent the Internet. The report also noted that the five main public service channels (PSBs), while continuing to lose viewer share, continued to attract 52 per cent of all viewing.[12]

In a democracy informed public debate depends on a number of factors. Most obviously, there has to be freedom of expression, constrained only by agreed restrictions on such matters as libel, incitement to crime, interference with the judicial process and unjustified invasion of personal privacy. The exact boundaries in all of these areas are matters of ongoing controversy, as has been illustrated most clearly in recent years by the collapse of the UK Press Complaints Commission, the establishment of the Leveson Inquiry and the aftermath of that inquiry, which has yet to be fully worked through.

What is also crucial to democratic debate is pluralism. There needs to be a wide range of outlets for the dissemination of news and opinion. Given the strong UK commitment to balance and impartiality in broadcasting (contested terms admittedly), the survival of a combative and heterogeneous press sector is crucial.

In Scotland, the broadcasters, despite some anxieties about the future of both the licence fee and advertising, are reasonably secure, though the election of fifty-six Scottish National Party MPs to Westminster in 2015 implied the possibility that some restructuring of Scottish broadcasting might be revisited. That security does not apply to newspapers, where an apparent plethora of titles – whether Scottish or Scottish versions of English papers – masks very real problems in sustaining the financial model which has served them to date. Cutbacks in staff have occurred on a regular basis, and once all the supposed inefficiencies have been removed, there must come a point where the ability of newspapers to provide comprehensive news services and to mount sustained investigations will be seriously undermined.

The Holyrood Parliament has taken a limited interest in this situation. To some extent it has been constrained by the parameters of the devolution settlement, with broadcasting and press mergers/competition policy being matters reserved to Westminster, unlike arts and film policy. However, as mentioned above, a Holyrood committee did mount an inquiry into the health of the local press in 2010. It resulted in the abandonment of a proposal which would have allowed local authorities to move much of their informational advertising online, and in the process deprive local (mainly weekly) titles of an important source of revenue. Sooner or later the future viability of the Scottish daily and Sunday press will also have to be seriously discussed, given the implications for Scottish democracy.

The election of a Conservative government in the May 2015 election and the overwhelming victory of the SNP in Scotland will pose particular challenges for the BBC. In the first place, in their manifesto the Conservatives promised to freeze the licence fee, and the minister subsequently appointed to the relevant department is on record as being unhappy with the fee as a method of financing the Corporation. Secondly, there will be the need to work out a *modus operandi* which ensures that in news and current affairs a balance is struck which reflects the different political balances at both Westminster and Holyrood, something that may be less of a challenge for STV.

If the SNP win a majority at the Holyrood election in 2016, it is likely that the arguments in favour of a Scottish BBC (or even a Scottish Broadcasting Corporation) will intensify. A way forward might be for the BBC to seize the initiative and restructure itself as a genuinely federal organisation, but that would require a radical change in its nature.

The debates around the referendum and the election leave little doubt that much of Scottish civil society is speaking more assertively about the nation's distinct political identity than has been witnessed in recent memory. Despite the growth of online alternatives, the current evidence suggests that the media as a whole are only partially providing the platforms required for fully informed, fair-minded discussion about the final destinations for Scottish, and indeed British, democracy to sustain the journeys on which both are now embarked. It is an open question whether these media will have the financial, intellectual and imaginative resources to rise to this formidable challenge.

Notes

1. McCrone, *Understanding Scotland, passim.*
2. Scotland's Census, 2011.
3. Scottish Government, 2008.
4. House of Commons, 2009.
5. Scottish Government, 2010.
6. Reid, *Deadline: The Story of the Scottish Press, passim.*
7. Circulation figures are derived from the data produced by the Audit Bureau of Circulations. See also note 10.
8. Brock, *Out of Print*, p. 234.
9. Hutchison, 'The history of the press', p. 66.
10. These calculations are derived from ABC figures. Because Scottish dailies – other than the *Record* – now classify themselves as regional rather than national, their figures relate to the period July to December 2013; other figures are for February 2013 to February 2014.
11. MG Alba, 2014.
12. Ofcom, 2014.

Bibliography

Brock, George, *Out of Print* (London: Kogan Page, 2013).

House of Commons Scottish Affairs Committee, 1 July 2009, <http://www.publications. parliament.uk/pa/cm200809/cmselect/cmscotaf/401/401.pdf> (last accessed 14 May 2015).

Hutchison David (2008), 'The history of the press', in Neil Blain and David Hutchison (eds), *The Media in Scotland* (Edinburgh: Edinburgh University Press, 2008), pp. 56–70.

McCrone, David, *Understanding Scotland: The Sociology of a Nation* (Abingdon: Routledge, 2001).

MG Alba, 2014, <http//www.mgalba.com/about/index.html> (last accessed 21 November 2014).

Ofcom, Communications Market Report, 7 August 2014, <http://stakeholders.ofcom. org.uk/binaries/research/cmr/cmr14/2014_CMR_Scotland.pdf> (last accessed 21 November 2014).

Reid, Harry (2006), *Deadline: The Story of the Scottish Press* (Edinburgh: Saint Andrew Press, 2006).

Scotland's Census 2011, <http://www.scotlandscensus.gov.uk/news/census-2011-detailed-characteristics-ethnicity-identity-language-and-religion-scotland-%E2%80%93> (last accessed 24 February 2014).

Scottish Government, 2008, <www.scottishbroadcastingcommission.gov.uk/news/final-reportnews.html> (last accessed 14 May 2015).

Scottish Government, 2010, <http://archive.scottish.parliament.uk/s3/committees/ellc/reports-10/edr10-07.htm> (last accessed 21 November 2014).

3

Broadcasting and the Press: Some Key Moments

David Hutchison

Elsewhere in this section of the book are a chapter on the editorial stances adopted by the various newspapers, an analysis of the broadcasting output and a discussion of the performance of the Scottish commentariat. This chapter focuses on key moments in the run-up to the vote, specifically the publication of the White Paper on 26 November 2013 and the two television debates in August 2014, and considers how the mainstream press and broadcasting responded. As far as the White Paper is concerned, I draw on material published at greater length elsewhere.[1]

For the analysis of the White Paper coverage, the early evening and late evening news and current affairs programmes of the BBC, ITV and Channel 4 at UK level and the output of BBC Scotland and STV transmitted to the domestic audience were examined, a total of ten programmes.

The first observation to be made is that the output reflected in almost textbook form the general approach of public service broadcasting in the UK, whether financed by licence fee or advertising, that is to say it has an obligation to seek to report events factually and to treat matters of current controversy in an even-handed way. Partisanship of the kind found in the press is unacceptable; judgements may be offered by journalists but committed commentary can only come from protagonists and, to an extent, from 'experts'. And in a matter of controversy these 'experts' should cast light on the subject matter, not intensify partisanship.

All of the programmes led with the White Paper and gave it substantial coverage. Channel 4 News (also provided by ITN, the news service of ITV) was the only one not to do so; instead it led with a thirteen-minute item on a different UK political story before turning to the White Paper.

In the presentation of the contents of the document there was again a similarity. A correspondent, and not the programme anchor him/herself, outlined what it contained, while clips from the launch event were used as illustration. By way of balance, there was brief comment from the leader of the Better Together campaign, Alistair Darling. Anchors then either interviewed fellow specialist journalists on different aspects of the White Paper or introduced filmed packages.

Not all of these reports were from Scotland. STV's early evening bulletin ran interviews with London taxi drivers and Channel 4 had one of its reporters in Spain discussing the relationship between the Scottish and forthcoming Catalan referendums.

Experts/pundits, many of them familiar certainly to Scottish domestic viewers, appeared across the output.

All of the programmes had substantial interviews with Alex Salmond and with Alistair Darling or the Scottish Secretary, Alistair Carmichael. The Salmond interviews tended to focus on the issues of access to the pound sterling for an independent Scotland and its entry to the EU. Defence and the SNP determination to remove nuclear weapons from Scotland, while remaining a member of NATO, also featured, as did the White Paper's proposal to improve childcare. This last led to some sharp questioning as to why, since childcare is a devolved matter, the proposed improvements could not be implemented now: the First Minister's answer was that it was only within a Scottish budget that such a plan could be afforded. He took pains to emphasise that the British government's debt had been built up under the chancellorships of the current incumbent, George Osborne, and the leader of the Better Together campaign, Alistair Darling. In several of the interviews he referred to Scottish oil revenues disappearing 'into the maw of George Osborne'.

The interview which veered from this general trend was conducted by Gordon Brewer on BBC's *Newsnight Scotland*. Brewer tackled the currency issue but concentrated on the fact, as he presented it, that once committed to the pound there would be no escape for Scotland; he also raised the impact on the standing of the UK in the world if Scotland left the union. This was the sole interview in which there was real friction. A number of British broadcast interviewers have a reputation for being rather aggressive towards politicians. However, what was striking about the Salmond interviews here examined is that they were not particularly abrasive: the First Minister laid out his case and was rarely interrupted. The only exception was the Brewer interview where Salmond reacted rather testily when Brewer referred to a poll of a large number of senior pupils in Aberdeenshire which showed a substantial majority against independence. The interviewer rather sarcastically suggested that it might reflect the fact that for many young people the campaign for independence was a throwback to the nineteenth century with little relevance to the twenty-first.

The interviews with Alistair Darling focused on the issues already referred to, and the former Chancellor dismissed the White Paper as a 'work of fiction'; he emphasised the difficulties in securing a currency union and the financial consequences of an ageing population.

The main difference between the coverage by UK and Scottish programmes was that coverage by the latter was far more extensive, sometimes wearyingly so. Both sets of programmes reflected what was taken to be the general view that the

White Paper had not answered some of the central questions, but journalists did hedge their bets on the likely outcome of the September vote.

The following day's front pages of all of the Scottish newspapers and the Scottish editions of English titles led with the White Paper. However, the English editions of the latter did not; they led with allegations made at the trial of former employees of the celebrity cook Nigella Lawson that she was a cocaine user, or on a migration story.

The Scottish broadsheets' extensive coverage set out for readers the basic content of the document. Columnists in *The Herald* and *The Scotsman* argued the cases for and against independence. *The Herald* declared in an editorial that the White Paper 'goes some way to filling the vision vacuum' although 'big questions remain unanswered', while *The Scotsman*'s leader suggested that there was now a challenge to the Better Together campaign to clarify its position on several issues. With its eye on part of its regional audience, the *Press and Journal*'s front page headline highlighted the White Paper's pledge that post independence more power would be devolved from Edinburgh to Orkney, Shetland and the Western Isles. The paper's editorial, like that in *The Herald*, argued that key questions 'remain in the air'. *The Courier*, as had done *The Scotsman*, in its leader urged readers to study the White Paper, which it described as a 'curate's egg'. The most overtly hostile coverage was in the *Daily Record*. The front page headline referred to some of the SNP's post-independence aspirations and asked 'Did he (the First Minister) FORGET ABOUT THE PRICE TAG?' The White Paper's contents were reported inside but that was followed by a piece headlined DARLING PULPS ALEX'S FICTION. In its critical editorial the *Record* declared 'On key issues . . . the answers rang hollow'.

The tone of editorials and columnists in these Scottish titles varied but two recurring themes did emerge: that a number of key questions remained to be answered by the Yes side and that the Better Together campaign needed to articulate a more convincing case for the union than it had offered so far.

The Scottish edition of *The Sun* took the same editorial line. The paper provided more extensive coverage than the *Record*'s, and gave space to both Salmond and Darling to argue their cases. The London edition of the paper, however, carried one report which was hostile to independence and no editorial. There was an interesting contrast in the two editions of the *Daily Express*. Coverage was light in the London edition compared to the Scottish one, but, while both ran hostile editorials, the London one expressed the hope that 'the campaign to keep the UK intact relies more on optimism and positivism about a common future than on creating a fear factor that suggests Scots could not hope to run their own affairs in a satisfactory manner'.

THE GREAT PRETENDER was the front page headline in the Scottish edition of the *Daily Mail* and the same page featured a cartoon of Alex Salmond in *Braveheart* outfit. The report beneath was unambiguous in its hostility to independence, a hostility replicated throughout the paper's coverage, although it would have been possible to discern what the basic ideas in the White Paper were. Both Darling and Nicola Sturgeon, then Deputy First Minister, were given columns to outline their positions. The rather long editorial was very critical of the 'menu without prices' and ended by describing the break-up of the UK as 'Scotland's nightmare – a desolate prospect that this dodgiest of dossiers fails to camouflage'. The London edition ran an equally hostile editorial and a two page report in similar vein.

The *Telegraph* was also hostile to the SNP's vision, and in its north of the border edition its Scottish editor, Alan Cochrane, one of the commentators most hostile to independence and the SNP, used his column to pour scorn on what he regarded as an empty document. The editorial carried by both editions asked why, when the ties with England would remain so close, there was any point in independence at all. However, the most striking piece in the *Telegraph*, carried by both editions, was written by the novelist and commentator Allan Massie. While critical of the SNP's refusal to acknowledge the difficulties it faced, he argued that for Better Together 'appeals to the head may not be enough'. Massie put the case for a quasi-federal future, an option not on offer in the referendum vote.

The Times in both its editions carried a cartoon showing Salmond as Mickey Mouse in front of a hillside with the inscription 'Holyrood'. The paper's leading article argued that the White Paper 'asks all the right questions but fails to give many satisfactory answers'. In the Scottish edition there was a column by Alex Massie (son of Allan) which was partially sympathetic to the independence movement, while in the London edition there was a piece by John McTernan, a Labour Party political adviser, which emphasised Scottish attachment to UK institutions.

Both of these broadsheets provided the basic facts, though in more extensive form in their Scottish editions. Of those without such editions, *The Guardian*'s coverage included a report, an editorial which referred to 'many unanswered questions' and a couple of columnists sympathetic to the Scottish desire for more autonomy. The *Financial Times* in its editorial said that 'while the *Financial Times* strongly favours the continuation of the union, we accept that there is an arguable – if flawed – case for independence'. The editorial went on to focus on the difficulties on the currency front. *The Independent*'s (not *The i*'s) approach – report, cartoon and editorial ('Salmond fishing') – was more hostile.

As can be seen from the foregoing, the themes which arose north and south of the border in editorials and commentary pieces were fairly similar.

Nonetheless, what is very striking is that no paper was offering support to the independence movement; individual columnists certainly did so in *The Herald* and *The Scotsman*, space was offered to Salmond and Sturgeon, but there was no support in editorial columns in the papers examined here. However, what was clear at that juncture was that the tone of editorials in a non-daily title, the *Sunday Herald*, was more sympathetic than what was found elsewhere, so it was not a total surprise when, as noted in the previous chapter, that paper later in the campaign became the sole paper to support the Yes side. It has to be acknowledged too that those on the Yes side who believed that the No camp, with the connivance of some media outlets, was running a 'Project Fear' could find evidence for that belief in some of the press coverage reviewed here.

There were many discussion programmes on radio and TV in the run-up to the vote but arguably the most important were two television debates between Darling and Salmond. The first of these took place on 5 August and lasted for two hours (less commercials). It was transmitted only north of the border though it was available online in the rest of the UK. The debate was moderated by STV's political editor and, rather surprisingly, the audience was allowed to cheer and boo the answers as the protagonists questioned each other and responded to questions from the floor. There had been low expectations for Darling's perfor-mance, but as he pushed Salmond repeatedly on what Plan B for the currency was, it became clear that he would not come out as badly as had been anticipated. Salmond for his part put Darling in a corner on the question of the promised new powers for the Scottish Parliament but the First Minister did not do nearly as well as expected. Newspaper headlines reflected that impression:

Darling draws first blood (*Herald*)
Salmond and Darling in head to head battle (*Scotsman*)
ALEX TAKES A POUNDING (*Record*)
Salmond fails to find an answer (*Telegraph*)
First round to Darling as Salmond comes unstuck (*Times*)
A BLOODY NOSE FOR SALMOND (*Mail*)

Only *The Sun* ran a rather different headline:

STALE MATES

And that paper suggested in an editorial that 'it was impossible to pick a winner. The first battle has ended in a draw – the contest is far from over.' By contrast the *Record*'s editorial focused on the currency issue and ended 'Alex Salmond, currency is your weakest link. If you do not come up with answers in the next six weeks, then it is goodbye.'

Alan Cochrane claimed in the *Telegraph* that 'the incredible vacuum at the heart of Alex Salmond's economic policy was laid bare in the most humiliat-ing fashion'. Although neither *The Herald* nor *The Scotsman* was taking a pro-independence editorial line, commentators in their pages did. So, in the latter, George Kerevan (later a successful SNP candidate in the Westminster 2015 election) continued to insist that what was on offer in the vote was 'the prospect of a structured, stable partnership of sovereign nations within the British Isles'. In *The Herald* Ian Bell (a longtime nationalist) chose to pour scorn on the unionist parties' promises of further powers for Holyrood: 'The idea is to render Scotland quiescent and preserve the essence of the present relationship with the UK.'

Overall the tone of reporting across the press veered from triumphalist to puzzled. The refusal of all of the UK political parties to enter into a currency deal seemed to have become the focal point of discussion. That was also reflected in subsequent broadcasting overage.

The second debate, on 25 August, was staged by the BBC and was transmitted throughout the UK. It lasted for an hour and half with no breaks for comments from journalists (which had been a feature of the previous encounter). As with the STV debate, it was moderated by a journalist who took questions and comment from a lively audience. The protagonists made opening and closing statements and cross-examined each other. The issues covered included the currency, social policy, oil reserves and possible new powers for Holyrood, a similar agenda to the STV one. The general impression was that Salmond had the edge, and this was reflected in newspaper headlines the next day:

Salmond strikes back (*Herald*)
Heat turned up in second TV debate (*Scotsman*)
SALMOND BOUNCES BACK (*Record*)
Sound and fury as Salmond fights back (*Telegraph*)
Salmond the bruiser rallies to dominate final TV debate (*Times*)
Not tonight, Darling (*Sun*)

Only the *Mail*'s headline struck a rather different note:

THE GREAT TV DEBATE TURN-OFF

The general view across the press was that Salmond had won the debate, although there was much emphasis on the amount of shouting at each other the protagonists indulged in, and much editorial comment to the effect that the Yes side had still not won the argument for independence. In its editorial the Scottish edition of the *Mail*, having criticised the BBC for putting together an audience which was in fact 'a partisan crowd', declared that 'The unedifying spectacle did little to advance either side's cause. Had it been conducted in a pub rather than Kelvingrove Art Gallery and Museum, the public would have lifted their drinks and moved back to let the bouncers move in.'

In *The Times* Alex Massie commented on Darling's performance: 'By the end of the evening, Mr Darling's repeated concentration on the risks of independence began to feel a little weary, a little frayed, a little stale'. *The Scotsman* employed the ubiquitous Strathclyde University psephologist John Curtice to comment on both debates; of the second he said that 'perhaps the most important theme of the evening was risk', risk attendant upon leaving and risk attendant on staying in the UK. He ended his piece thus: 'A much better night for Mr Salmond. But will it be enough to sway many voters?' The *Record*'s reporting concentrated on the 'noise' generated in the exchanges, and its editorial commented that 'The ugly tenor of the debate' could cause the Yes side serious problems. *The Sun*'s coverage, however, presented Salmond as the clear winner and the editorial declared 'Many of the don't knows watching at home and waiting to be convinced will have found his passion hard to resist and the Better Together's chief's dithering doom-mongering just as hard to admire'.

One important aspect of the campaign was that the two leading tabloids, the Scottish versions of *The Sun* and the *Daily Record*, both faced divided readerships, and may not have been at all sure how the majority of their readers would vote, so there was obviously a danger that too partisan an approach would alienate too many customers. One intriguing way in which the *Record* handled this situation was to hand over six pages in its editions of 4 and 5 September to each side, the Thursday pages supposedly being edited by Alistair Darling and the Friday ones by Alex Salmond. The Thursday edition carried pro-union pieces by Bob Geldof, Gordon Brown, Ed Miliband, J. K. Rowling and a Shetland JP, the Friday one articles by businessman Jim McColl, the actress Elaine C. Smith and a Glasgow-based paediatrician. It is doubtful whether many readers were converted by either side's arguments; what was important was that the paper was signalling that, although it was committed to the No camp, it acknowledged the strength of the arguments on the Yes side.

There is clearly a marked contrast overall with the way in which many papers offered the SNP support when it sought re-election to Holyrood in 2011. But support for the SNP running Scotland's domestic affairs, usually on the grounds that it had done a competent job as a minority government and deserved to be given another chance, has never led on to support for independence (though in April 2015 the Scottish edition of *The Sun* backed the SNP in the Westminster election while its London-based stablemate urged support for the Conservatives). The lack of press support was a serious problem for the Yes side. It had to hope that the more balanced broadcast coverage worked against this general hostility and the virulence of some of the papers opposed to independence. On the other hand, the public may have tired of the unpleasantness of some of the coverage, even in papers they regularly purchased, particularly as they contrasted it with the ways in which some of the more polished performers on the Yes side handled themselves in television discussions and debates. Could it even be the case that unremitting hostility was self-defeating, for after a time voters might have resented such coverage, particularly coverage by English newspapers in their Scottish editions, which might ultimately have seemed not just anti-SNP or anti-independence but anti-Scottish? And if that was in fact what happened, how many percentage points was it worth to the Yes side? A similar question might be asked about the 2015 general election campaign. When David Cameron argued that the choice facing Britain was a government led by him or a Labour government under a weak leader in hock to a large number of SNP MPs, did that approach, noisily amplified as it was by several newspapers, not only persuade wavering Labour voters in England to cast in their lot with the Conservatives but also lead to some Scottish voters defecting from their original parties of choice to the SNP?

Note

1. Hutchison, 'The media and the referendum: uncharted waters, perilous seas?'.

Bibliography

Hutchison, David, 'The media and the referendum: uncharted waters, perilous seas?', in Klaus Peter Müller (ed.), *Scotland 2014 and Beyond – Coming of Age and Loss of Innocence?* (Frankfurt am Main: Peter Lang, 2015), pp. 117–35.

4

Scotland's Changing 'Community of the Communicators': The Political Commentariat and the Independence Referendum

Gerry Hassan

Introduction

This chapter explores the characteristics, role and influence of the Scottish political commentariat. It develops previous research on this group into the terrain of the recent independence referendum debate.[1]

A central concept in this research is the term 'elite narratives', used to give sense to a privileged and influential small group of participants in public life and the collective set of perspectives they deploy about contemporary Scotland. Mackenzie's concept of 'the community of the communicators' is also utilised, to place and understand the role of the commentariat in public life, the critical issue of who speaks and has authority, and who does not, issues of differential access and the marked gaps, and spaces and silences within public discourses.[2]

The Making of the Commentariat

The concept of 'the commentariat' is of recent invention and importance. For example, it took Anthony Sampson, in his series *Anatomy of Britain*, the first of which was published in 1962, until the final update *Who Runs This Place?*, published in 2004, to use the term.[3] Sampson presents a world where politics and public life have been remade by the media, and compares 1962 Britain with the present:

> No sector increased its power in Britain more rapidly than the media. Editors, journalists and cameras penetrated nearly all institutions – including Parliament, the monarchy, the political parties and Whitehall – demanding answers to irrelevant questions, debunking their traditions and clamouring for openness. They were not separate limbs or membranes in the anatomy so much as part of the lifeblood, or nervous system.[4]

This edition has a section on the 'Commentariat',[5] with Sampson writing, 'Many are now more famous than politicians, taken more seriously, better paid and more in demand as dinner guests'. He continues, 'Many columnists are conscious of being intellectually superior to politicians with first-class degrees which in earlier times would have taken them into academia. They can be more candid than politicians bound by party discipline and discretion.'

Sampson identified the commentariat's characteristics: 'Its members come from a more limited background than politicians: most were educated at Oxbridge, live in Islington and Kensington, and frequently attend media-political parties where they meet other communicators within the Westminster bubble.' He noted that this had also become intergenerational and familial, through the establishment of 'media dynasties like the Dimblebys, Prestons, Toynbees and Johnstons, brought up with an instinctive feel for media politics'.

This particular view does not make a clear distinction between journalists and commentators. It emphasises that there is a privileged group of insiders who operate very close to those whose activities they also comment on and discuss. A few years after Sampson's observations, Julia Hobsbawm and John Lloyd offered eight criteria in answer to their own question, 'What do commentators do?':

- They entertain.
- They set agendas and erect signposts for other journalists.
- They say they tell the truth and alert the people to the lies and falsehoods told to them, above all by politicians.
- They do battle.
- They spot, or set, agendas.
- They form, or speak to, constituencies.
- They change their minds.
- They have the power to destroy ministerial and other public careers, or at least substantially affect reputations.[6]

This arguably overstates matters and contains an agenda, most obviously in the third point, 'They say they tell the truth . . .' John Lloyd arguably took the same position in *What the Media Are Doing to Our Politics*, where he wrote that 'British press and TV news are at least as cynical as their US equivalents. They trash politicians at least as much.'[7] He makes the charge of the media as 'an alternative establishment' explicit: 'The conflict between politics and the media is generally supposed, certainly by the media, to be unequal', and concludes that 'the battle is unequal the other way round. Politics and politicians depend on the media for access to people.'

There are numerous reasons for the emergence of the commentariat in the UK, the US and elsewhere.[8] First, it is part of the interface and blurring between fact and comment in the media. Second, there are more media spaces and outlets to fill with the pressures of 24/7 broadcasting. Third, in an age of complex, technical questions it is easier and cheaper to commission from a commentator than to support expensive investigative journalism. Fourth, there is the discon-nection of large parts of academia and intellectual life from politics and public life; this is seen in an advanced state in the US where academia has become increasingly one of orthodoxy in privileged universities, and insecurity with a commensurate anxiety about status and the role of dissent.[9] It should be noted, however, that the American political environment is very different from that of the UK and most of the Western world in having competing and partisan 'conservative' and 'liberal' commentariats, with each usually naming and challenging the other as the problem.[10]

Focusing on the UK situation, some assume that commentators are journalists; some are and some are not – the roles are different but overlap. The commentariat are typically freelance, hail from a range of backgrounds and work across a number of spheres, whereas most journalists are professionally trained and tend to work for a media organisation that offers them some (although arguably less than previously) rights, security and resources. Most members of the commentariat are not experts, although a few, Polly Toynbee for one or in a different way, Peter Oborne, are exceptions, the first having a track record in social justice and the second in understanding the political classes. Frank Furedi has written of 'The devaluation of the status of the intellectual and the authority of knowledge'[11] that has contributed to the rise of this new class of generalist opinion formers.

The Scottish Political Commentariat

The Scottish political commentariat has never really been fully defined as Sampson mapped out, in terms of where it stays, its beliefs and inter-relationships. A rare example was the *Sunday Herald*'s 'Power Map' on political and media con-nections published in 1999,[12] which highlighted the close relationship between the media and Scottish Labour at that time.

For the purposes of this research, three broad criteria were employed to select, and then interview, members of the Scottish commentariat – they wrote a print column or blog or had a public profile; their views were cited or referenced by others as of some significance, and they were perceived by others as influential or contributing towards the shaping of public debate.

The Composition of the Scottish Political Commentariat

Fifty members of the commentariat were interviewed between November 2011 and March 2012, including nearly all of the media players who could be seen as significant public figures in debates in Scotland over the last twenty years.[13] Their average age was 52.8 years at the time; 41 were male (82 per cent) and 9 female (18 per cent); in ethnicity all of them were white; and in terms of their media or institution setting 33 were from the mainstream media (66 per cent), 6 were policy entrepreneurs (12 per cent), 4 were bloggers (8 per cent), 4 were academics (8 per cent), and 3 worked for a think tank (6 per cent); 29.5 (59 per cent) were organisation-based, 18.5 (39 per cent) were independent and 2 (4 per cent) were retired; 46 (92 per cent) of them were on the record and 4 (8 per cent) off the record.

As far as Sampson's point about dynasties is concerned, the Scottish commentariat are inter-connected and interwoven through personal and professional relationships and connections. There were two married couples and one formerly married couple, and a large group connected through media and public institutions since the 1970s and 1980s, many having known each other professionally and personally for over 30 years. This powerful ethos of belonging and inclusion, whilst supportive and affirming, can result in a gate-keeping culture where people promote and look out for one another, and can lead to the creation and sustenance of closed conversations which exclude new voices.

An Outline of the Commentariat and the Role of Collective Memories

Exits and entrances

Considering the range of this group, how they became commentators is unsurprisingly varied. One critical issue about becoming a commentator is that of entrances and exits. People have to be able to solicit or manufacture entrances or exits to allow for change and churn – and this can happen by a variety of methods. George Kerevan suggested that 'commentators like me ... didn't really exist before, I don't think, before the '60s' (interview). He also took the view that people entered through accident and chance: 'I think how people become a columnist in Scotland is a bit serendipitous but maybe a bit, and I say there is a bit, of cronyism, I mean it is quite often who people know' (interview).

Lorraine Davidson, who used to write for *The Times*, observed that a certain group grew up politically engaged: 'I mean there is probably something about our generation that we are very vocal because we grew up where it was the norm, where it was expected that you would go out and you would take a stand on things' (interview). She suggested that this has resulted in an absence of younger people in their twenties and thirties having a public media voice, 'I am not sure that people twenty years younger than us, they haven't sort of lived through these sort of big changes, they are probably more polite in how they have debates' (interview).

Remembering the near past

This brings us to the defining experiences of the Scottish commentariat – the decade of Thatcher and Thatcherism in the 1980s. Concepts of 'collective memories'[14] and Andrew O'Hagan's 'civic memory'[15] are relevant in understanding how part of Scotland, and in particular the political commentariat, understood the 1980s and their role in wider public perception of this period.

It can also be located in a longer perspective of, in William McIlvanney's words, a 'pop-up picture school of history' in which Scots 'see our past in a series of gestures rather than a sequence of actions' and as 'wilful fragments'.[16] This remaking of recent history contributed to the dominant version of the 1980s evoking a host of characteristics and key events. These include the imposition of Thatcherism on an unwilling Scotland, the closing down of traditional industries, the totems of the poll tax and the Scots as 'guinea pigs' and the closing of the Ravenscraig steel works (even though this actually occurred under John Major's government).

Thatcherism as Scotland's 'other'

William McIlvanney gave voice to this during the 1980s in an influential address entitled 'Stands Scotland Where It Did?', when he said about Margaret Thatcher, 'if we allow her to continue, she will remove from the word "Scottish" any meaning other than geographical'.[17] One senior BBC journalist reflecting on this commented:

> Obviously you get even the title of that 'Stands Scotland Where It Did?' and just kind of rhetorical pomposity, a big macho 'Stands Scotland Where It Did?' The language is very revealing and extreme, and Jimmy Reid was very guilty of this as well. (interview)

Neal Ascherson, talking of Scottish Labour MPs in the 1980s, stated that 'They had to watch in impotence as Mrs. Thatcher demolished Scotland's steel, engineering and mining industries, decreed the sale of council housing . . . and used Scotland as testing ground for the disastrous poll tax'.[18] Neil Oliver, in the BBC TV series *A History of Scotland*, described this world in retrospect: 'Moribund dinosaurs like shipbuilding, coalmining and steel, living on state finance, starved to death in no time. Even now, a generation of Scots talks bitterly about 'what Margaret Thatcher did to Scotland'.[19]

The Scottish commentariat version of Thatcherism and the 1980s has become part of 'the official story' of Scotland, of 'Thatcherism in a cold climate'.[20] One source said that the Scotland of the present was a land shaped by 'William McIlvanney's 1980s account of Scotland', suggesting that this may pose a problem now because it was a story 'of simplicity, good and evil, heroes and villains' (background interview). Lorraine Davidson reflected that opposing Thatcherism was about something existential:

> It wasn't just about jobs to people it was about communities . . . it was the soul of Scotland and she was just ripping it apart . . . It motivated you in a way that I am not sure that young people now have that kind of motivational sort of hate figure. (interview)

Scotland as a political community

A central part of the more recent story is an account of Scotland as a centre-left political community, of social democratic and even socialist values. Pivotal to this is the role of the commentariat and whether they followed or influenced a centre-left account of Scotland that came more to the fore in the 1980s and onward. Were they following voters and the wider environment, or did interventions of the commentariat shape and legitimise the story of a centre-left Scotland? This is about the interaction between popular narratives and the notion of 'elite narratives'.

There is also the related dimension of how the commentariat frame and understand public life, the wider polity and power, and whether they have a multidimensional understanding of these factors. Do they have a curiosity and scrutiny which pushes behind the public facade and 'official story', or do they support and sustain the 'official story?' It is of interest to discover if they wish to find out and challenge convention and comforting stories, or if there are elements of collective orthodoxy and groupthink. The commentariat may also be part of what some call the incestuousness of Scottish public life – the blurred boundaries and potential conflicts of interests that call to mind Sampson's point referenced earlier. These aspects are not unique to Scotland, or even small countries: 'the Westminster village' displays some of the very same characteristics.[21]

A few of those interviewed commented, sometimes negatively, on others whom they viewed as being part of the commentariat. One subject opined that one of the problems with Scotland was the view articulated by another named member of the commentariat; another that there was predictability with the dominance of some who promoted 'the same views for what seems like an eternity' (interview). Another put the view that one named journalist 'had written the same column for the last 20 years' (interview).

One interviewee talked of the ease with which once someone gains status as an active member of the Scottish commentariat, it is then possible to remain in position and to rely on established contacts: 'there is maybe a laziness about our journalism that you go to the usual suspects because there is something comfortable about, you know, the debate' (interview). She viewed this as narrowly focused, commenting that in relation to public debate in Scotland, 'it is the usual suspects, you kind of know who is popping up next, you know where they are coming from, you know their whole history, so I think and I wonder, it's bloody incestuous isn't it?' (interview). She felt that the result was the development of an insider group's shared sense of identity, a collective memory and history, which is also excluding and can lead to a tendency to look backwards, reminiscing, for example, about 'the STUC conference in 1984' and about what a public figure did in the past along the lines of '"Oh, do you remember when Campbell Christie did this or that?"' (interview).

The 'settled will' of the commentariat

Another interviewee observed a remarkable constancy in part of the commentariat class, saying that 'if you look at people who were around writing columns 30 years ago, they are not all still around obviously – but a good number of people, you know. Ian Bell is still around, Allan Massie is still around . . . [Iain] Macwhirter has been around for a long time now. Joyce

McMillan has been around for longer than she would care to acknowledge perhaps. Ruth Wishart . . .'

This leads to the question of whether the commentariat have influence and how that influence is gauged. They do not have direct power in terms of ownership and economic control, but power in Steven Lukes' sense of how decision making is framed, across more than one dimension.[22] Quoted in the Hobsbawm and Lloyd publication on the commentariat, Peter Oborne was dismissive of the concept that he had power:

> I don't agree with the premise that the commentariat is powerful. I broadly think it is hard to see examples of it having any effect at all. I only have in mind the readers. I don't have any power at all.[23]

Similarly, in the same volume the business journalist Anthony Hilton downplayed his role, claiming that 'I never feel powerful. I am writing for my mother'.[24] The Oborne disclaimer superficially undermines his own thesis of the rise of 'the political classes', of which the commentariat is a key part,[25] and it may be that his personal disclaimer is an attempt to retain the perceived integrity of an outsider whilst enjoying the status of being an insider.

The Commentariat and the Independence Debate

The independence debate has to be contextualised in the evolution of Scotland's recent history, and the ways in which Thatcherism, Blair and New Labour, and a distinct 'narrative of difference' have been increasingly articulated in politics and media.[26] The commentariat interviews were undertaken when the independence debate, post-2011, was beginning to take shape; the UK and Scottish governments were in negotiations, prior to the Edinburgh Agreement between the two which set out the framework for the referendum.

The interviews demonstrated the predominance of the idea of Scotland as being anti-Tory, centre-left and imbued with progressive values. Many in the commentariat emphasised the narrative of difference – of seeing England as 'other' and overwhelmingly Tory (with the acknowledgement of the existence of significant Labour regions, such as the north-west and east, for example). Along with that was the truncated, selective account of Scotland post-1979 – Thatcher and Blair, and the potent feeling that British politics was inexorably moving to the right, and in parallel with that the articulation of a Scottish national dimension which has become associated with commitment to social democratic politics.

The independence debate has illustrated the boundaries and qualities of Scotland as a political community and the exit and entrance points of permissible debate within the commentariat. Numerous examples illustrate this. Take the then Scottish Labour leader Johann Lamont's 'something for nothing' speech of September 2012, where she openly questioned the sustainability of Scotland's universal public policies such as free university tuition fees and free care for the elderly (*STV News*, 25 September 2012). This brought forth criticism from a wide spectrum of the commentariat, with several comparing Lamont to Thatcher and New Labour.

Iain Macwhirter commented that Lamont's intervention was like 'Nick Clegg without the apology' and 'the second longest suicide note in history', after Labour's disastrous 1983 election manifesto (*Herald*, 27 September 2012). Ian Bell called it 'the triumph of Blairism in a party that no longer seems sure what it means by a welfare state'; he went on to write that 'The principle of universality is a bastion. Once it is breached, everything is up for grabs' (*Sunday Herald*, 30 September 2012). Joyce McMillan stated that Lamont's 'fatal slip' left Salmond as 'one of the few Western leaders of our time with the courage and gaiety to buck the trend and to dare to offer a politics of hope rather than fear, meanmindedness and decline' (*Scotsman*, 28 September 2012).

This debate illustrated powerfully the boundaries and totems of a large part of Scotland's political community, of the use of Thatcher and Blair and the narratives of their politics to create demarcation lines of what is possible and not possible to discuss in public. Lamont's 'something for nothing' speech may or not have been ill-considered, with little strategic preparation, and may have been careless in its language, but it ventured into terrain which deserved more than being characterised and dismissed in the terms just quoted.

The independence debate has to be understood in this context. So high profile interventions late in the campaign included historian Tom Devine talking of independence as a way of maintaining Scotland's 'social democratic agenda' and saying that 'It is the Scots who have succeeded most in preserving the British idea of fairness and compassion in terms of state support and intervention' (*Observer*, 17 August 2014). The day after the referendum Devine gave a classic example of 'othering' Britain, describing it as 'a failed state' (*Newsnight*, 19 September 2014).

Macwhirter, similarly, offered a reading of the last 40 years of Scottish politics as Scots rejecting 'the SNP's crass materialistic "It's Scotland's Oil" campaign in the 1970s, just as they later rejected "loadsamoney" Thatcherism in the 1980s'. He further described the mood of the Scottish electorate over this period as rejecting 'self-interest', 'communitarian' and embracing the values of 'New Testament morality' (*Sunday Herald*, 31 August 2014).

This is typical of the tone and language of a significant part of the independence debate: one which characterises Scotland not just as a political community, but one with a distinct moral and ethical framework which draws from a deep religious strand of memory and tradition, sometimes implicitly and sometimes explicitly.

The construction of this dominant elite narrative has of course to acknowledge the existence of counter-narratives, particularly from pro-unionist and centre-right perspectives. These encompass many high profile commentators such as Alex Massie and Alan Cochrane, but they have to be situated and understood in the context of Scottish politics as a counter-narrative and an insider–outsider perspective. Positioning oneself on the centre-right automatically leads to a perspective outside of Scotland's 'community of the communicators', and outside the anti-Tory story of Scotland post-1979 which has influenced the independence debate.

One commentator said after the vote: 'Scotland has bought into the great anti-Tory story. And now there is another compelling one: "We are all Nationalists and Scotland is different". It is hard to argue with such certainty as Labour have found post-referendum' (interview). A pro-union voice reflected on their sense of isolation stating that 'there are only three fully paid-up members of pro-unionist opinion in the press: Alex Massie, Alan Cochrane and Chris Deerin' (interview).

It should be emphasised that the independence debate has not seen the degree of popular and elite narrative consensus which characterised, for example, the devolution proposals and referendum of 1997. In fact, part of the debate can be seen as exposing the division within elite narratives, and yet at the same time, there has been a slow shift of a significant part of the commentariat over to a pro-independence position, Macwhirter, Lesley Riddoch, Ruth Wishart and Ian Bell, being the most obvious examples.

An important part of this shift involves presenting independence as a politics of continuation, of a defence of traditional Scottish values which are under threat from the rightward drift of British politics, and the need to take a stand against that drift via independence. In many cases, this involves an explicit referencing of the 'golden era' of the British welfare state: seen in Tom Devine's public rationale for voting Yes, or Joyce McMillan's rejection of No before embracing Yes.

What does all of this mean for independence and the political commentariat's interpretation of it? First, Scotland is already significantly autonomous. That is a statement of the obvious, but this autonomy has led to a kind of quasi-independence in how Scotland talks, thinks and interprets itself at least at the level of the commentariat and part of its political discourse: I have called this 'an independence of the Scottish mind'.[27] This is, of course, a heavily qualified, conditional and contested form of independence and self-government, but the trend and direction seems very clear despite the presence of articulate counter-narratives.

Second, there is an element of self-referencing in a collective reinforcement loop. Scotland's 'community of the communicators', to use Mackenzie's phrase, are a small, select group who know each other and have experienced many of the events of the last few decades via shared, reinforced and collective moments. There is thus a sense of a common lineage of key dates, watersheds and personnel, and how these are referenced and interpreted. There is to an extent a missing ingredient of self-criticism and objectivity to question and critique.

Third, the Scottish construction of autonomy has involved little curiosity about other nations' experiences in recent years, pre- or post-crash. In my interviews, undertaken post-crash, as the independence debate was getting underway, references were nearly all Scottish. What was conspicuously missing was Westminster, the crises of the British political classes, Europe, or a wider connection to debates around contemporary capitalism.

Fourth, there is the issue – drawing from Mackenzie's 'community of the communicators' – of noting who are being privileged and gaining authority and permission to speak, and have voice. Scotland's political commentariat, for all its progressive credentials and aspirations, is a very select and partial representation of society: one heavily gendered, generationally skewed, and geographically concentrated in a Glasgow–Edinburgh cluster. Gaps, spaces and silences in public life can be clearly noted regarding who is not invited to speak and who is systematically excluded.

The narrow bandwidth of public conversations, authority and expertise utilised in programmes such as *Newsnight Scotland*, *Scotland Tonight* and *Scotland 2014* underwent an element of change in the independence referendum, but still reflected a very partial Scotland. Thus, the ubiquity of male-only panels (*Newsnight Scotland* twice running eight men-only discussions), or *Scotland Tonight* having four men talk about 'the missing Scotland' – a subject heavily gendered but which four middle-aged, middle-class men were deemed fit to comment upon. The Scotland presented on these platforms is one that is still, for all the change produced during the referendum, defined by three Gs: gendered (predominantly male), generational (skewed towards those of middle and older age), and geographic (drawing from a narrow stratum of the Central Belt).

The Future of the Commentariat

The independence debate happened at a time of transition and change: for politics, society and media. It could be that the referendum will be seen as the last hurrah of the political commentariat as we have known it. There has been a significant amount of change and churn in the political activism of Scotland in the independence debate with new voices, agencies and self-organising groups being formed and achieving impact and status.

The impact of social media in a wider political sense has yet to be fully analysed, but on a range of criteria their reach can be gauged: the number of unique visits and traffic to sites, the use of crowdfunding models, and increasing reference and appearances in mainstream media. All of this is occurring as traditional newspaper circulations are in decline, and the BBC and STV have faced repeated accusations of reporting the referendum either in a way which is biased, or more credibly, without much courage or imagination.

Underneath the relationship between supposed old and new media there is a deeper set of relationships. One traditional media retort in the campaign has been to ask, 'Is the influence of social media a positive in this campaign?' – a question that can be seen as attempting to undermine and challenge their emerging role. At the same time, a frequent response of social media participants is to dismiss traditional media, as (this from pro-independence supporters) part of a 'unionist conspiracy', with phrases such as 'BBC bias' thrown about as if a given. The dynamics between these two discourses is about who can best lay claim to legitimacy and to question the legitimacy of the other, and about voice, audience and reproduction.

What the independence debate has demonstrated is a political culture in significant transition, along with the public sphere, institutions and civic culture, and within that the role of the media and commentariat. The commentariat sit at an intersection of soft power, status and authority, mixing the roles of generalist, occasional expert, insider, interpreter and navigator of political information and analysis: characteristics and qualities now in significant flux. The future place, influence and make-up of Scotland's political commentariat will depend on the different contestations of the referendum result, Scottish and UK politics post the 2015 UK general election and post the 2016 Scottish parliamentary election, along with trends in the global, UK and Scottish economies, wider politics, and media developments.

One future set of trends poses a more disputatious, diverse and fragmented public sphere, and sees this as an opening from the previous age of gatekeepers and highly managed exits and entrances. But many other possible futures can be sketched out, including ones where new forces of authority and expertise seek to control and manipulate knowledge and information in an age of new political, media and capitalist elites.

It is beyond this chapter to offer an informed judgement on such future trends. But the future of Scottish commentary can be said to be one where Scottish autonomy and a qualified independence will be central, where a language of difference and distinctiveness remains, and where the issue of how to implement and understand centre-left ideas and values will be a cornerstone of any foreseeable near future.

Note

1. Hassan *Independence of the Scottish Mind*; Hassan, 'The Scottish political commentariat, the independence referendum and elite narratives'.
2. Mackenzie, *Political Identity*.
3. Sampson, *Who Runs This Place?*
4. Ibid., p. 207.
5. Ibid., pp. 234–6.
6. Hobsbawm and Lloyd, *The Power of the Commentariat*, pp. 18–26.
7. Lloyd, *What the Media Are Doing to Our Politics*, p. 101)
8. See Gouldner, *The Future of Intellectuals and the Rise of the New Class*.
9. Jacoby, *The End of Utopia*; Hedges, *Death of the Liberal Class*.
10. Goldberg, *Liberal Fascism*.
11. Furedi, *Where Have all the Intellectuals Gone?*, p. 72.
12. Fraser, 'Politics gets personal'.
13. The main body of interviews with the fifty members of the political commentariat were conducted between November 2011 and March 2012; a follow-up sample, numbering eight, were interviewed January to February 2014, and a third

smaller group of four were interviewed post-referendum in September to October 2014.

14. Zerubavel, 'Social memories: steps in a sociology of the past'.
15. O'Hagan's, 'Civic memory: making Scotlands of the minds'.
16. McIlvanney, 'Freeing ourselves from inner exile'.
17. McIlvanney, 'Stands Scotland where it did?', p. 246.
18. Ascherson, *Stone Voices*, p. 107.
19. Oliver, *A History of Scotland*, p. 364.
20. McCrone, 'Thatcherism in a cold climate'.
21. Oborne, *The Triumph of the Political Classes*.
22. Lukes, *Power: A Radical View*.
23. Hobsbawm and Lloyd, *The Power of the Commentariat*, p. 9.
24. Ibid., p. 19.
25. Oborne, *The Triumph of the Political Classes*.
26. Hassan, *Caledonian Dreaming*.
27. Hassan, *Independence of the Scottish Mind*.

Bibliography

Ascherson, N., *Stone Voices: The Search for Scotland* (London: Granta Books, 2002).

Fraser, D., 'Politics gets personal', *Sunday Herald*, 27 February 2000.

Furedi, F., *Where Have all the Intellectuals Gone? Confronting 21st Century Philistinism* (London: Continuum, 2004).

Goldberg, J., *Liberal Fascism: The Secret History of the American Left: From Mussolini to the Politics of Meaning* (New York: Broadway Books, 2009).

Gouldner, A.W., *The Future of Intellectuals and the Rise of the New Class* (New York: Seabury Press, 1979).

Hassan, G., *Caledonian Dreaming: The Quest for a Different Scotland* (Edinburgh: Luath Press, 2014).

Hassan, G., *Independence of the Scottish Mind: Elite Narratives, Public Spaces and the Making of a Modern Nation* (London: Palgrave Macmillan, 2014).

Hassan, G., 'The Scottish political commentariat, the independence referendum and elite narratives', paper to ECPR Annual Conference, Glasgow University, September 2014.

Hedges, C., *Death of the Liberal Class* (New York: Nation Books, 2010).

Hobsbawm, J. and J. Lloyd, *The Power of the Commentariat* (London: Editorial Intelligence, 2008).

Jacoby, R., *The End of Utopia: Politics and Culture in an Age of Apathy* (New York: Basic Books, 1999).

Lloyd, J., *What the Media Are Doing to Our Politics* (London: Constable, 2004).

Lukes, S., *Power: A Radical View*, 2nd edn (Basingstoke: Palgrave Macmillan, 2005).

McCrone, D., 'Thatcherism in a cold climate', *Radical Scotland*, June/July 1989, 7–11.

McIlvanney, W., 'Stands Scotland where it did?' in *Surviving the Shipwreck* (Edinburgh: Mainstream, 1992), pp. 241–53.

McIlvanney, W., 'Freeing ourselves from inner exile', *The Herald*, 6 March 1999.

Mackenzie, W. J. M., *Political Identity* (Harmondsworth: Penguin, 1978).

Oborne, P., *The Triumph of the Political Classes* (London: Simon and Schuster, 2007).

O'Hagan, A., 'Civic memory: making Scotlands of the minds', National Theatre of Scotland lecture, 21 August 2011, <http://nationaltheatrescotland.wordpress.com/2011/08/24/andrew-ohagan-civic-memory/> (last accessed 31 August 2014).

Oliver, N., *A History of Scotland* (London: Weidenfeld and Nicolson, 2009).

Sampson, A. (2004), *Who Runs This Place? The Anatomy of Britain in the 21st Century* (London: John Murray, 2004).

Zerubavel, E., 'Social memories: steps in a sociology of the past', *Qualitative Sociology*, 19(3) (1996), pp. 283–99.

5

The Scottish Press Account: Narratives of the Independence Referendum and its Aftermath

Marina Dekavalla

The 2014 independence referendum was a major topic in the Scottish press for over two years. From the SNP's majority win at the 2011 Scottish election, which put it in a position to realise its longstanding policy of holding a referendum on independence, to the Edinburgh Agreement in October 2012, which gave the Scottish Parliament the power to hold the referendum, and the long campaign that led to 18 September 2014, all stages of the trajectory received considerable coverage in Scottish newspapers.

Even if they no longer enjoy the large readerships they previously commanded and many of them are struggling to remain profitable in a highly competitive market, Scottish newspapers have traditionally held an important position in the public sphere.[1] There has always been a close relationship between the Scottish press and national identity,[2] especially as Scottish affairs do not usually receive the same amount of attention in the UK-wide media.[3] In the 1997 devolution referendum, voters surveyed said that they had paid considerable attention to the media during the campaign, and particularly read indigenous Scottish newspapers.[4]

Scottish papers still see themselves as sharing a special relationship with their readerships by being close to the issues that matter to them.[5] They also believe they are influential in Scottish politics and policymaking and saw the 2014 referendum as an opportunity to reaffirm their position in the national debate.[6]

This chapter focuses particularly on editorial coverage, which expresses the official views of the newspapers, during the week before the referendum and the week after it. The days before the vote are important because coverage can still inform political decision making when the referendum is most topical, and this is also when newspapers declare their position on the vote. The days following the referendum are significant in demonstrating how newspapers responded to the outcome and how they see future developments.

A prominent issue in the political agenda in the final week of the campaign was the Better Together party leaders' 'vow' promising increased devolved powers for Scotland in the case of a No vote. The increased devolution option was not officially on the ballot paper but had been previously discussed by the leaders of all three main UK parties during the campaign. It was then re-affirmed a few days before the vote in a joint commitment signed by their leaders and published on 16 September in the *Daily Record*. As will be seen, this move was discussed across the press that week. The week after the referendum saw the resignation of Alex Salmond, the Scottish First Minister, and an ongoing debate on the way forward after voters decided that Scotland should stay in the UK.

The Analysis

The study analyses the discourse of the editorials in five daily morning and five Sunday titles. *The Scotsman* and *Scotland on Sunday*, *The Herald* and *Sunday Herald*, the *Daily Record* and the *Sunday Mail* are all indigenous titles produced and read primarily in Scotland. The *Daily Record* and its stablemate the *Sunday Mail* are popular papers, while the others are quality titles. The *Scottish Sun* and *Scottish Sun on Sunday*, the *Scottish Daily Mail* and *Scottish Mail on Sunday* are the Scottish editions of London papers with the highest circulations in Scotland according to ABC figures.[7] Although they are right-of-centre, the *Mail* is a consistent supporter of the Conservative Party while the *Scottish Sun* has supported a range of parties including the Conservatives, Labour, and the Scottish National Party (SNP).[8]

The analysis includes all the editorials about the referendum published in the two weeks before and after the vote: thirty-nine in the week before and twenty-six in the week following the day of the vote. All the editorials from each title were read in sequence in order to explore the way each newspaper constructed the narrative of the referendum. Although editorials are opinion pieces expressing the official view of the newspaper, they still provide accounts of events in this process. Like news, they construct narratives, or 'stories about reality'.[9] In order to deconstruct these narratives, Greimas's theory of semiotic analysis was used.

Greimas's narrative semiotics is a structuralist approach developed in the 1960s. Structuralism studies 'systems, relations and forms – the structures – that make meaning possible in any cultural activity or artefact'.[10] Adapted from Propp's analysis of Russian folk tales, Greimas's theory was also originally used to describe the structure of different types of narrative.[11]

In the following decades, Greimas and his colleagues developed their approach to study any type of discourse and established 'a theory (and a methodology) that, within the limits of its own principles of relevance, would be able to account for the widest range of the forms in which society produces meaning'.[12] Like much of structuralism, the point of applying Greimas's framework to texts is to reveal new ways of looking at how they function and to highlight how their ideological position is reflected in structure – this is the purpose of the analysis here.

The Quest for Change

Although Greimas's framework has many components, perhaps the best-known is the actantial model. This describes the roles of different characters in a text. The key actants in any narrative are the subject and the object and they are linked by 'an axis of desire':[13] the subject wants to have the object and its quest to get it is the narrative's 'programme of acquisition'.[14]

All the Scottish indigenous papers apart from the *Sunday Herald* provided a very similar narrative of the referendum in their editorials both before and after the vote. In this, the subject or main character is Scots/Scotland, often referred to in the editorials as 'we'. The object that this subject desires is change, which translates into increased powers for the Scottish Parliament or a better country:

> 1. The three leaders – one of whom will be PM after the general election in May – have recognised that Scotland wants change . . . And we support this guarantee of change because we believe most Scots want more powers for Holyrood. (*Daily Record*, 16 September 2014)[15]

In this excerpt discussing the 'vow' published on its front page, the *Daily Record* presents it as a fact that Scotland 'wants change' – this statement is not questioned. The UK party leaders did not propose the change; they merely recognised the will of the people. The second sentence then specifies what kind of change is being described. For the *Record* increased devolution is the object of Scots' desire.

Similarly in *The Herald*, Scots are presented as 'wanting change' – this desire permeates the whole nation, not just Yes voters:

> 2. But the supporters of independence do not hold the monopoly on caring passionately about Scotland and wanting change to help bring about a more just, equal and prosperous society. (*Herald*, 16 September 2014)[16]

Change for *The Herald* is defined as a 'better, stronger and fairer' country and a 'more just, equal and prosperous society'. The same definition of change is adopted by *Scotland on Sunday*:

> 3. New powers on offer will give Holyrood the toolkit to build the country we all want to live in . . . A better Scotland is within our grasp. A more confident, assured and can-do Scotland. An optimum Scotland. (*Scotland on Sunday*, 14 September 2014)[17]

Here all Scots are said to want to live in a changed country, which is 'better', 'more confident, assured and can-do'. New powers for Holyrood are not the ultimate goal of Scots' quest though. In Greimas's framework, the subject often needs to fulfil certain requirements before it can perform a quest: it may need to acquire knowledge (knowing) and/or power (being able). Knowledge and power are preliminary or 'modal' objects: they are acquired through preliminary tests, before the subject is ready to embark on its main quest, and these tests may be successful or unsuccessful.[18]

In excerpt 3, new powers for Holyrood are such a modal object (Greimas's 'being-able-to'), whose achievement will allow ('give the toolkit' for) the main quest to take place. According to this narrative, increased devolution is one way of achieving competence for the main quest. The other way (the second alternative modal object) is independence:

> 4. That change may be through independence or through the guarantee of new powers for the Scottish Parliament. (*Daily Record*, 18 September 2014)[19]

The vote was therefore presented as a choice between independence and increased devolution, both being alternative roads to achieving competence for pursuing change. Although the option of increased devolution was not on the ballot paper, newspapers which adopted this narrative identified a No to independence with increased devolution and presented this as their preferred option on the days leading up to the vote. They gave a range of justifications for this preference:

> 5. Instead of facing the future as a country split right down the middle, 50–50, we can move forward with an overwhelming majority getting behind the creation of a powerhouse parliament at Holyrood. We can face the future united, not divided. (*Scotland on Sunday*, 14 September 2014)[20]
>
> 6. The hard truth is that independence carries considerable risks with the promise of uncertain benefits. Instead of taking such a gamble with Scotland's wellbeing, our nation has the chance to seek transformative change by pursuing greater autonomy within the UK. (*Herald*, 16 September 2014)[21]
>
> 7. In the past week, the Scottish financial sector has spelled out the adverse consequences of independence for our banks and insurance companies. Other business leaders also warned of increased costs. It is clear that the risks are real and the costs unknown . . . The [promised] powers will not be as complete as some would wish. But, with a No vote, Scots will undoubtedly have more power over their own affairs. (*Scotsman*, 18 September 2014)[22]
>
> 8. Yes, Scotland can have more control over its future. And it can do so without breaking the ties that bind us to the people of England, Wales and Northern Ireland. (*Daily Record*, 18 September 2014)[23]

At this stage in the narrative, Scotland, the main character, has to choose between two modal objects that could potentially make it competent to pursue the change it desires. The first, independence, is 'risky': it is a 'gamble' in excerpt 6, it is likely to have 'adverse consequences' and 'unknown costs' in excerpt 7, it will cause division among Scots in excerpt 5, and it will break Scotland's bond with the rest of the UK in excerpt 8. Increased autonomy, through a No vote, will unite people towards the same goal (excerpt 5) and will 'undoubtedly' give Scots more power/control over their own affairs/future (excerpts 7 and 8).

In addition to these advantages, there are powerful helpers to assist if Scotland chooses to pursue the modal object of increased devolution. In Greimas's model,[24] the acting subject may have helpers in its quest for the object (whose actions assist the quest) or opponents (who obstruct the quest). In this case, the three main UK party leaders have already committed to help; and after a No vote, the SNP would also join the cause. This is stressed in the weeks both before and after the referendum:

9. In the event of a No vote, the three main pro-UK parties will bear a heavy responsibility: to meet the great expectations of millions of Scottish voters of gaining extensive further devolution. (*Herald*, 19 September 2014)[25]

10. One of the SNP's great contributions to Scotland's story has been as 'The Power For Change' – Nationalists can reclaim this role after a No vote, in the Scottish national interest. (*Scotland on Sunday*, 14 September 2014)[26]

11. There is little doubt the SNP, while reaffirming their belief that, in the words of Alex Salmond, 'the dream will never die', will nevertheless park the independence issue for the foreseeable future. They will instead direct their political energies to fighting for greater home rule for Holyrood, within the confines of the UK. (*Scotland on Sunday*, 21 September 2014)[27]

12. All the UK parties have pledged extensive new powers for the Scottish Parliament. Sturgeon has promised to work with them to get that done. That is the right thing to do because she must govern for all of Scotland, not just the 45 per cent who voted for independence. (*Daily Record*, 25 September 2014)[28]

Although the SNP campaigned for independence, it is not seen as an opponent of further devolution according to this narrative. It is rather assumed that it will work with the main UK parties, even before anyone in the party suggested this might be their plan (excerpts 10 and 11). *The Herald*, on the other hand, agrees that the SNP will be a helper in achieving more powers, not necessarily by collaborating with the other parties but by putting pressure on them through continuing to pursue independence:

13. The SNP has made it abundantly clear that it intends not to let its hopes of independence die even for a weekend. That should set alarms bells ringing once again in Downing Street. (*Herald*, 22 September 2014)[29]

In any case, the opponent to achieving this modal object is not the SNP. This role is taken by the main UK parties in the week after the vote. The *Sunday Mail* expresses concern about whether the UK parties will keep their promise to help as early as the Sunday after the vote:

14. Scotland has spoken, but if our faith is broken, if their [UK party leaders'] word is worthless, they can be assured that we'll speak again. (*Sunday Mail*, 21 September 2014)[30]

However, the *Sunday Mail* and its sister paper, the *Daily Record*, both traditional supporters of the Labour Party, avoid placing any doubt on Labour's commitment to help. Instead the *Record* suggests that David Cameron is more likely to backtrack from the joint vow:

15. For Cameron to reverse out of such a public pledge would leave him despised, loathed and mistrusted across the UK, not just in Scotland. (*Daily Record*, 22 September 2014)[31]

Labour leader Ed Miliband continues to be a helper in the editorials of the *Record* throughout the week following the referendum:

16. And he [Miliband] is under the spotlight like never before as he pushes to make good on his vow to hand more powers to Holyrood. But actions like this show he is a man of substance where it matters. (*Daily Record*, 23 September 2014)[32]

For the *Scotsman* and *Herald*, though, the opponent to achieving the modal object of further devolution is the disagreement between and within the main parties. Ed Miliband is presented as obstructing rather than promoting the cause, due to considerations about the electability of his party:

17. But already there are divisions that cast serious doubt, not only on how quickly this pledge can be honoured but whether the party leaders can secure the support of their backbenchers for such legislation . . . Mr Cameron wants changes to move in parallel with plans to make sure only English MPs can vote on English laws – a major constitutional change for the UK. Mr Miliband, fearing that this could neuter the power of any future Labour administration, wants a slower process with further debate. (*Scotsman*, 22 September 2014)[33]

18. All three have brought forward proposals, but Labour's in particular are simply not ambitious enough. If the defenders of the Union fail to meet voters' demands, they will face their day of reckoning at the ballot box. A Labour Party that is seen as hampering meaningful change out of fear of diminishing the relevance of its 40 Scottish MPs risks losing them at next year's General Election. (*Herald*, 19 September 2014)[34]

A significant absence in this narrative is that of an anti-subject. This would be an actant who is also pursuing the same object and competes with the subject.[35] In this narrative there is no other actant equivalent to the main character (Scotland): the other nations of the UK do not have a protagonistic role. The referendum is presented as being only about Scotland and what Scotland wants. On the few occasions when England appears in the narrative, it is presented as an opponent to further devolution for Scotland, but not as a subject in itself:

19. It should also be evident that more powers for Scotland might well satisfy constitutional demands north of the Border, but they are also likely to exacerbate constitutional grievances elsewhere, particularly the perception that the Scottish awkward squad is getting a special deal to the disadvantage of everyone else in the Union. The most significant of those grievances is that England is the only part of the Union without any devolution, so MPs from Scotland can vote on, some would say trample on, English domestic issues. (*Scotsman*, 23 September 2014)[36]

This is significant because a constitutional issue that involves change for the whole of the UK is presented as being primarily Scotland's problem – the other nations are not presented as having their own wishes in relation to this change, other than reacting to Scotland's pursuit of further devolution.

The Quest for Independence

The *Sunday Herald* was the only newspaper in the sample (and among the press overall) that openly supported independence and, as a result, it adopts a different narrative in its editorials. This can be divided into two phases, whereby the acting subject remains Scots/'we', but the object that this subject pursues changes. In the first phase, in the week before the vote, Scots desire independence:

> 20. We want to have mastery over our own affairs and be governed by those we elect. We want democracy to be what it's meant to be: the means by which people collectively have a say in the society in which they live. We want to be a nation like so many successful others around the world, reliant on our own plentiful resources, responsible for our own actions. We want for the buck to stop with us . . . Despite an almost constant bombardment of negativity and the testimony of so-called experts, support for independence has remained robust and continues to rise. (*Sunday Herald*, 14 September 2014)[37]

The opponent in this quest for independence is primarily the No campaign ('the naysayers' in excerpt 21), the 'so-called experts', in excerpt 20, who supported the No campaign's case. Another opponent is the media:

> 21. Meanwhile, the media tried to bolster the naysayers. In the last week alone, Scots have been described as stupid, selfish and smug. That much we have come to expect from the ignorant metropolitan blethers, more concerning, however, is the attitude of the BBC, which we are told exemplifies what's good about Britain. (*Sunday Herald*, 14 September 2014)[38]

However, with the referendum outcome the quest ultimately fails:

> 22. We fought for independence and we failed to win the ultimate prize. (*Sunday Herald*, 21 September 2014)[39]

In the second phase of the narrative, the subject's object of desire becomes 'constitutional change':

> 23. Although the referendum itself is over the fight for significant constitutional change is not. Add the Yes vote to those in the No camp persuaded to give their support by the last-minute promises of Westminster leaders and there is a clear majority for just such a change, even if there is still no consensus on just what that change might be. (*Sunday Herald*, 21 September 2014)[40]

The Yes movement is the only helper in this second phase of the pursuit, while opponents include senior Tories and the main UK party leaders, who are likely to break their promises:

24. The Yes movement has a role to play in holding Westminster to account on their much-lauded vow, which although low on detail did include some promises which already look under threat. Senior Tories have already suggested that the promises to maintain the Barnett Formula and to introduce a fairer system of allocating our own money to Scotland are contradictory . . . We can now see that the promises of a backbench MP have little clout with Coalition partners who have a history of breaking their word. (*Sunday Herald*, 21 September 2014)[41]

Contract Failure

The third narrative of the referendum was found primarily in the *Scottish Daily Mail/Mail on Sunday*. The subject here is once again Scots, and in particular 'decent', 'sensible', and 'cautious' Scots:

25. Which is why today the Mail makes a heartfelt appeal to the decent, sensible, cautious Scots, who represent the overwhelming majority of a great nation. (*Scottish Daily Mail*, 17 September 2014)[42]

The SNP is presented as a 'sender', that is another actant who tells the subject that the object is worth having and pursuing.[43] If the subject accepts this mission to conquer the object, the 'manipulation' or 'contract' phase of the narrative is successful and the quest begins. Here the sender-SNP tries to persuade Scots to desire independence:

26. Nationalists are also guilty of inventing grievances and whipping up hatred where almost none existed before. It is a tribute to Alex Salmond's political skill and the brutal slickness of his campaign that he has apparently persuaded so many Scots to take the leap in the dark towards independence. (*Scottish Daily Mail*, 17 September 2014)[44]

The Scots Salmond had 'apparently persuaded' on the eve of the vote by 'inventing grievances' and 'whipping up hatred' are not the 'sensible, cautious' Scots of excerpt 25. These are presented as not having wanted a referendum in the first place:

27. The responsibility we have been handed – we did not seek it – has been heavy. It has fallen to our luck to be the ones to wield the casting vote on the most successful political and social union in history. (*Scottish Daily Mail*, 19 September 2014)[45]

Eventually the attempt of the sender/SNP to persuade the subject fails. The *Mail* sees the outcome of the referendum as definite evidence that the 'manipulation' stage of the narrative has failed:

28. The result was clear, an absolute rejection of the SNP's separatist agenda by 55 per cent to 45 per cent . . . The referendum result means nothing less than the death of its [the SNP's] raison d'être – separation. (*Scottish Daily Mail*, 22 September 2014)[46]

In the week after the referendum, the subject is no longer Scots, but the Scottish Parliament and the object becomes increased devolution:

29. The Scottish Parliament needs additional powers, not for the sake of self-important politicians, but because a parliament that may spend money but bears no responsibility for raising money is only half a parliament. (*Scottish Mail on Sunday*, 21 September 2014)[47]

However, the *Mail* does not dedicate a lot of space in its post-referendum editorials to this new mission. Instead it dedicates space to commenting on the SNP's perceived resistance to accepting the outcome of the referendum (on 22 and 24 September) and on the role of Alistair Darling during the campaign (on 23 September).

Finally the *Scottish Sun* shares with the *Mail* a representation of the SNP as a sender who tried to persuade Scots to want independence but failed:

30. Scotland's verdict is in: We're better together. It's No to independence. No to Alex Salmond's dream of a breakaway Scotland. No to severing the 307-year-old Union. (*Scottish Sun*, 19 September 2014)[48]

31. He [Salmond] is an inspiring leader who fought like a lion to achieve his lifelong dream but couldn't convince Scotland that independence was anything other than a giant gamble. (*Scottish Sun*, 20 September 2014)[49]

The *Sun* uses much more positive language than the *Mail* to describe Salmond and the SNP – as in excerpt 31, its editorials express admiration. However, it is clear throughout the narrative that independence was *his* vision: it is neither presented as something Scots wanted by themselves nor as a modal object that would lead them to a better country. In its editorial on the day before the vote, the *Scottish Sun* declared its commitment to supporting Scots whichever decision they made but also highlighted the uncertainties of independence:

32. It may pay off. It may not. (*Scottish Sun*, 17 September 2014)[50]

After the referendum, it shifts its focus to the pursuit of new powers for Scotland. By contrast to the discourse of the *Mail* though, here the new powers are clearly presented as something that the Scots desire:

33. The 1.6 million voters who backed independence on Thursday wanted a more powerful Scotland. Many of the 2 million No voters did too – on the basis of David Cameron, Ed Miliband and Nick Clegg's last minute vow on new powers. (*Scottish Sun on Sunday*, 21 September 2014)[51]

The SNP becomes a helper towards this goal, fighting against potential obstacles from the Westminster parties:

34. The country needs someone who will fight to make sure the powers promised by the Westminster parties to Scotland are delivered – but who will also be aware of the need to heal the divisions opened up by the independence debate.

Sturgeon has the strength for the first part and the good sense for the second. (*Scottish Sun*, 25 September 2014)[52]

Therefore the *Scottish Sun*'s narrative also bears similarity to the 'quest for change' narrative, especially in the week after the referendum. This newspaper's position in the referendum debate was in fact more complex than that of the other titles in the sample: the *Scottish Sun* had backed the SNP in the 2013 Scottish election and there was speculation that it would also come out for independence at the referendum, following comments on Twitter by its owner Rupert Murdoch during the campaign.[53] On the other hand, such a move would have been quite radical for a newspaper that has deep-seated interests in England and Westminster. Eventually the paper did not advise readers to vote either way. This complex situation may be part of the reason why its discourse seems to be sitting between that of the Scottish indigenous press and the more unionist discourse of the *Mail*.

Conclusion

Writing soon after the 1997 devolution referendum, which led to the establishment of the Scottish Parliament,[54] suggests that 'it is an open question whether ultimately the new constitutional settlement will push the wider British polity in the direction of federalism, or instead lead to Scottish separation'. The newspaper editorials' discourse ahead of and directly after the 2014 independence referendum focused exactly on this 'open question': the ballot was not presented as being about a choice between independence and the status quo (which strictly speaking it was), but between independence and further devolution.

For the indigenous Scottish titles, the referendum was a step towards Scots' quest for change (except for the *Sunday Herald* where the quest was unambiguously for independence). The content of this change was presented as positive but abstract: a better country, more fairness, more control over Scotland's affairs. Independence was not seen as the only road towards this change. The editorials emphasised the risks involved in independence and suggested that neither independence nor increased devolution would automatically bring on a better, fairer country: both would require hard work and political strategy.

These newspapers' preferred road to change was through further devolution because it was deemed safer to pursue more control within the guarantees provided by membership of the UK. Although the indigenous press had unanimously supported devolution in 1997,[55] this time independence seemed too bold a step.

The Scottish editions of London titles studied here saw the referendum as an attempt by the SNP to persuade Scots that independence was the way forward – an attempt which ultimately failed. The referendum was not presented as part of Scotland's own journey towards a goal, at least not until the week after the vote. The main difference between the *Scottish Daily Mail* and the *Scottish Sun*, is that the *Sun* did not position itself against independence and expressed admiration for the SNP and its efforts. In the week after the campaign the discourse of the *Scottish Sun* resembled more that of the indigenous titles. The *Scottish Daily Mail* on the other hand was categorically against independence and focused more on the defeat of the SNP after the referendum than on future steps.

Clearly the close relationship Rupert Murdoch had been building with the SNP in previous years had an influence on the *Sun*'s stance, perhaps combined with a desire not to alienate its substantial Scottish readership, many of whom could be voting Yes.

Although media effects on voting are complex and difficult to prove, it would be fair to say that newspapers' construction of the referendum narrative confirmed and potentially reinforced a pre-existing uncertainty about independence in the public sphere. Evidence from the 2013 Scottish Social Attitudes (SSA) survey[56] shows that although neither independence, nor increased devolution, nor the status quo had the outright support of the majority of voters, fewer people opposed increased devolution than opposed the other options. It was generally considered as the least risky option that would at the same time boost 'the degree of pride that people might have in their country'.[57]

The narratives of the referendum presented in this chapter seem to fit rather well with the attitudes reported in the survey. Change is indeed what most Scots appear to have wanted and the representation of independence and more devolution as two alternative roads to change was established enough in public discourse for them to be included in SSA questions in the previous years. Increased devolution was the preferred (or least opposed) option of both the people and the majority of the press.

It thus appears reasonable to suggest that most of the indigenous Scottish titles, true to their self-perception as being close to what their readers think,[58] reflected/confirmed/reinforced in their editorials what was understood to be the public opinion over the previous years. Perceptions of how the referendum campaign, as it unfolded after 2013, impacted on these attitudes appear to have influenced the pro-independence stance of the *Sunday Herald* and the more non-committal approach of the *Scottish Sun*. However, it seems that, in the run-up to the vote, there was still a significant degree of scepticism in what both people and the press thought.

Notes

1. Smith, *Paper Lions*.
2. Schlesinger, 'Scottish devolution and the media'.
3. McNair, 'The Scottish media and politics', p. 234.
4. Denver, 'Voting in the 1997 Scottish and Welsh devolution referendums', p. 831.
5. Dekavalla, 'The Scottish newspaper industry in the digital era'.
6. Ibid.
7. www.abc.org.uk
8. Hutchison, 'The history of the press'.
9. Bird and Dardenne, 'Myth, chronicle and story', p. 346.
10. O'Sullivan et al., *Key Concepts in Communication and Cultural Studies*, p. 302.
11. Greimas, *Narrative Semiotics and Cognitive Discourses*.
12. Ibid., p. 37.

13. Greimas, *On Meaning*, p. 73.
14. Greimas, *Narrative Semiotics and Cognitive Discourses*.
15. *Daily Record* (16 September 2014), 'Now we know what's on offer on Thursday', p. 4.
16. *Herald* (16 September 2014), 'Once in a lifetime opportunity to cast a future that meets the aspirations of Scots', p. 14.
17. *Scotland on Sunday* (14 September 2014), 'Scotland can be changed for the better with a No vote', p. 36.
18. Greimas, *On Meaning*, p. 80.
19. *Daily Record* (18 September 2014), 'Choose well Scotland', p. 1.
20. *Scotland on Sunday* (14 September 2014), 'Scotland can be changed for the better with a No vote', p. 36.
21. *Herald* (16 September 2014), 'Once in a lifetime opportunity to cast a future that meets the aspirations of Scots', p. 14.
22. *Scotsman* (18 September 2014), 'Time to write ourselves into the history books', p. 24.
23. *Daily Record* (18 September 2014), 'Choose well Scotland', p. 1.
24. Geimas, *On Meaning*.
25. *Herald* (19 September 2014), 'After the poll, the real work begins', p. 18.
26. *Scotland on Sunday* (14 September 2014), 'Scotland can be changed for the better with a No vote', p. 36.
27. *Scotland on Sunday* (21 September 2014), 'Yes movement has power to shape the new Scotland', p. 36.
28. *Daily Record* (25 September 2014), 'Nicola must back all 100 per cent of us to be a success', p. 8.
29. *Herald* (22 September 2014), 'Promises to Scots that must be kept', p. 18.
30. *Sunday Mail* (21 September 2014), 'We'll speak again. That is a promise', p. 12.
31. *Daily Record* (22 September 2014), 'There's no going back Mr Cameron', p. 8.
32. *Daily Record* (23 September 2014), 'Man with a plan', p. 8.
33. *Scotsman* (22 September 2014), 'Delivering on pledges is crucial to healing wounds', p. 24.
34. *Herald* (19 September 2014), 'After the poll, the real work begins', p. 18.
35. Greimas, *On Meaning*, p. 108.
36. *Scotsman* (23 September 2014), 'Labour have to see fairness for all in the Union', p. 22.
37. *Sunday Herald* (14 September 2014), 'One day, one vote, that's all it will take', p. 26.
38. *Sunday Herald* (14 September 2014), 'One day, one vote, that's all it will take', p. 26.
39. *Sunday Herald* (21 September 2014), 'We dared to dream . . . we still do', p. 35.
40. Ibid., p. 35.
41. Ibid., p. 35.
42. *Scottish Daily Mail* (17 September 2014), 'A special message to Scottish readers from the Mail in England', p. 14.
43. Greimas, *On Meaning*.
44. *Scottish Daily Mail* (17 September 2014), 'A special message to Scottish readers from the Mail in England', p. 14.
45. *Scottish Daily Mail* (19 September 2014), 'Now we are in the eye of the storm. All we can be sure of, Yes or No, is huge change', p. 16.
46. *Scottish Daily Mail* (22 September 2014) 'Voters have spoken, the SNP must listen', p. 14.
47. *Scottish Mail on Sunday* (21 September 2014), 'Time for the politicians to get to work', p. 25.
48. *Scottish Sun* (19 September 2014), 'Now unite for change', p. 10.

49. *Scottish Sun* (20 September 2014), 'True colossus', p. 4.
50. *Scottish Sun* (17 September 2014), 'Britain's got talent v the Ecks factor', p. 1.
51. *Scottish Sun on Sunday* (21 September 2014), 'New front in the battle for more powers', p. 6.
52. *Scottish Sun* (25 September 2014), 'No soft touch', p. 6.
53. Martinson, 'Rupert Murdoch hints at support for Scottish independence'.
54. Schlesinger, 'Scottish devolution and the media', p. 71.
55. Denver, 'Voting in the 1997 Scottish and Welsh devolution referendums'.
56. Curtice, 'So where does Scotland stand on more devolution?'.
57. Ibid., p. 8.
58. Dekavalla. The Scottish newspaper industry in the digital era'.

Bibliography

Bird, Elizabeth and Robert Dardenne, 'Myth, chronicle and story: exploring the narrative qualities of news', in Daniel Berlowitz (ed.), *Social Meanings of News* (London: Sage, 1997), pp. 333–50.

Curtice, John, 'So where does Scotland stand on more devolution?', posted on 18 February 2014, ScotCen, <http://www.scotcen.org.uk/blog/what-does-scotland-think-about-more-devolution (last accessed 6 November 2014).

Dekavalla, Marina, 'The Scottish newspaper industry in the digital era', *Media, Culture and Society*, 37(1) (2015), 107–14.

Denver, David, 'Voting in the 1997 Scottish and Welsh devolution referendums: information, interests and opinions', *European Journal of Political Research*, 41 (2002), pp. 827–43.

Greimas, Algirdas Julien, *On Meaning: Selected Writings in Semiotic Theory* (London: Pinter, 1987).

Greimas, Algirdas Julien, *Narrative Semiotics and Cognitive Discourses* (London: Pinter, 1990).

Hutchison, David, 'The history of the press', in Neil Blain and David Hutchison (eds), *The Media in Scotland* (Edinburgh: Edinburgh University Press, 2008), pp. 55–70.

McNair, Brian, 'The Scottish media and politics', in Neil Blain and David Hutchison (eds), *The Media in Scotland* (Edinburgh: Edinburgh University Press, 2008), pp. 227–42.

Martinson, Jane, 'Rupert Murdoch hints at support for Scottish independence', *The Guardian*, 10 September 2014, <http://www.theguardian.com/politics/2014/sep/10/rupert-murdoch-hints-support-scottish-independence> (last accessed 6 November 2014).

O'Sullivan, Tim, John Hartley, Danny Saunders, Martin Montgomery and John Fiske, *Key Concepts in Communication and Cultural Studies* (Abingdon: Routledge, 1994).

Schlesinger, Philip, 'Scottish devolution and the media', in Jean Seaton (ed.), *Politics and the Media: Harlots and Prerogatives at the Turn of the Millennium* (Oxford: Blackwell, 1998), pp. 55–74.

Smith, Maurice, *Paper Lions: The Scottish Press and National Identity* (Edinburgh: Polygon, 1994).

6

Scottish TV Coverage of the Referendum Campaign from September 2012 to September 2014

John Robertson

M edia coverage of the Scottish referendum campaign in 2012–14 has attracted a great deal of claim and counter-claim regarding alleged imbalance and bias. The research presented here, which was carried out with the help of three colleagues, is an assessment of the extent to which the BBC and to a lesser extent ITV/STV met the commonly agreed standards of fairness and impartiality deemed to be central to public service broadcasting in the United Kingdom, and which are regularly reiterated in BBC and Ofcom codes of practice.[1]

Both television and radio news broadcasting were considered in the research.

Television News

The survey of TV coverage of the referendum campaigns reported here covers the period from 17 September 2012 to 18 September 2013 and includes every weekday evening (6–7 p.m.) news broadcast by BBC 1, *Reporting Scotland*, ITV and STV, and shorter weekend broadcasts in that period. A total, therefore, of approximately 640 hours, minus advertising breaks in ITV and STV broadcasts, was watched, transcribed and coded. The evening TV programmes were chosen as the news broadcasts with the largest audiences in Scotland and in the UK. The distribution and quantity of messages of different types are presented in a tabular format with selected text examples to illustrate types of message.

Our purpose was to answer the following questions, which emerged as salient issues from first and second readings of the transcripts:

1. How prevalent were referendum topics in the first year of the campaigns?
2. What was the relative balance of statements given to the views of Yes and No representatives, arguments and evidence?
3. What was the relative balance of independent, scientific or academic evidence presented in support of the Yes and No campaigns?
4. To what extent did No arguments precede the Yes ones and vice versa?
5. What was the ratio of arguments finishing broadcasts unchallenged in favour of the Yes and No campaigns?

6. To what extent were arguments equated with the apparently personal wishes of political personalities rather than as collective positions?
7. What was the relative balance of offensive statements made to Yes and No campaigners and broadcast?
8. What forms of evidence dominated the discourse – economic, political, social?
9. Overall, and to what extent, did reporting favour the Yes or No campaign?

Methodology

The methodology adopted was essentially the same for both studies reported here. The coding which led to the evidence reported below emerged from a grounded theory/phenomenological approach which allows the data to speak.[2] The final coding is the product of two phases, passing through all the data, of coding by the lead researcher and subsequent moderation by colleagues. Coding of human language cannot of course be utterly objective, but the team has done what it can towards that end.

The unit of measurement adopted here, termed a 'statement', refers to a set of words taken together to make a point which is recognisably separate from other points made in the same sentence or paragraph. Typically these will be sentences, clauses within sentences, list items within sentences and sometimes full paragraphs. It is accepted here that different coders may at times disagree on the boundaries of a 'statement'. The lead researcher coded all of the material to ensure a degree of consistency but selected sections were second- and third-coded to increase the self-awareness of the first coder. The coding was done 'cold' with no pre-reading of the full set of transcripts which might have contaminated the coder with initial impressions of the relative frequency of different codes.

A content analysis of the relative presence of types of political message contained within broadcasts in the first year of the Scottish independence referendum campaigns applied the following coding categories which emerged from pilot coding exercises:

• *About/Descriptive*: Statements about independence which could not be otherwise coded as pro- or anti-
• *Pro-independence*: Statements which could clearly be associated with the pro-independence or Yes position
• *Anti-independence*: Statements which could clearly be associated with the anti-independence or No position
• *Pro-Ind/Sci/Acad Evidence*: Statements which made use of academic, scientific or 'independent' evidence to support the pro-independence or Yes campaign
• *Anti-Ind/Sci/Acad Evidence*: Statements which made use of academic, scientific or 'independent' evidence to support the anti-independence or No campaign
• *Anti-Pro Order*: An opening sequence of statements in which an anti-independence or No statement preceded a pro-independence or Yes response

- *Pro-Anti Order*: An opening sequence of statements in which a pro-independence or Yes statement preceded an anti-independence or No response

- *Personalisation of ideas as AS's wishes*: Labelling pro-independence statements as representing the wishes or desires of Alex Salmond rather than as those of the 'Scottish government' or the 'SNP' or the 'Yes campaign' or any other collective

- *Personalisation of ideas as BT individuals' wishes*: Labelling anti-independence statements as representing the wishes or desires of Johann Lamont or Alistair Darling or any other individual rather than as those of the 'British government' or 'critics' or the 'No campaign' or any other collective

- *Abusive of Pro*: Broadcasting the use of insulting language aimed at pro-independence campaigners

- *Abusive of Anti*: Broadcasting the use of insulting language aimed at anti-independence campaigners

- *Economic evidence*: Presenting evidence relating to the economic consequences (trade, taxes, cost of living, employment) of independence for either side

- *Social evidence*: Presenting evidence relating to the social consequences (health, education, welfare, arts) of independence for either side

- *Political evidence*: Presenting evidence relating to the political consequences (NATO, EU, defence, constitution) of independence for either side

- *Finishing with Pro evidence unchallenged*: Finishing a broadcast item with a clearly pro-independence or Yes piece of evidence left unchallenged

- *Finishing with Anti evidence unchallenged*: Finishing a broadcast item with a clearly anti-independence or No piece of evidence left unchallenged

Table 6.1 presents data which can be used to reveal the distribution, over 12 months, of different types of message within broadcasts, allowing comparison of the relative presence of each category and enabling comparison between channels for the same categories.

News reports relating to the referendum were fairly regular occurrences on the two Scottish channels over the twelve months. In sharp contrast, the UK-wide broadcasts rarely reported on this topic. The BBC 1 figures are inflated by the *Reporting Scotland* headline alerts which followed the 'national' headlines and which were seen only in Scotland. This apparent lack of interest in a major constitutional challenge to the very existence of the UK, by its two dominant news programmes, is the first observation to be taken from the above data.

The simple numerical preponderance of anti-independence statements over pro-independence statements by a ratio of about 3:2 on *Reporting Scotland* and on *STV News* is also clear. One obvious explanation lies in the editorial decision to allow all three anti-independence parties to respond to each SNP statement, thus creating an unavoidable predominance of statements from the former even when these were kept short. Anti-independence statements were heavily concentrated on economic affairs such as alleged increased unemployment or closures after independence.

Table 6.1 Results: total and average figures for each coded category.

Code	RepSc	STV	BBC1	ITV	RepSc+BBC1	STV+ITV
Reports	141	141	51	11	192	152
About/Descriptive	85	79	24	3	109	82
Pro-independence/SNP	171	172	40	7	211	179
Anti-independence/SNP	262	255	55	10	317	265
Pro-Ind/Sci/Acad Evidence	4	7	0	0	4	7
Anti-Ind/Sci/Acad Evidence	22	20	1	0	23	20
Anti-Pro Order	66	61	13	1	79	62
Pro-Anti Order	24	53	19	3	43	56
Personalisation of ideas as AS	28	32	7	2	35	34
Personalisation of ideas as BT individuals	0	0	0	0	0	0
Abusive of Pro-independence figures	18	18	1	0	19	18
Abusive of Anti-independence figures	3	3	0	0	3	3
Economic evidence	38	23	9	3	47	26
Social evidence	18	10	7	0	25	10
Political evidence	14	9	15	2	29	11
Finishing with Pro evidence unchallenged	8	17	2	0	10	17
Finishing with Anti evidence unchallenged	28	34	12	0	40	34
Coded items	789	793	205	31	994	824

Health-related matters were the other dominant theme. For example, the case of a Scottish patient seeking free care only available in England was highlighted and linked to the relative lack of GP control in Scotland. This began a mini-series of reports that particular day by *Reporting Scotland* reporters and containing statements from Labour spokespersons on alleged failings in the Scottish NHS. No balancing cases were reported of a patient flow in the other direction although such cases were reported in the press ('Now English asthma patients are denied life-changing drug offered to Scots', *Daily Mail*, 9 November 2012). The use of single cases to suggest wider concerns is of course problematic.

The use of evidence from sources other than the parties themselves and which might be presented as 'independent', 'academic' or 'scientific' is a measure of quality in political debate. Notably, there was very little use of such evidence in the reporting overall and, where there was, there was a clear tendency to use anti-independence over pro-independence evidence. Though a rare phenomenon overall, reporting tended to link pro-independence evidence from Scottish government sponsored committees to their sponsorship, while UK advisory groups such as the Office for Budget Responsibility, the Institute for Fiscal Studies (IFS) and several parliamentary, Treasury, or House of Lords committees were typically treated as independent, despite linkages to UK government and other government departments, or their nature as units with a vested interest in the union. Indeed the IFS was referred to as a 'well-respected think tank' (*Reporting Scotland*, 19 November 2012) whereas a Glasgow University academic was 'outed' as having been 'bought' by the Yes campaign to support the independence case (*Reporting Scotland*, 22 August 2013).

The sequence of statements whereby anti-independence arguments preceded pro-independence responses, as opposed to the reverse order, is of interest. There was a clear majority (66:24) of the former on *Reporting Scotland*, where 'bad news' about independence came first and obliged a defensive response from a pro-independence spokesperson, but a much narrower majority (61:53) on *STV News*. The *Reporting Scotland* imbalance tends to normalise the No/anti-independence position and put the onus on the Yes/pro-independence position to justify itself.

Personalisation of political issues is a long-established strategy and can be used to weaken arguments, shifting focus from collective reasoning or shared values to supposed personal desires and personality traits. Historically, this tendency or strategy has been used to undermine numerous political figures in the UK including Neil Kinnock and John Major. In the above data, the repeated association of the Yes/pro-independence campaign with the personal desires of Alex Salmond was regular and frequent. No such equation between No/anti-independence figures' personal drives and the No campaign was made. Likewise, the broadcasting of personally insulting comments by anti-independence representatives (especially Johann Lamont) aimed at Alex Salmond, almost entirely, was predominant, though a few counter-jibes by Salmond against Lamont and the Labour Party were also presented. Notably, the use of insults aimed at Salmond declined and had become less common in the second six months of the survey. The tendency by opposition politicians to attempt to undermine the Yes campaign by labelling its ambitions as the product of Alex Salmond's desires is largely outwith the control of the editorial role. However, it was common for reporters and presenters to adopt the same style.

The distillation of the debate over independence into a largely economic one was also clear. Particularly notable is the role, here, of political editors in framing the discussion in this way, advising the viewer that the debate over living standards, employment and taxation was the pre-eminent one.

The closing statements in reports might be felt to leave a lingering impression and thus carry more weight than material presented earlier. In many cases, reporters would round-off with a compromise assessment so as to leave the two campaigns in a kind of balance. Quite often, however, a statement strongly supportive of one side would be left hanging as the final thought. This was more likely, especially on *Reporting Scotland*, to be an anti-independence statement.

Comparing *Reporting Scotland* with *STV News*, the former seemed less balanced and fair to the Yes campaign if only in the tendency to give pro-independence statements a greater frequency of opening and closing debates. Overall, however, both featured a preponderance of anti-independence statements, a majority of anti-independence evidence and a heavy personalisation of the debate around the character of Alex Salmond, with the latter often portrayed as selfish and undemocratic. However, if we characterise viewers as likely to watch both *BBC 1* and *Reporting Scotland* or both *STV* and *ITV News*, in succession, the two experiences diverge further than is apparent in comparing one programme with another. The *BBC1*, *Reporting Scotland* alerts were commonly short and punchy with an attack, typically a Westminster scare story, on the Yes campaign, mostly left unanswered and unchallenged, so that the viewer of the paired BBC news programmes experienced an even less balanced reporting of news.

Good Morning Scotland

The second piece of empirical research described here was a qualitative content analysis of the broadcasts of BBC Radio Scotland's *Good Morning Scotland* (GMS) throughout April 2014. This is a three-hour radio programme, except on Saturdays, when it is only two hours long and presented as *Newsweek Scotland* (latterly that became the Saturday edition of GMS and in 2015 a Sunday edition was added). The codes which emerged by the end of the third phase of listening and reading of the texts were:

Negative About Yes: *Statements which were negative for the Yes campaign*
Negative About BT: *Statements which were negative for the BT campaign*
Positive About Yes: *Statements which were positive for the Yes campaign*
Responses from Yes: *Statements which were made in defence of the Yes campaign*
Positive About BT: *Statements which were positive for the BT campaign*
Responses from BT: *Statements which were made in defence of the BT campaign*
Challenging Questions to Yes: *Interviewer questions which challenged the Yes campaign*
Challenging Questions to BT: *Interviewer questions which challenged the BT campaign*
Good News First: *Where positive information for the Yes campaign came before negative information for Yes*
Bad News First: *Where negative information for the Yes campaign came before positive information for Yes*
Interrupt of Yes: *Where statements (by Yes supporters of the interviewer) were interrupted*
Attempted Interrupt of Yes: *Where statements (by Yes supporters of the interviewer) were almost interrupted*
In Quick on Yes: *Where statements (by Yes supporters of the interviewer) were followed very quickly*
Total Interrupts Against Yes: *Total of the above three categories*
Interrupt of BT: *Where statements (by BT supporters of the interviewer) were interrupted*
Attempted Interrupt of BT: *Where statements (by BT supporters of the interviewer) were almost interrupted*

In Quick on BT: *Where statements (by BT supporters of the interviewer) were followed very quickly*
Total Interrupts Against BT: *Total of the above three categories*
Problems with Evidence Against Yes: *See notes below*
Problems with Evidence Against BT: *See notes below*
Uncodable: *Statements which could not be fitted to any of the above categories with confidence*

Table 6.2 *Good Morning Scotland*: April 2014: overall frequency of coded categories.

Code	Total
Negative About Yes	376
Negative About BT	147
Positive About Yes	306
Responses from Yes	283
Positive About BT	70
Responses from BT	176
Challenging Questions to Yes	44
Challenging Questions to BT	34
Good News First	8
Bad News First	15
Interrupt of Yes	24
Attempted Interrupt of Yes	5
In Quick on Yes	5
Total Interrupts Against Yes	34
Interrupt of BT	10
Attempted Interrupt of BT	1
In Quick on BT	0
Total Interrupts Against BT	11
Problems with Evidence Against Yes	30
Problems with Evidence Against BT	3

Table 6.2 shows the overall frequency of coded categories.

The differences between the coding for this survey and for the previous two were unplanned and, as argued for elsewhere by reference to grounded theory, allowed the data to suggest the coding. The extended, more combative and interactive nature of radio discourse by contrast with TV news will have been a factor, resulting in, particularly, more subtle gradation of the types.

Discussion

At the outset it must be pointed out that no imbalance in the crude number of statements favourable to the Yes campaign and those favourable to the Better Together (BT) campaign is evident in these results. Indeed if we add positive statements about Yes to responses from Yes, plus negatives about BT (736) and compare this total to the total of positive statements about BT and responses from BT plus negatives about Yes (622) we get a ratio favouring the Yes campaign by 7:6. This is different from the results in the earlier study of television news coverage which revealed a 3:2 ratio favouring BT. However, this crude measure ignores the fact that many of the positive statements about Yes were reactive and made in response to the quite large number of opening negative statements about the Yes campaign (376) while opening negative statements about BT were much fewer (147). So, we have a situation where statements favouring Yes are numerous but commonly reactive and overshadowed at times by large numbers of negative statements about Yes positioned (obviously) ahead of the former.

With fifteen broadcasts opening with bad news for the Yes campaign as opposed to eight beginning with good news for the Yes campaign, there is a clear imbalance which may be combining with the large overall number of negative statements about Yes to create a fairly regular (1 in 2) climate unfavourable to the Yes campaign.

A further piece of evidence emerging from these broadcast transcripts which seems clearly to favour BT was the tendency of interviewers and interviewees to interrupt, almost interrupt and to cut in quickly to break flow of statements in support of the Yes campaign. The totals give a ratio of almost exactly 3:1 in favour of BT.

The most marked case of aggressive interviewing was James Naughtie's interview of Deputy First Minister Nicola Sturgeon on 24 April, on the subject of pensions and welfare in post-independent Scotland, where Naughtie made seven full interruptions and one failed interruption, while Sturgeon attempted only two later in the interview. Naughtie had been 'helicoptered' back into the Scottish public sphere with a view to 'beefing-up' the exchanges with politicians. At one point Naughtie delivered four interruptions in close sequence, two questions which flirted with offence rather than professional challenge and a concluding comment which flirted with patronising dismissal – 'Carry on get back to the point, yah'. Interestingly, Sturgeon's earlier interview (8 April) with regular presenter Gary Robertson, responding to former NATO chief Lord George Robertson's speech on Scotland and NATO, was marked by quite aggressive interviewing too, with eight interrupts, attempts or cut-ins for two by Sturgeon.

The contrast with Naughtie's very passive interview of Robertson, also on the 8 April, was marked. Lord Robertson's doom-laden predictions on the consequences of Scottish independence for the free world were met with no interrupts or quick cut-ins and only the most polite of suggestions that the former's language was a bit over-the-top. George Robertson's batting aside of this suggestion and further dramatic claims attracted only a quiet 'thank you' from Naughtie, who was to repeat this approach interviewing former (1960/80s) Pentagon adviser on nuclear weapons strategy Frank Miller, on 11 April, where the latter's apparent commitment to mutually assured destruction went unchallenged. The repeated treatment of Sturgeon with multiple interruptions and irritable tones is notable and worthy of reflection. No accusation of deliberate discriminatory practice is suggested but this form of aggressive interviewing directed at a confident and articulate woman and not matched in interviews with male equivalents such as Lord Robertson or the former Pentagon advisor is unsettling.

There was 'tough' interviewing of two Better Together supporters, leader of the Opposition Ed Miliband and LibDem minister Ed Davey. Davey, interviewed by Gary Robertson, had to deal with eleven quite challenging questions, four interrupts, with only one return interrupt from Davey. Robertson did provoke Davey with challenges to his reasoning, on energy markets, as in: 'So you would make a political choice to disadvantage Scotland?' In a similar way, James Naughtie grilled Miliband quite thoroughly with thirteen questions, three interrupts by Naughtie but four interrupts of Naughtie by Miliband. Naughtie certainly did not behave with the kind of undue respect accorded by him and others to Lord Robertson or former Pentagon adviser Miller. When Miliband promised a better future when he became PM, Naughtie replied quickly – 'You're not exactly miles ahead in the polls'.

Taken together, we have evidence here of tough professional journalism directed at both sides, but during the month in question there were seven tough interviews of those offering evidence of a positive nature regarding Scotland's future, but only two grillings of Better Together supporters and four very soft interviews of those bringing bad news for Yes voters. If we add the seven tough interviews of Yes supporters, or evidence-givers, to the four soft interviews of BT supporters and compare these with the two tough interviews of BT supporters, we get a 9:2 ratio.

Quite a marked imbalance of 30:3 or 10:1, in favour of BT, in the relative use of 'Problems with Evidence Against Yes' as opposed to 'Problems with Evidence Against BT', subject to critique of its quality, is perhaps the clearest marker of underlying bias in the broadcasts. Note, it is not suggested here that this derives from conscious conspiracy on the part of editors, reporters or interviewers but rather from a subconscious internalisation of establishment perspectives and values.

On 4 April, the repeated association of Kenny Anderson of Anderson Construction with Business for Scotland contrasted with the highly respectful and uncritical treatment of Keith Cochrane of Weir Group, the previous day. The BT alignment of the latter, reported elsewhere in the media, was not mentioned. This seems a clear example, perhaps accidental, which enables the portrayal of one set of evidence, favouring BT, as untainted by ideology while the other is presented as clearly biased in favour of the Yes campaign. This is particularly notable given that the second report was actually from the Bank of Scotland and not from the Yes campaign itself. The former, Weir's own research study, was produced by Oxford Economics and characterised by Weir Group's CE as 'independent'.

Conclusions

What this study has demonstrated – at least as far as the material analysed here is concerned – is that there was an imbalance in the reporting of the referendum on television and radio in Scotland.

However, it is important that the author of this chapter acknowledges that when the initial findings were published, BBC Scotland reacted in a very determined fashion and, in an extended critique, challenged both methodology and findings. Though the author posted an equally extended riposte, and defended the report against all substantive criticisms, he did agree that there had been a number of minor factual errors, but nothing which undermined the basic thrust of the research or its conclusions. It is also worth considering the comments made by the retiring chair of STV, Richard Findlay, as he took up his new post as chair of Creative Scotland. Discussing the referendum campaign, he said, 'There is always a difficult line to walk; we certainly walked it at STV; The BBC could look at itself a little more carefully sometimes. Sometimes it does get tied up in its own bureaucracy.' These are cautious remarks but they are critical.[3]

Notes

1. BBC Editorial Guidelines on Impartiality; Ofcom Broadcasting Code, Section Five.
2. Glaser and Strauss, *The Discovery of Grounded Theory*; Glaser, *Theoretical Sensitivity*; Glaser, *Basics of Grounded Theory Analysis*; Strauss and Corbin, *Basics of Qualitative Research Techniques*; Strauss and Corbin, *Basics of Qualitative Research Techniques*, 2nd edn; Dey, *Grounding Grounded Theory Guidelines for Qualitative Inquiry*; Charmaz, *Constructing Grounded Theory*.
3. (*Herald*, 21 January 2015, p. 11).

Bibliography

Alotaibi, N. N., 'Media effects on voting behaviour', *European Scientific Journal*, 9(20) (2013), pp. 1857–81.

Ansolabehere, S. and S. Iyengar, *Going Negative: How Campaign Advertising Shrinks and Polarizes the Electorate* (New York: The Free Press, 1995).

BBC, Editorial Guidelines on Impartiality 2015, <http://www.bbc.co.uk/editorialguidelines/page/guidelines-impartiality-introduction/> (last accessed 16 September 2015).

Biocca, F., *Television and Political Advertising: Signs, Codes, and Image* (Abingdon: Routledge, 2014).

Briggs, A. and P. Cobley (eds), *The Media: An Introduction* (Harlow: Longman, 2002).

Charmaz, K. (2006), *Constructing Grounded Theory: A Practical Guide through Qualitative Analysis* (London: Sage, 2006).

Chomsky, N., *Necessary Illusions: Thought Control in Democracies* (South End Press, 1989), online summary <http://www.thirdworldtraveler.com/Chomsky/Necessary_Illusions.html> (last accessed 16 September 2015).

Cromwell, D., 'Scotlandshire: BBC Scotland coverage of the independence referendum with Professor John Robertson, Medialens, April 2014, <http://www.medialens.org/

index.php/alerts/alert-archive/2014/759-scotlandshire-bbc-scotland-coverage-of-the-independence-referendum.html> (last accessed 16 September 2015).

Dey, I. (1999), *Grounding Grounded Theory Guidelines for Qualitative Inquiry* (San Diego: Academic Press, 1999).

Faber, R. J., A. R. Tims and K. G. Schmitt, 'Negative political advertising and voting intent: the role of involvement and alternative information sources', *Journal of Advertising* 22(4) (1993), pp. 67–76.

Gauntlett, D., Ten things wrong with the 'effects model', 2004, <http://www.theory.org.uk/effects.htm> (last accessed 16 September 2015).

Glaser, B. G. and A. L. Strauss, *The Discovery of Grounded Theory: Strategies for Qualitative Research* (New York: Aldine de Gruyter, 1967).

Glaser, B. G., *Theoretical Sensitivity* (Mill Valley, CA: Sociology Press, 1978).

Glaser, B. G., *Basics of Grounded Theory Analysis Emergence vs. Forcing* (Mill Valley, CA: Sociology Press, 1992).

Herman, E. and N. Chomsky, *Manufacturing Consent* (New York: Pantheon Books, 1988).

Kitzinger, J. (2002), 'Impacts and influences', in A. Briggs and P. Cobley, P (eds), *The Media: An Introduction* (Harlow: Longman, 2002), pp. 272–81.

Lee, M., *Inventing Fear of Crime and the Politics of Anxiety* (Abingdon: Willan, 2007).

Noelle-Neumann, E., *The Spiral of Silence: Public Opinion – Our Social Skin* (Chicago: University of Chicago Press, 1993).

Ofcom, Broadcasting Code 2015, Section 5, 'Due impartiality and due accuracy and undue prominence of views and opinions' <http://stakeholders.ofcom.org.uk/broadcasting/broadcast-codes/broadcast-code/impartiality/>.

Sauer, T., *Nuclear Inertia: US Weapons Policy After the Cold War* (London: I. B. Tauris, 2005).

Schmitt, J. and D. Rosnick, '"Misunderestimating" living standards', Center for Economic and Policy Research, January 2008 <http://www.cepr.net/documents/publications/living_standards_2008_01.pdf>.

Strauss, A. and J. Corbin, J., *Basics of Qualitative Research: Grounded Theory Procedures and Techniques* (Newbury Park: Sage, 1990).

Strauss, A. and J. Corbin, *Basics of Qualitative Research Techniques and Procedures for Developing Grounded Theory*, 2nd edn (Thousand Oaks: Sage, 1998).

Williamson, L., Brown, M., Wathan, J. and V. Higgins, *Analysing the Fear of Crime using the British Crime Survey: Secondary Analysis for Social Scientists* (London: ESRC, 2013).

YouGov, Trust in the media, 2011, <http://yougov.co.uk/news/2011/11/14/trust-media/> (last accessed 16 September 2015).

7

'Liked', 'Shared', Re-tweeted:
The Referendum Campaign on Social Media

Margot Buchanan

I n the months leading up to 18 September 2014, social media were set ablaze by the polarised debate surrounding the Scottish referendum on independence. While the benefits of social media as platforms for political campaigning had been recognised for several years, the referendum debate on Facebook and Twitter was notable for the high level of public participation and activity. The competing Yes Scotland and Better Together official campaigns were joined on Facebook and Twitter by a number of pages and accounts established by groups which mostly favoured Scottish independence. Some of these were aligned to political parties such as the Scottish Socialist Party, the Green Party and the Scottish Labour Party (Labour for Independence). Others were established by issue-focused groups, such as Women for Independence/Independence for Women. Public participation in the independence debate on Facebook and Twitter was so extensive that on 10 December 2014 it was announced that the Scottish referendum was the UK's most discussed subject on Facebook, and one of the most featured topics on Twitter.

Debate on Scotland's future did not end on 18 September, however, but was continuing on social media even as 2014 drew to an end. Post-referendum activity, particularly on Facebook, suggested that those Scots who had supported the Yes campaign had no intention of bringing the debate to an end. This chapter looks at debate on Facebook and Twitter before and after polling day.

By 2014, the use of social media as vehicles for political communication was securely established: Facebook and Twitter were successfully deployed by Barack Obama during his 2008 campaign for the presidency of the USA and comprehensively used in the 2010 UK general election. Social media allow politicians – as well as private individuals and special interest groups – total control over their self-representation and the content and initial dissemination of their campaign messages. Referendum campaigning on Facebook and Twitter began more than two years before Scottish voters went to the polls. An early start is a significant factor on social media, as it enables campaigns to have an established profile online, to begin disseminating messages and to build a strong support base well before the immediate pre-poll period; UK politicians and parties adopted the same tactics in preparation for the 2010 general election.[1]

Better Together established its Facebook and Twitter accounts in May 2012, describing itself in one short sentence: 'The patriotic all-party & non-party campaign for Scotland in the UK'.[2] The succinct definition suggested that a No vote in the referendum was patriotic and in Scotland's best interests, thus making a clear distinction between patriotism and the nationalism associated with the Scottish National Party and the Yes campaign. Yes Scotland, the main pro-independence campaign, launched its Facebook page in May 2012 and its Twitter account in April 2012, defining itself as:

> an alliance of the Scottish National Party, Scottish Green Party, Scottish Socialist Party and other groups and individuals who believe that it is fundamentally better for all of us if decisions about Scotland's future are taken by the people who care most about Scotland – that is by the people of Scotland.[3]

This definition indicated that the desire for Scottish independence was not driven solely by the SNP and its supporters but also by a range of other political parties in Scotland. It suggested that these parties had only Scotland's best interests at heart, unlike the Westminster government.

Communication on social media is, however, multi-modal; it is not only textual, but also visual and oral through the use of photographs, images and the embedding of video clips. The core arguments were summarised in the logos that headed each movement's Facebook page and Twitter profile and were therefore significant in imprinting the campaigns' images in the minds of online audiences. Yes Scotland Facebook and Twitter accounts featured the image of a woman wearing tartan and a bonnet and holding a Scottish thistle, named Bella Caledonia, superimposed on a St Andrew flag. It resonated with Scottish national and political history and included the invitation 'LET'S WORK TOGETHER AS IF WE ARE LIVING IN THE EARLY DAYS OF A BETTER NATION' (a quotation from Alasdair Gray, a Scottish writer, artist and independence supporter), delivered in the print style of famous Scottish architect Charles Rennie Mackintosh, and thus referencing the achievements of some historic Scottish figures. While the image resonated with Scottish iconography, the text was both inclusive and forward looking. It also included a small square containing the word 'YES' in one corner; this was adopted as the profile badge for the campaign, both online and offline, and supporters were able to adopt it during the campaign to replace their personal profile photograph which accompanied every action they performed on social media.

The Better Together campaign logo, like its description, was much simpler: the image of a heart with the text 'LOVE SCOTLAND VOTE NO' superimposed. The 'O' in NO featured a cross, representing the cross with which voters would mark their preferences on their voting papers, while the heart-shaped image and use of the word 'love' served to soften the negative connotations of 'no'. These elements worked to present a No vote not only as a positive act, but also an emotional one. The profile image further included a black circle bearing the words 'NO THANKS', again with a cross in the centre of the 'O' in 'NO'; Better Together used this as a campaign badge offline and profile image online. Again, campaign supporters could adopt the badge as their profile photograph to both identify themselves with, and to participate in, the unionist campaign. Both campaign logos used capital letters – online code for emphasis or shouting.

Such analysis of the profile images which headed the main opposing campaigns' social media presence may seem overdone, but these images were the first page visitors would see each time they visited either of the campaigns' Facebook pages or Twitter accounts. It was important that they were memorable and representative of the ethos of each movement, particularly on social media platforms where much emphasis is placed on self-representation in the form of photographs and profiles; Castells notes, 'The most powerful message is a simple message attached to an image'.[4] These campaign profiles and images were doubly significant: first, traditional broadcast platforms such as newspapers and television would present mediated campaign messages and second, newspaper sales were continuing to fall, and many people, especially those in the younger age groups, accessed news on social media. Both campaigns had to ensure that their social media presence was effective, but particularly so to teenagers since the franchise was extended to include, for the first time, people aged sixteen.

While Facebook and Twitter provide extremely cost-effective methods of political campaigning, their strength lies in the opportunities they offer the general public. Facebook's 'Comment', 'Like', 'Share' and Twitter's 'Favourite', 'Reply' and 'Retweet' buttons invite responses from private individuals; these responses are subsequently automatically circulated to their Facebook friends and Twitter followers, and the flow of information converges from the vertical, that is from the top down, to the horizontal, that is between peers.[5] In this way, information may spread across the Web in ever increasing circles like ripples in water, reaching not only identified circles of friends and acquaintances, but also potentially reaching friends of friends and followers' followers. As a result, campaigns will also reach people who are not politically affiliated or interested in politics.

Polat[6] argues that online discussions can increase the level of participation in political debate; in social media terms this suggests that individuals' level of activity on the sites is as influential as the number of friends and/or followers they have. The more active a platform user is, the more often they will disseminate political messages, particularly if users adopt the relevant campaign badge as their profile photograph. This practice is a formidable asset in political campaigning, but also encourages higher levels of engagement in political debate. It benefits democratic societies such as the UK, where falling levels of voter involvement in politics have been viewed as a major source of concern.[7] A 2004 parliamentary inquiry into democracy in Britain recommended that politics in the UK should be more participatory and inclusive[8] to encourage greater citizen engagement in politics; elements which are at the core of all forms of communication on social media platforms. Political campaigning on social media therefore extends political debate and ensures a plurality of voices is heard in the public domain, although the extent of polemical argument surrounding the referendum on Facebook and Twitter indicated that any suggestion that these platforms have created a virtual Habermasian public sphere is premature; Habermas's[9] concept is based on reasoned debate and the requirement of consensus being reached.

Pre-Referendum

Social media, like other platforms on the Web and on the Internet, elide both temporal and spatial boundaries. As a result, contributions from private individuals to the referendum debate were not confined to people who lived in Scotland and therefore able to vote on 18 September, but also included comments and discussions from people around the globe. Keen interest in the debate came from people living in Spain, Austria, Canada, the USA and the rest of the UK, indicating that in a networked and mediated society, political debate can become international and that the Scottish referendum was the subject of interest from around the globe. International support for Scottish independence came as early as February 2014, with one comment posted on the Yes Scotland Facebook page by a Spanish citizen, linking the Scottish independence campaign with Catalonia's campaign for independence from Spain. International support for each side of the campaign was regularly offered, with further contributions made by people living in the rest of the UK, reflecting Boyd's[10] suggestion that social media have created a new, technically enabled form of 'mediated publics' which enable individuals to meet publicly.

Such contributions also indicate the significance of social media in terms of the dissemination of news and information. Within the UK, where sales of newspapers are falling, traditional news platforms had to select which, from a plethora of referendum stories, should be published or broadcast; outwith the UK, the referendum was unlikely to dominate the news agenda. Social media users on Facebook and Twitter can therefore be regarded as conducting 'random acts of journalism'[11] by sharing and re-tweeting campaign messages on platforms that are available across the globe. Lascia uses the phrase to define the actions of private individuals who disseminate in the public domain images and information of events via digital technologies. In the referendum campaign, these platforms further enabled social media users to participate in the debate without having to negotiate the media gatekeepers who decide which voices are heard in the public domain, and to challenge statements made by leading political figures.

With seven months to go until the referendum, the Better Together campaign was gaining both momentum and support from key political figures: US President Barack Obama; José Manuel Barroso, then President of the European Union, who suggested that an independent Scotland would find it very difficult to join the EU; and UK Chancellor of the Exchequer George Osborne, who rejected the proposal that an independent Scotland would be able to adopt the pound as its currency, with public support from Mark Carney, the Governor of the Bank of England. All of these interventions were given extensive coverage in the traditional media, as were what may be described as celebrity endorsements for Scotland remaining part of the UK from sportsmen and women, pop stars and actors.

While private individuals had little recourse or opportunity to comment upon or challenge these arguments on mainstream media platforms, they were able to voice their opinions on Facebook and Twitter. At this point it is worth noting that the number of written responses to tweets in general was fairly low in comparison with the level of communication and interaction on the Facebook groups. This may have been due to the 140 character restriction on the length of tweets. Better Together supporters welcomed the arguments made by high profile celebrities. These endorsements, along with other policy announcements by the campaign, often led to derogatory and insulting comments directed at the leader of the Scottish National Party and First Minister of Scotland, Alex Salmond. Personal criticism of him included comments such as 'Salmond is outed as an idiot, all over SNP' and 'this sleekit, arrogant man', while one individual posted 'I think Salmond, Swinney and the awful Sturgeon need to look at what they're trying to do to my country'.

Celebrity endorsement also resulted, however, in severe criticism for famous people who publicly offered support to either side of the campaign; author J. K. Rowling was subjected to insulting comments from Yes supporters for her financial contribution to and support for the Better Together campaign, while unionists were equally ferocious in their condemnation of the tennis star Andy Murray following a tweet he posted just hours before the polls opened that appeared to indicate he supported independence. Murray's tweet was not explicitly pro-independence, but did imply criticism of the negativity of the Better Together campaign followed by the final phrase 'Let's do this'.

Scottish businessman Bill Munro, founder of Barrhead Travel, was targeted and verbally abused by independence supporters in March 2014 after sending an email to all of his staff to the effect that he would be voting No on 18 September because of the consequences separation would have on the firm, and predicting that Scottish independence would be a complete disaster. This was taken by pro-independence supporters as an attempt to influence his staff's votes on polling day. A boycott of Barrhead Travel was threatened with some posters predicting the firm would 'go bust' or into administration.

Many pro-independence supporters were labelled 'cybernats' for their extensive use of the Internet, especially those who employed it to verbally abuse opponents – despite the SNP's many attempts to disassociate themselves from these supporters on the grounds that they damaged the campaign. The level of criticism aimed at both Alex Salmond and Andy Murray by Better Together supporters indicated, however, that such behaviour was common to both sides of the debate and it must be emphasised that the posting of offensive and inflammatory comments online, known as 'flaming', was a well-established practice of many Internet users and not confined to political debate.

The division between social media contributors was therefore deep, but not necessarily due to the issue of national identity. Leith and Soule[12] argue that the notion of Scottish national identity is complex; it is not grounded solely on a person's place of birth. 'National identity is not a fixed point or some *a priori* essence',[13] they say; Scottish national identity comprises both civic and non-civic aspects.[14] The referendum debate on Facebook, in particular, bore out this theory. There were several groups supporting Scottish independence, as noted above. These were linked by a focus not on national identity, but on social change and the vision that an independent Scotland would be a more socially responsible and caring society; that it would focus on what were seen as traditional Scottish values. This was directly associated with the Yes Scotland logo, while also indicating that the Yes campaign was not linked solely to the SNP. These groups explicitly rejected the neo-liberal policies and austerity cuts of the Westminster government, linking them to increased inequality and poverty in Scotland, as illustrated by the growing dependence on food banks, and perceived as the result of Westminster social policies.

One contributor to the Women for Independence/Independence for Women Facebook page commented 'I am not a nationalist, a separatist, racist or any other kind of negative label you decide to use. I'm a mum. I want better for my kids'.[15] Other contributors commented that Scottish votes in a general election had little effect on the outcome and that Scotland was condemned to be forever ruled by a government it had not voted for. Independence supporters expressed concern over the possible impact on Scotland of the anti-immigration and anti-Europe policies of UKIP (the United Kingdom Independence Party) which had made significant advances in England. This suggested that many of those who campaigned for a Yes vote did so not because they supported Scottish independence per se but because they considered it would deliver Scotland from future Conservative austerity cuts (at this time the Conservatives were expected to win the 2015 general election, while the Labour Party had also pledged to pursue an austerity programme, should it win) and the increasing gap between rich and poor.

One pro-independence group which proved to be a dominant presence within the debate on social media was Wings Over Scotland. Originally established as a website in 2011, Wings Over Scotland, which was not affiliated to the Scottish National Party or any other political party, joined social media platforms in 2012. The group's website and social media presence were established and maintained as political sites by its creator, Stuart Campbell, who uses the title 'Reverend'. Wings Over Scotland was also registered with the Electoral Commission as a permitted participant in the referendum. The group and its website were crowdfunded; it was financed by online donations from supporters. The level and strength of support was such that in 2014, when the group sought £53,000 of funding from supporters, the target was reached within nine hours; the final sum was almost double the amount sought. Wings Over Scotland's logo comprised a blue stylised representation of a lion sitting on a pair of wings superimposed on an outline map of Scotland, suggesting the group was protective and guarding Scotland. Campbell, a Scottish born video game designer and former video games journalist, defined the group on Facebook as 'a Scottish political media digest and monitor which also offers its own commentary'.[16]

Campbell's political commentary as he surveyed the mainstream media platforms before and after the vote can mainly be described as acerbic. Wings Over Scotland appeared to monitor discourse across the spectrum of newspaper, radio, television media platforms. Campbell selected items that he considered to be presenting inaccuracies or misrepresentations by unionist campaigns and mainstream media; he highlighted them on the group's own website and in its Facebook and Twitter feeds and presented facts and figures that challenged those presented by independence opponents. The multi-modal affordances of digital media meant Campbell could post links to both the anti-independence material and the information which contradicted these campaign messages. In general, these posts and tweets were aimed at countering many of the anti-independence campaign claims in mainstream media. In July 2014, the Facebook page featured the headline 'Lying Labour liars tell lies shock'.[17] The link led to the Wings Over Scotland webpage that featured a tweet by the Labour Party's 'Truth Team' which claimed that the SNP's six Westminster MPs had voted against an energy price freeze proposed by Labour; Campbell said the SNP MPs' names were not on parliamentary records as having voted against the price freeze.

The second story to be featured was based on Scottish Labour's depute leader Kezia Dugdale's column in the *Scottish Daily Record* of the same date which claimed that that thousands of Scottish voters in the English town of Corby had voted against independence in a mini-referendum; Campbell reported that only 576 Scots had participated. His ripostes garnered comments such as 'GASP! SHOCK! Labour tell lies?' and 'It would be news if LABOUR TELLS THE TRUTH!'

Despite the Better Together campaign having adopted a more positive name in the approach to the referendum, its arguments remained predominantly negative. Supported by key European politicians, it focused on Scotland's dependence on the rest of the UK and its inability to sustain a healthy economy. 'A vote for Scotland to stay in the UK is a vote to protect Scotland & the welfare of the Scottish people', said John Reid of Better Together on Twitter (7 June 2014), a comment illustrative of the predominant discourse of the No campaign; Scotland needed to be supported and protected by the Westminster government.

The overt message given by the Better Together campaign was that not only was Scotland incapable of being independent, but that a Yes vote would result not only in the financial industry in Scotland, a significant employer, moving their business to England but also that other major companies would follow suit; the old age pension would be adversely affected and pensioners would suffer; furthermore, the country would also be globally isolated. While these campaign messages could be found on all news platforms, again social media enabled private citizens to comment on them. There was severe criticism by anti-independence campaigners and Westminster government agencies and many in the Scottish business community of the SNP's claim that it would be able to share the pound as Scotland's currency, and its reliance on oil revenues; a comment reportedly made by Queen Elizabeth that the Scots should 'think carefully' about independence was used to suggest that she wanted Scotland to remain part of the United Kingdom.

The negativity of the No campaign's arguments played to people's fears for their future under independence while the Queen's comment played to their emotions, as Yes supporters were quick to point out. Conversely, Yes supporters were criticised for placing emotion, in terms of national identity, before practical concerns.

Political judgement is influenced by emotions;[18] positive emotions are triggered by people striving towards a certain or shared goal; negative emotions, such as anxiety and anger, are stirred when people find themselves on unfamiliar ground in what they perceive as a high risk environment.[19] Many contributors to the Facebook accounts expressed anxiety over the claims and assertions made by the unionist campaign concerning prospective job losses and the loss of major employers as well as the suggestion that the old age pension would be negatively affected. Scotland had been part of the United Kingdom for centuries; an independent Scotland would have been unfamiliar and untried territory and the prospect could be seen as daunting, inducing further anxiety. These factors, combined with the strong ties with England and affection for the Queen felt by older generations, in particular, would have encouraged anxiety on several levels.

It is worth noting at this point that social media platforms are not solely the realm of young people; their comprehensive use by those in older demographics has grown steadily as social media have become a significant means of communication. Debate between supporters of each campaign was therefore at times emotional, aggressive and derogatory, but in equal measure it was also reasoned, polite, thoughtful and insightful; lengthy discussions developed in which numerous participants dropped in and out of the conversation over several days. The debates were highly interactive, although they were not linear; due to the simultaneity of posting comments online, participants called each other by name, answered questions and mainly adhered to the subject under discussion.

As the hours ticked away to 18 September, the Better Together campaign announced that the leaders of the three pro-union parties, Labour, the Conservatives and the Liberal Democrats, had pledged that the Westminster government would grant more powers to the Scottish government. This pledge was heralded by mainstream media as a major concession and promise to Scotland and became known as 'the vow'; many No supporters considered it would be the *coup de grace* for the Yes campaign. The announcement supported the campaign's 'Best of Both Worlds' slogan. Responses on Facebook, however, revealed a high level of cynicism in both Better Together and independence supporters. Many of the politically astute pointed out that in fact the leaders were unable to fulfil the promises made in the declaration without the consent of the Westminster

Parliament, and forecast that Prime Minister David Cameron would find it difficult to gain the support of his backbenchers.

While criticism of 'the vow' by pro-independence supporters could be expected, the Better Together Facebook page was flooded with mainly critical posts. One woman commented 'How can they guarantee something that needs to go to a Westminster vote – and which the Tories have already said they'll vote against! I despair I really do', while another remarked 'Good luck getting this past the LORDS and back benchers. Disgraceful underhanded tactic'. The number of bitter and critical posts indicated that while pro-union supporters opposed independence, they did not believe that the promises made were likely to be fulfilled. They further suggested a higher awareness of parliamentary procedures than politicians possibly anticipated.

However, many Better Together supporters welcomed the development, seeing it as a positive step, a good reason to vote No, and a powerful weapon against the Yes campaign; many other unionist supporters condemned the strategy. They considered it to be an act of desperation in the final hours before the vote, when results of a poll, conducted by ICM for the *DailyTelegraph* newspaper and published on 13 September, suggested that the Yes campaign had gained a seven-point lead over the Better Together campaign. These reactions may not have been what the No campaign anticipated, and were not reflected in mainstream media reports, but they indicated the significance of social media platforms to political campaigning: private individuals were able to voice their reactions to political strategies on a public platform. In particular, these comments publicly demonstrated a level of cynicism in regard to politicians and their campaign pledges.

Post-Referendum

This cynicism was writ large in the days following the vote. The various campaigns issued cautious statements about the result: Yes Scotland thanked those who had supported them and acknowledged the depth of sadness being experienced by their supporters. The campaign also looked to the future – thanking everyone who had voted, and inviting No and Yes voters to work together to 'build a better nation'. Better Together was magnanimous in victory and stated on 19 September 'Scotland has voted for unity. Let's move forward together to achieve faster, better, safer change for Scotland within the United Kingdom'. But any expectation that the matter was resolved proved to be mistaken and the division between independence and union supporters on social media deepened in the days immediately following the referendum. Pro-independence supporters expressed both anger, over what was deemed to have been a dishonest campaign by Better Together, and, as Westminster politicians indicated that the promises made in 'the vow' would not immediately be implemented, contempt for No voters who had trusted the assurance and whom they labelled 'naïve'. Simultaneously, Yes voters began adopting a new independence logo as their profile photographs on social media; a white 45 per cent on a blue background was used to identify them as belonging to the 45 per cent of Yes voters in the referendum. This development both annoyed and dismayed unionist voters.

Yes supporters on the Wings Over Scotland website also revealed the depth of their disappointment at the result, but there was much discussion of conspiracy theories around the voting procedures; this began the day after the vote and it was clear that feelings were running high amongst disappointed independence supporters. 'With no security on the boxes being uplifted or delivered it leaves a wide open opportunity for box exchange to pre-ready votes', said one independence supporter, while another commented 'I'm not concerned at the counting of the vote . . . I'm worried about the integrity of the ballot papers themselves' – just two examples of many of the similar concerns voiced. Campbell, however, expressed little patience with such sentiments and posted the comment 'We lost. There was no conspiracy. Now let's get to work winning', as he sought to focus bitterly disappointed independence supporters on the pursuit of their ultimate aim instead of harbouring resentment and challenging the result. As was the case with other pro-independence groups, he made it plain that the fight was far from over, and that the referendum was not the end of the issue. 'Of course, candles can still be relit, so long as they have a wick', he commented, indicating that so long as support for independence remained undiminished, the fight would be continued.

Meanwhile, as internal strife developed within the Conservative Party and its focus shifted to what became known as EVEL (English Votes for English Laws), the cynicism which had been expressed about the Better Together campaign's pledges of more powers for Scotland proved to have been prophetic. Despite the very rapid establishment of the Smith Commission, and a detailed timetable for the Commission's report and action plan, the failure of the Westminster government to immediately fulfil the undertakings made in 'the vow' sparked social media condemnation of the three political parties. The Labour Party in Scotland, however, was the focus of severe criticism. The Labour for Independence group stated that a public meeting would be held in October to decide its future, an announcement that generated more than 900 responses, mostly from disillusioned Labour Party supporters who voiced their rejection of the party for its contribution to and leading role in the Better Together campaign; 'Labour is dead to me', 'Labour is finished in Scotland' are sentiments that were repeated time and again. This outpouring of anger at Labour's leading role and close association with the Conservatives in the No Thanks campaign and in 'the vow' suggested that the Labour Party in Scotland, just months before the UK 2015 general election, was facing a major backlash from many of those who previously supported it; many of those who had voted No indicated that they had joined the SNP and in the weeks that followed, membership of the SNP did indeed grow exponentially.

Yes campaigners, meanwhile, refused to end the debate about Scotland's future, and continued to focus on their ultimate goal. For these groups, as noted earlier, the vote had not been solely about independence per se but also about a very public rejection of the neo-liberal policies of the Westminster government. Yes Scotland posted 'Our tears belong to yesterday. It's time to start building today for a better nation tomorrow. Our conversation continues' (20 September), and the movement for change rolled forward. Yes Scotland and other pro-independence groups began reaching out once more to the public on social media. The National Collective, the Common Weal, Women for Independence/Independence for Women all announced the continuance of their campaigns for substantial change in Scotland, using social media to garner further support. Their activities extended to the development of a network of branches and the organisation of rallies throughout Scotland, taking their movement for change from social media to the streets. Facebook and Twitter were used to co-ordinate offline action. Women For Independence/Independence For Women not only established branches around the country, but also opened food banks and used social media to organise collections for them. The National Collective announced it had already made plans to continue the Yes campaign's 'legacy', adding:

> When you get a popular revolution driven by hope and optimism like this, that energy will not dissolve into nothing. It can only grow. In the aftermath of a normal election, the losing party is disheartened and their supporters deflated. The difference here is that whilst the official No campaign has finished and will no doubt try to delete all evidence of it ever existing, people still make the Yes movement and we will continue to campaign and dream.[20]

The Common Weal also pledged to continue to pursue its goal, while Wings Over Scotland pledged to continue its campaign for an independent Scotland. Those who had voted No, meanwhile, continued to express a combination of dismay and bitterness that a democratic vote had not, as expected, settled the debate and that independence supporters were continuing to campaign for change both online and offline.

As 2014 came to a close, therefore, the movement for Scottish independence and social change was still very much active, both on social media and at grassroots level in communities around the country. The referendum result did not end pro-independence campaigning; this new and unexpected development widened the division between Yes and No voters; many of the latter were very distressed that the vote had not brought closure to an issue which had divided the country. The link between social media and the continuance of campaigning is inescapable, as the former played a significant role in making the second possible. They were the hubs which had enabled both sides of the referendum debate to disseminate their campaign messages without mediation by mainstream media, and to reach out to private individuals. They were successfully used to engage Scottish citizens in politics to an unprecedented extent; they provided platforms which enabled private individuals to have a voice in the public domain.

Castells observes that 'communication happens by activating minds to share meaning'[21] and the post-referendum period indicated that, having been engaged in the debate over Scotland's future, many independence supporters rejected any suggestion that they should accept defeat and submit to the results of the democratic vote. Instead, they used social media to continue campaigning. This creates considerable implications for future plebiscites, raising questions about the finality of election and referendum results and creating distress and uncertainty amongst those who supported the winning campaign. Simultaneously, however, these platforms not only provided outlets for hundreds and thousands of Scots to express their disappointment and in many cases devastation at the result of the referendum, but also directed them in ways that enabled them to continue the momentum built up during the campaign in productive ways.

Notes

1. Buchanan, 'Facebook: privacy and power in social space', p. 238.
2. Better Together, 2014.
3. Yes Scotland, 2014.
4. Castells, 'Communication, power and counter-power in the network society', p. 242.
5. Castells, 'Communication, power and counter-power in the network society', p. 70.
6. Polat, 'The Internet and political participation', p. 451.
7. Kelso, 'Parliament and political disengagement', p. 364.
8. House of Commons, 'Connecting Parliament with the public', p. 12.
9. Habermas, *The Structural Transformation of the Public Sphere*.
10. Boyd, 'Social network sites', p. 2)
11. Lascia, 2003, blog.
12. Leith and Soule, *Political Discourse and National Identity in Scotland*, p. 154.
13. Ibid., p. 154.
14. Ibid., p. 154.
15. Independence for Women, Facebook, 2014.
16. Wings Over Scotland, 2015.
17. Wings Over Scotland, 24 July 2014.
18. Huddy and Gunnthorsdottir, 'The persuasive effects of emotive visual imagery: superficial manipulation or the product of passionate reason', in Castells, *Communication Power*, p. 147.
19. Ibid., p. 147.
20. National Collective, Facebook, 20 September 2014.
21. Castells, *Communication Power*, p. 137.

Bibliography

Better Together, 2014, <https://www.facebook.com/bettertogetheruk?fref=ts> (last accessed 31 December 2014).

Boyd, D., 'Social network sites: public, private or what', *Knowledge Tree*, 13 May 2007, <http://tkt.flexiblelearning.net.au/tkt2007/?age_id=28> (last accessed 30 November 2014).

Buchanan, M., 'Facebook: Privacy and power in social space', unpublished PhD thesis, University of Stirling, 2011.

Castells, M., 'Communication, power and counter-power in the network society', *International Journal of Communication*, 1 (2007), pp. 238–66.

Castells, M., *Communication Power* (Oxford: Oxford University Press, 2009).

Habermas, J. [1962], *The Structural Transformation of the Public Sphere*, trans. T. Burger and F. Lawrence (Cambridge: Polity Press, 1989).

House of Commons, 'Connecting Parliament with the public', 2004, http://www.publications.parliament.uk/pa/cm200304/cmselect/cmmodern (last accessed 18 March 2015).

Huddy, L. and A. Gunnthorsdottir, 'The persuasive effects of emotive visual imagery: superficial manipulation or the product of passionate reason', *Political Psychology*, 21(4) (2000), pp. 745–78.

Kelso, A., 'Parliament and political disengagement: neither waving nor drowning', *Political Quarterly*, 78(3) (2007), pp. 364–73.

Lascia, J. D., 'Blogs and jotrnalism need each other', 8 September 2003, <http://www.jdlasica.com/2003/09/08/blogs-and-journalism-need-each-other/> (last accessed 31 December 2014).

Leith, M. S. and D. P. J. Soule, *Political Discourse and National Identity in Scotland* (Edinburgh: Edinburgh University Press, 2011).

Polat, R. K., 'The Internet and political participation: exploring the explanatory links', *European Journal of Communication*, 20 (2005), pp. 435–59.

Yes Scotland, 2014, <https://www.facebook.com/YesScotland?fref=ts> <https://twitter.com/YesScotland> (last accessed 31 December 2014).

Wings Over Scotland, 2014, <https://www.facebook.com/WingsOverScotland?fref=ts> (last accessed 26 February 2015). <https://twitter.com/search?q=wings%20over%20scotland&src=tyah> (last accessed 26 February 2015). <http://wingsoverscotland.com/> (last accessed 3 March 2015).

8

Sport, Gender and National Identities

John Harris and Fiona Skillen

Introduction

Sport and the Scottish independence referendum were inextricably intertwined. The possible impacts of a Yes vote had been the subject of many debates within sports organisations and in the media during the build-up to 18 September. How would funding for national UK bodies be split? What would happen to National Lottery funding so crucial to many community sports groups? And what about elite sport, what would bodies such as UK Sport do should Scotland become independent?

2014 was an unprecedented year for sport in Scotland with the nation hosting both the Commonwealth Games and the Ryder Cup – two of the biggest sporting events in the world. These high profile sporting events brought issues of national identity and politics sharply into focus. As Jim White noted:

> never mind all the alarmist stuff about bank flight and currency uncertainty, sport offers the most positive message the No campaign could offer . . . the history of sport in Scotland is the best evidence of how successfully the Union has worked. (*Telegraph*, 17 September 2014)

Others might have suggested that the Yes campaign was slow to exploit the already existing national sporting opportunities, such as Scotland's ability to enter its own teams into competitions such as the Commonwealth Games and the football World Cup.

This chapter will examine some of the main issues which emerged during 2014 relating to the world of sport and the referendum. It will look at the ways in which the media focus on athletes to identify them with the nation and will look specifically at the role of the Commonwealth Games within the referendum campaign. It will also consider the incident that created the most controversy, and will then reflect upon two significant events in the sport of golf which took place in Scotland around the time of the referendum. Before focusing specifically on the summer of 2014 though, it is important to briefly reflect back on a couple of other major sporting events where discussion and debates around national identities were most visible as Scottish athletes competed as part of the wider collective of Great Britain and Northern Ireland in the Olympic Games.

The Olympic Games

Prior to the much anticipated Commonwealth Games taking place in Glasgow, the discussion of the contested terrain surrounding Scottish and British identities within international sport became the focus of much debate and discussion. In the summer of 2012 many Scottish athletes found themselves at the centre of discussions surrounding sport as a means of national representation when London hosted the Olympic Games. For members of Team GB, then, this was really a 'once in a lifetime' opportunity to compete at a 'home' games. Despite the somewhat pessimistic outlook and last-minute concerns about the security arrangements in place, the Games were a remarkable success and generated a 'feel-good' factor amongst many Britons. In his speech arguing the case for the preservation of the union (delivered at the Velodrome in the Olympic Park in London on the day of the opening ceremony of the 2014 Winter Olympics at Sochi), the British Prime Minister David Cameron noted of London 2012 that 'it was the summer that patriotism came out of the shadows' (*Spectator*, 7 February 2014). Something of a media vortex emerged around the games as all media across Britain led with stories of the event with titles such as 'Scots play leading role as Team GB rack up medals' (*Herald*, 1 August 2012) appearing in the Scottish media. As the home nation continued to win medals there was a popular presentation of Britishness carrying on from the positive legacy of a royal wedding in 2011 and the Queen's diamond jubilee celebrations one year later.

There was much to celebrate for Scottish athletes during this period. The cyclist Sir Chris Hoy surpassed Sir Steve Redgrave's record to become Britain's most successful Olympian. Andy Murray, who had recently been defeated in the final of Wimbledon, won gold in the tennis. The popular rower Katherine Grainger, born in Glasgow and who took up rowing at university in Edinburgh, finally secured a gold medal after taking silver at the previous three Olympics. Grainger, who had been based in the south of England for most of her long and successful career, had a postbox in Aberdeen painted gold in her honour. This was one of a number of postboxes across the country painted gold to celebrate the achievements of Team GB's Olympic and Paralympic gold medalists.[1]

Two years later, at the beginning of 2014, a smaller group of athletes were to represent Team GB at the Olympic Winter Games in Sochi. Scottish athletes accounted for almost one third of Team GB for this event. Here, in both men's and women's curling, all of the players were Scottish and both of these teams came home with medals. Their successes contributed to half of the medals won by Team GB which, although a modest total, actually equalled the previous record for the most medals won by a British team at the inaugural Winter Olympics in 1924. With the referendum looming ever closer, it was clear that competing claims for these medal winners was going to become an ever-present issue. The women's Skip, Eve Muirhead, noted that 'We are proud to represent Great Britain at the Olympics, and we are proud to represent Scotland in other competitions' (*Daily Mail*, 20 February 2014).

Here, in both the men's and women's curling competitions, Team GB were the subject of much media attention with numerous references to the success of 2002 when a team of Scottish women claimed the gold medal for Great Britain and Northern Ireland. O'Donnell has noted how much of the media creatively and inventively appropriated the relatively unknown sport of curling, and the gold medal winning British women's team, as 'the quintessence of all that is Scottish'.[2]

Twelve years on and the increasing sensitivities surrounding the referendum were clearly visible as any comments from the athletes were seized upon and taken as evidence of being either for or against independence. The women's team, in particular, was the focus of much attention and the group was often questioned about their views on the referendum. Muirhead's comment that competing for Team GB was 'extra special', given that nine times out of ten she would be representing Scotland, was seized upon by some as a pro-union stance (*Express*, 25 February 2014). These athletes, like their counterparts in other sports who were to compete in Glasgow a few months later, were in a no-win situation and had to be very careful not to be pulled into the independence debate.

Living and training in Scotland, the only part of the wider collective where curling is really played, these women would represent Scotland in European and World Championships and Team GB in the Olympic Games. The sport is governed by the Royal Caledonian Curling Club, but is funded by a system of elite sport performance supported by UK Sport, thereby demonstrating the many layers involved in the governance of the sport.

In performance terms, these were heady times indeed then, with record break-ing results at London and Sochi accompanied by many heart-warming narratives to celebrate the power of sport in a range of media (e.g. *Herald*, 1 August 2012; *Scotsman*, 22 January 2014). Glasgow's successful bid to host the Commonwealth Games in 2014 meant that in Scotland sport remained firmly in the spotlight. Coming so soon after the London 2012 Olympics there could really have been no better time to stage a Commonwealth Games in a part of Britain, although the impending referendum made this a potentially contentious event where sport and politics might collide.

The Commonwealth Games

In the months leading up to the Glasgow Commonwealth Games there was a growing expectation in some parts of the media that the referendum would overshadow the event. Some journalists speculated that the date of the referendum, 18 September, had been deliberately chosen by First Minister Alex Salmond in order to maximise on burgeoning Scottish national pride stimulated by the Commonwealth Games and Ryder Cup (*Guardian*, 21 March 2014). The London 2012 Olympics had seen a swelling of British patriotism

(*New Statesman*, 12 August 2012) and, significantly for Salmond, unionism. Could the combination of the Commonwealth Games, Ryder Cup and Homecoming 2014 neutralise these feelings?

Much of the press seemed to think so, and voices supporting independence speculated about what potential impact a 'good' Games would have on national feeling, and perhaps most significantly, on those who were still undecided about which way to vote. Among articles outlining the implications at policy level, *The Herald* noted a 'Whole new ball game for sportscotland in event of a yes vote' (14 August 2014). Concern focused almost exclusively on the Yes camp and what tactics they might employ to 'hijack' the event for their own ends. Indeed there was good reason to suggest that the SNP, and First Minister Alex Salmond in particular, would seek to maximise the impact of the Commonwealth Games on their campaign. Salmond, had of course, used international sporting events as a platform for nationalist politics. In the build-up to the 2012 Olympics he had released a controversial statement wishing Team GB all the best and singled out the Scots within the team, 'to all 54 Olympians and 23 Scottish Paralympians'. He went on to encourage all fellow Scots to cheer on what he described as the 'Scolympians' (*Telegraph*, 27 July 2012). In July 2013, at the final of the men's singles championship at Wimbledon, Salmond, whilst sitting behind UK Prime Minster David Cameron, unfurled a flag of St Andrew as Andy Murray received his trophy.[3] Murray, it has been joked in sections of the press, was characterised as British when he was winning and Scottish when he was losing (*New Statesman*, 6 July 2013). The First Minister clearly saw this as an opportune moment to make the point once and for all that Andy Murray was Scottish, a tactic which Murray himself later said he 'didn't like' (*Telegraph*, 8 June 2014).

In January 2014, former First Minister Jack McConnell called for a 'truce' between both sides of the independence debate for the duration of the Commonwealth Games (BBC News, 8 January 2014). In his speech in the House of Lords McConnell stated that in such a potentially close-run vote it would be tempting for both sides to use the Games as a platform for their campaigns. He stressed the need to focus on 'Glasgow and Scotland winning some gold medals', ensuring that none of the organisers or competitors were 'distracted or concerned [that] what they say, do or achieve might be exploited or used by either side in the aftermath' (BBC News, 8 January 2014). Shona Robison, Commonwealth Games and Sport Minister, struck back arguing that there was absolutely no evidence that politics would, or indeed could, overshadow the events of the Games. Salmond too was quick to respond, stating that the Commonwealth Games 'are going to be the most enormous success for Scotland. It's right and proper that people will debate politics, but the idea that politics will overshadow the Games is nonsensical' (*Guardian*, 8 January 2014).

By early July, neither side had agreed to McConnell's truce.

> I hope that everybody will see sense around the Games and do all they can to avoid politicising them. But I think the fact that they haven't said clearly in

advance [that they won't] will mean they will be pushed by the media and others
to do so . . . and I think that's very unfortunate. (*Independent*, 10 July 2014)

However, only a few days later, Salmond had reconsidered his position. He
decided to impose a 'self-denying ordinance' that forbade him from talking about
the referendum, something which he did with only limited success. He said that
he had imposed this ban on himself in order to avoid any 'argy-bargy, with
George Osborne and David Cameron' (*Telegraph*, 23 July 2014).

For most of the Games both sides steered clear of overtly political statements,
appearing to adhere to an 'unofficial truce'. Nonetheless the prominence given
to politicians within the media coverage of key events ensured that the nation's
attention was rarely away from the referendum, and one journalist went as far as
to describe the issue as 'the elephant in the stadium' (*Independent*, 11 July 2014).

While the politicians attempted to keep politics out of the Games some
of the competitors were less inclined to do so. In the run up to the opening
ceremony, Team Scotland released a statement:

> We believe that all our athletes are entitled to express their opinions on any
> subject, but we have advised them to bear in mind that there is heightened
> interest in the independence referendum later this year. I am sure some of them
> will nail their colours to the mast and, indeed, some of them have already done
> so. All we would do is remind them that it's important not to let anything
> become a distraction. (*Independent*, 19 July 2014)

Amongst the first athletes to 'nail their colours to the mast' were Judo champion
Connie Ramsay (Yes) and boxer Stephen Simmons (No). Both athletes were
vocal in their beliefs regarding the referendum and were keen to utilise the media
platform the Games provided to voice their opinions (*Independent*, 10 July 2014).
Ramsay was part of a group of Scottish athletes who in May had launched a Sport
for Yes vote campaign (*Herald*, 15 May 2014). During the fortnight of competition other athletes joined those above in voicing their opinion on the referendum issue, but of the 310 Team Scotland competitors only a handful publicly lent
their voices to the debate.

2014 was Scotland's most successful Commonwealth Games ever, with a
medal haul of thirty-three. In the immediate aftermath there was a suggestion
that the success of the Games, both in terms of Team Scotland's medal tally and
the staging of the event, would have an impact on feelings of national pride and
therefore buoy a pro-nationalist vote. Gerry Hassan commented,

> Of course the Commonwealth Games will have an effect on the independence
> referendum. It couldn't be otherwise. And part of the independence argument is
> an argument about: can Scots feel they have the confidence to do this? Do they
> feel they have the optimism?[4]

However, Hugh O'Donnell pointed out that there was little evidence of previous sporting events affecting political success or failure. For him, 'people do

not "live in their nations full time", they live in their local areas, their homes, families and workplaces' (BBC News, 2 August 2014). The Commonwealth Games therefore could impact on how people felt about Scotland but that impact was temporary and always in relation to 'bigger' or more tangible immediate issues, such as employment, education, health and financial security. Indeed polls conducted in the days after the closing ceremony showed little change in the way people intended to vote. One poll conducted by Survation found that more than 80 per cent of those asked said 'the Games had made no difference to how they would vote'. While the crucial 'undecided' voters were generally unmoved (82 per cent), 14 per cent said that Scotland's performance and organisation in the Games had persuaded them to vote Yes, and 4 per cent moved towards No (*Scotsman*, 3 August 2014).

So the Commonwealth Games were an undoubted success but also highlighted the role of sport as politics with a small 'p'. The huge cheers from the Scottish crowd for the athletes from the other home nations, including England, had shown that the fears of them being roundly booed were unfounded. Yet perhaps for those expecting some major controversy linking sport to the referendum the most news-worthy story came from a rather unlikely source as Andy Murray entered the debate.

Tweeting into Trouble

Most athletes adopted a strategy of not making public their views on the refer-endum as the day of the vote drew closer. This was due in part to the increasing tension apparent where anyone who dared raise her/his head above the parapet was subject to hostile commentary, and those who engaged with the debate through the medium of Twitter might be subject to the twenty-first century disease of 'trolling', where personal and at times highly abusive commentary would be directed at them. Andy Murray, as we have highlighted above, was one of the most high-profile athletes from Scotland. His performances over the past couple of years had seen him become a site of contention between different sides of the referendum debate.[5] Murray, like others among the most famous Scottish athletes, does not reside in Scotland so did not have a vote but on the day that Scotland went to the polls he tweeted: 'Huge day for Scotland today! no campaign negativity last few days totally swayed my view on it. excited to see the outcome. lets [*sic*] do this!'

This late intervention by Murray, who only a few months previously had acknowledged that he was embarrassed by Alex Salmond's unfurling of the Scottish flag at Wimbledon, became a massive news story. O'Donnell[6] has noted that the suggestion that Murray is British when he wins but Scottish when he loses is a myth that has also been used in relation to the performances of a number of other athletes from Scotland. In his autobiography Murray reflected upon this dual identity:

> Let me say, here and now, that I am Scottish. I am also British. I am *not* anti-English. I never was. I'm patriotic and proud to be Scottish, but my girlfriend is

English, my gran who I love to bits is English and half her family is English . . .
I practise in England with English players, I play Davis Cup for Britain – but I
love being Scottish. There is nothing wrong with that.[7]

Some of the English press was very critical of Murray when he joked that he
would be supporting 'anyone but England' in the 2006 football World Cup and
this experience clearly influenced his guardedness with the media for many years.
Murray was a clear winner in the public vote for the BBC's Sports Personality of
the Year award in 2013 and, prior to the tweet referred to above, had seen a massive increase in his popularity within a British context since the summer of 2012.

Murray's entry into the debate led to headlines such as 'Andy Murray branded
"irresponsible" for revealing "extremely ill-advised" Scottish Independence view
on Twitter' (*Independent*, 18 September 2014). The player's views on the issue
attracted international media attention well beyond the British press with an
article in the *Courier Mail* (Australia) referring to 'polls running tighter than a
bagpiper's blowhole' and the reaction of Middle England 'spitting out its tea and
dropping its crumpets simultaneously' (18 September 2014).

Murray's comments here must surely be the main reason why he was the most
searched-for sportsman in the UK online during 2014 (according to Microsoft's
search engine Bing), thereby placing him ahead of the South African Paralympic
and Olympic athlete Oscar Pistorius, who was jailed in October 2014 for killing
his girlfriend.

Interestingly, one of the main areas which the leading tabloid newspapers
decided to focus upon was the possible effect that Murray's tweet would have on
his mother winning the 'celebrity' television show *Strictly Come Dancing*. *The
Mirror* reported that as a result of her son's tweet the odds on Judy Murray being
the first to be voted off the show had been cut from 16-1 to 10-1 (19 September
2014).

Despite being a successful tennis coach in her own right, Judy Murray was
invited onto the show and described by the ubiquitous term 'celebrity' by virtue
of being Andy Murray's mother. Her son's comments did not seemingly impact
upon her tenure on the show where she remained in the competition for a number
of weeks despite clearly being one of the worst dancers on the programme. In
truth, then, despite much scaremongering immediately after her son's tweet, it
may only have had a very limited impact upon her participation in the show.

The sport of golf also represented an interesting site to further explore some
of the key issues surrounding the political terrain in Scotland and two significant
events were to take place within one week of the referendum. It is to these that
we now turn.

The Ryder Cup

As the memories of the Commonwealth Games faded and the date of the referendum drew closer, it was easy to lose sight of the fact that there was also another
major sporting event due to take place on Scottish soil just days after the vote.

The Ryder Cup had first been staged in 1927 as a golf match between the best players from the United States of America (USA) and Great Britain before being expanded to include Ireland in 1973 and finally the creation of a European team in 1979. It had been staged in Scotland only once before, when Muirfield in East Lothian was the site of the 1973 contest.

In some ways it felt a bit like an anticlimax in late September 2014, for Team Europe moved to an easy victory and the sole Scottish representative (Stephen Gallacher) played only a minor role. There was much to live up to after the dramatic contests in 2010 and 2012, which both went down to the final singles match, and although the 2014 Ryder Cup was a great success, it lacked much of the drama and excitement of many of the matches that had taken place before.

As a showcase for the host nation, in the country positioned as the self-styled 'home of golf', this was always going to be a significant part of wider tourism initiatives, irrespective of the vote on 18 September during the year of Homecoming 2014. Images of tartan were ubiquitous at Gleneagles as they had been for the opening ceremony of Glasgow 2014. For a while in the lead-up to the event it looked as though there would not be any 'home' players in the team for only the second time in the history of the event, but Stephen Gallacher's late run of form saw him granted one of the captain's three picks to become part of Team Europe. There was no fairytale match-winning story though for Gallacher, and the honour of claiming the winning points fell to Jamie Donaldson. That a Welshman, who lives in England, should become the match-winning hero for Team Europe in an event staged in Scotland offered a most fitting narrative to visibly show the many national (and indeed supranational) identities at play.

We are currently witnessing a continued Europeanisation of the Ryder Cup but this continues to be based upon a very strong British and Irish core.[8] Outside of the high-profile Ryder Cup, though, there was another important issue in the game of golf being discussed during the week of the referendum.

An Alternative Referendum

The decision on whether or not to support Scottish independence was not the only vote taking place in Scotland on 18 September, for the Royal and Ancient Golf Club of St Andrews was also deciding whether to admit female members. During the club's 260-year history it had followed a strict single-sex policy; women could play on the course at certain times but they could not become members, influence rule making or even enter the club house (BBC Sport, 18 September 2014).

For many the vote was important, not only in terms of women gaining access to the club, but also for the symbolism of this particular institution opening its doors to females. The Royal and Ancient (R&A), often referred to as the 'home of golf', is responsible for the governance of the sport throughout the world, with the exception of the USA.

Pressure had been mounting in recent years, beginning two years previously when the Augusta National Golf Club in the USA permitted female members, and culminating in 2014 when Alex Salmond, Maria Miller (former UK Culture Secretary) and Hugh Robertson (former Sports Minister) refused to attend the Open Championship at Muirfield (a male-only club), in protest at the inequalities within the sport (*Telegraph*, 18 September 2014). HSBC, one of the main sponsors of the Open, voiced its discomfort at the situation: 'it is a very uneasy position for the bank . . . we would like to see it solved' (*Herald*, 24 January 2014). Chief Executive of the R&A, Peter Dawson, admitted in July 2013, 'We do, I assure you, understand this is a divisive issue. It's a subject we are finding increasingly difficult, to be honest' (BBC Sport, 18 July 2013). In March, Dawson announced a ballot of members, stating, 'We've done this really because of our governance role in the game. Sport has been changing, society has been changing and golf is part of that. We think it's time this change is made' (BBC Sport, 26 March 2014).

For many, golf was still perceived to be 'outdated' and 'exclusive', although less than 1 per cent of the 3000 clubs affiliated to the R&A are single-sex. By opening up membership opportunities and promoting inclusion, rather than exclusion, it was hoped that this view could be changed. As Helen Grant, Minister of Sport, explained, 'With golf in the next Olympics, there is a huge opportunity for the sport to grow and this sends out the right inclusive message that golf is for everyone' (*Telegraph*, 18 September 2014). Catriona Matthew, former Women's Open Champion, went further, noting that:

> golf desperately needs to move with the times, to be seen as more inclusive, because this whole issue has been about perception as much as anything . . . It will make a symbolic difference. It will help to change the perception of golf as a stuffy, fuddy-duddy sport for old men in blazers. It will encourage more girls to get involved. It will say to other clubs – and other sports – that there needs to be more equality. (*Telegraph*, 18 September 2014)

And so the scene was set for the 'alternative' referendum.

In the days leading up to the vote a vox pop poll conducted in St Andrews predicted a positive outcome, but with only 60 per cent of the vote (*Telegraph*, 17 September 2014). When the results were announced late on the 18th, the result was indeed in favour of female membership, but with a much larger majority than previously expected at 85 per cent.[9] The club also approved an additional motion, which proposed allowing fifteen women to be fast-tracked through the membership process.

The issue of inequality in golf will remain a topic of debate in Scotland with both Royal Troon (due to host the Open in 2016) and Muirfield continuing to pursue single-sex membership. Nonetheless the change at the R&A may mark a significant change in the tide.

Concluding Remarks

Sport has long been recognised as a particularly powerful tool in the representation and promotion of national identities.[10] In Scotland, where Jim Sillars once described his country as a nation of 'ninety minute patriots', it is clear that sport matters[11] and that hosting two prestigious major sporting events in 2014 was a source of much national pride.

The referendum debate was ever-present in much of the discussion around Scottish sport and offered opportune sites for political capital to be gained. The media, as we have highlighted in some of the examples above, would also at times actively look for an angle whereby they could weave the issue of independence into narratives of sporting success. Alex Salmond's unfurling of the Scottish flag at Wimbledon, and David Cameron's choice of date and venue for his speech on preserving the union, both highlighted the ways in which sport matters and can be used by politicians.

Yet what was rarely considered in much of the media reporting were the ways in which these identities are fluid, contingent and relatively unfixed. Although sport provides seemingly fertile ground for the waving of flags and the banal nationalism embedded within many other aspects of popular culture, it is also a place where there are many different identities at play. The mediated suggestion of a virulent 'anti-Englishness' never materialised at the Commonwealth Games and the English athletes were perhaps afforded the second loudest cheers of all by the home fans. This is not to say that such sentiments are shared by all or that in a different context things will be the same. Towards the end of 2014 when Scotland played England in a men's football match at Celtic Park there has possibly never been a more pronounced jeering of the English (and British) national anthem at a sporting event on these shores.

2014 will go down in history not only as a significant year when the people of Scotland decided to remain part of the wider collective of the United Kingdom, but also as the biggest ever year for Scottish sport. The sun shone for much of the Commonwealth Games and the host nation surpassed the targets it had been set to be the most successful games ever for Team Scotland. If the weather co-operates and the host nation does well, then the main ingredients for a successful major sporting event are in place. Both men and women contributed to this success, as was also the case in the Olympic Winter Games earlier in the year where Scottish athletes accounted for half of all medals won by Team GB. As representatives of the nation, we saw female athletes play a prominent role in a range of media narratives during the summer of 2014 as they had during the reporting of other multi-sport events.[12] In Scotland, as in many other nations across the globe, female athletes remain under-represented and marginalised within much sports media reporting outside of such events, although their visibility took on an added significance in the summer of 2014 as national and political identities became ever more important. A continuing discussion of which nation many of these athletes represent – and of these associated gender questions – will remain a contentious topic in the years ahead.

Notes

1. See Harris, 'Dancing in the streets of Dunblane'.
2. O'Donnell, 'Scotland the we(e)?', p. 53.
3. Harris, 'Dancing in the streets of Dunblane'.
4. 'The Games People Play', BBC Scotland, 22 July 2014.
5. Harris, 'Dancing in the streets of Dunblane'.
6. O'Donnell, 'Scotland the we(e)?'
7. Murray, Hitting Back: The Autobiography, p. 126.
8. Harris, 'Europeanisation of the Ryder Cup.'
9. <randa.org>, 18 September 2014.
10. Blain et al., Sport and National Identity in the European Media.
11. See e.g. Reid, 'The stone of destiny'; Skillen and McDowell, 'The Edinburgh 1970 Commonwealth Games'.
12. O'Donnell, 'Scotland the we(e)?'; Reid, 'The stone of destiny'.

Bibliography

Blain, N., R. Boyle and H. O'Donnell, Sport and National Identity in the European Media (Leicester: Leicester University Press, 1993).

Harris, J., 'Dancing in the streets of Dunblane: Contested identities in elite Scottish sport', Catalan Journal of Communication & Cultural Studies, 6(2) (2014), 273–9.

Harris, J., 'Europeanisation of the Ryder Cup?', Sport&EU Review, 6(1) (2014), 14–19.

Murray, A. with S. Mott, Hitting Back: The Autobiography (London: Century, 2008).

O'Donnell, H. (2012) 'Scotland the we(e)?: A small country in a large world at the Salt Lake Winter Olympics', in C. Sandvoss, M. Real and A. Bernstein (eds), Bodies of Discourse: Sports Stars, Media, and the Global Public (New York: Peter Lang, 2012), pp. 37–54.

Reid, I., 'The stone of destiny: Team GB curling as a site for contested nationalistic discourse', Sport in Society, 13(3) (2010), pp. 399–417.

Skillen, F. and M. McDowell, 'The Edinburgh 1970 Commonwealth Games: representation of identities, nationalism and politics', Sport in History, 34(3) (2014), 454–75.

PART TWO

Views from the UK

9

English Television News Coverage of the Scottish Referendum

Andrew Tolson

Introduction

On Sunday, 14 September 2014, reporting of the Scottish referendum campaign on ITN's Channel 4 News included footage of a demonstration
outside the BBC's television studios in Glasgow. The demonstrators' main accusation was that the BBC was 'biased' against the Yes campaign and the footage
included prominent display of a placard calling for the BBC's political editor,
Nick Robinson, to be sacked. Understandably perhaps, the BBC's own reporting
of the demonstration was less extensive, with no identification of Robinson,
and only a passing reference to 'perceived bias at the BBC'. However, it was
discussed extensively with Blair Jenkins, chief executive of the Yes campaign, on
the following day's edition of *The Daily Politics*. Here Jenkins was at pains to assert
that the demonstration had not been organised by the campaign, but rather was a
spontaneous event, crowdsourced through social media. Although he was subject
to critical interrogation by his interviewer, Jo Coburn, Jenkins continued to
claim that there was an 'inability of London based journalists' to understand what
was happening in Scotland, and that Scottish journalists were being 'elbowed
aside' by their English counterparts.

Clearly this perception sets an agenda for a survey of English television news
coverage of the referendum. Was the BBC in fact guilty of bias, as charged? To
investigate this accusation, I have analysed nearly fifty hours of TV news coverage,
including every BBC 10 o'clock news from 3 September to 20 September, as
well as the subsequent programme, *Newsnight*, over the same period. I have also
looked at twelve editions of the BBC's *The Daily Politics* and three editions of
its Sunday morning equivalent, *The Andrew Marr Show*. For comparison I also
recorded and studied ITN's Channel 4 news, which was selected in preference
to other ITN news bulletins on the assumption that, with its greater length
(fifty-five minutes), it would contain more in-depth and detailed coverage of this
type of political event.

But before we can embark on this analysis, there is a problematic issue that must be addressed. This is because the title of this chapter, and indeed the brief I was given by the editors of this volume, begs an important question; namely, that there is something that can be defined as 'English' television news. All the news programmes I have studied for this chapter were made by organisations that officially adhere to the public service principle of geographic universality. In the UK context that of course means British, not English, broadcasting, and indeed all the programmes in my data, though produced in England, were shown simultaneously north of the border. The British TV institutions do provide some news programming that reflects geographic diversity, but (to the chagrin of many Scots) this is defined in regional, not national terms. In this context I took the view that there would be little point writing a chapter for this book based on English regional television simply because the Scottish referendum, not being 'local news', would not be covered there. So what we have here is TV coverage that is officially 'British', which makes the question of its possible 'Englishness' something interesting to investigate.

The chapter is organised into two main subsections, covering four aspects of the news coverage. Broadly these subsections are differentiated according to the kinds of editorial decision making they apparently contain. In the first section, editorial policy appears to be professionally controlled and deliberative. It concerns the explicit news agenda, in matters such as the placement of stories in bulletins, their respective length, and the topical focus on what, on any particular day, is 'making the news'. This also includes decisions about the 'major players' who are worth quoting and/or interviewing, and I have also added to this category some analysis of editorial commentary, such as that routinely provided by 'editors'[1] such as Robinson, either in live quasi-interviews with the news anchor, or in recorded pieces to camera. In all these contexts, one assumes, editorial practices are carefully considered.

However, in the second subsection, I also look at some journalistic practices whose communicative effects might be more open to debate. To what extent journalists themselves are aware of these effects is a matter for conjecture, but from an academic perspective they raise interesting questions about further levels of news presentation. For example, one thing that is immediately apparent in much of the BBC and Channel 4 news coverage of the referendum is that TV studios were abandoned in favour of external locations alongside iconic monuments (especially in Edinburgh). Did this immediately identify referendum news as somehow exceptional and what was the effect of choosing these specific locations? Another interesting factor was the choice of locations for 'roving reports', where journalists went in search of public opinion and were filmed questioning voters. Here Blair Jenkins's point becomes relevant, that often these were English journalists questioning Scottish voters. Of course, on one level, these journalists were following standard practices of 'vox pop' reporting, but on another level what was also constructed was a kind of drama of cross-cultural interaction.

Editorial Practices: News Agendas and Commentary

As far as the deliberative news agenda is concerned, the most obvious point to make is that everything changed following the publication of the YouGov poll on 7 September. The BBC actually previewed this as a 'breakthrough poll' in its Saturday evening news bulletin, and the Scottish referendum suddenly shot up its news agenda. In the previous week, the referendum had appeared as the fifth or sixth item in most BBC bulletins, though briefly up to fourth place with a visit to Glasgow by Ed Miliband on 4 September. The editions of *Newsnight* on 3 and 4 September had no coverage of the referendum at all (though it was the third item on Friday, 5 September). Similarly, Channel 4 news on 6 September had nothing on the referendum. At best, it is fair to say, the coverage was patchy. After 7 September, however, right through to polling day and beyond, the referendum was usually the number one story,[2] taking up by far the most amount of time. On Monday, 8 September the entire *Newsnight* programme was devoted to this topic, which it had twice completely ignored in the previous week.

Of course, it is easy to argue that this agenda shift reflected a new perception that the unity of the UK was under serious threat (and the role of opinion polls in driving news agendas is an interesting issue here). Furthermore, it was also apparent that this was a perception shared for the first time by the population of England, and in particular by its political establishment. Arguably it is the close relationship between that establishment and mainstream political journalism in the UK that underpinned the sudden agenda shift. Furthermore, it might be expected that the BBC, in particular, would have a vested interest in preserving the 'Britain' it had been founded to serve. However, it does not follow from these arguments that the BBC (or other broadcasting organisations) were uniformly 'biased' against the Yes campaign. Certainly there were aspects of the TV news agenda that were problematic for that campaign, particularly through the recycling of some critical issues and an interpretation of Scottish politics that linked it to the UK as a whole. However, as the debate intensified following 7 September, it was also the case the No campaign came under intense scrutiny, not only for its apparent failure to communicate with voters, but in particular for the shifting ground of its promises of enhanced devolution to the people of Scotland. And by 9 September, as we shall see, the characterisation of this as a reaction of 'panic' was actually shared by SNP politicians and the BBC's chief political editor.

There were two major problematic points for the Yes campaign on the British TV news agenda. The first was financial 'uncertainty', particularly around the currency question, following a critical intervention by the governor of the Bank of England which was given particular prominence (BBC News, 9 September). This was linked to reports of falling currency and share values, and what one No campaigner called Salmond's 'Black Wednesday', as banks and corporations, in the event of a Yes vote, threatened to move their headquarters to London (BBC News, 10 September). A second critical point was highlighted in an interview with George Robertson, former Labour Defence Secretary, on *Newsnight* (also on 10 September) on the implications of the Yes campaign's policy on Trident and its consequences for Britain's membership of NATO. The following week, *Newsnight* carried an interview with a minister in the Spanish government on the complexities of applying for EU membership (15 September) and this was followed the next day by an item on Channel 4 news featuring an American diplomat, on the likelihood of a diminished role for the UK in world affairs. Although alternative voices were sometimes heard (for example, in my data there are four brief interviews with representatives of Business for Scotland), the cumulative effect of these negative reports and interviews was to amplify the risks of voting Yes, which of course was very much part of the argument of the No campaign.

A second issue, which also complicated the question of Scottish independence, was a growing realisation that a Yes vote in Scotland would have major implications for politics in the UK as a whole. It is crucial to appreciate the significance of this dimension, for it gave other parts of the UK a stake in what was happening in Scotland which previously had been minimised (for example, the first televised debate between Salmond and Darling, on STV, was not even shown south of the border). There were two focal points here for the television news agenda. The first was constitutional, and the second was to do with the consequences of Scottish independence for UK-wide political parties. It is not necessary here to fully explore the often arcane constitutional questions: just to note, for example, that on 9 September *The Daily Politics* had former Conservative minister Kenneth Baker advocating a federal solution to 'huge constitutional change'; and on 15 September it included an interview with the shadow Welsh Secretary, Owen Smith, on the subject of further devolution for Wales. More radically, on 12 September the same programme gave a platform to Tory MP John Redwood's argument in favour of an English Parliament (also featured on *Newsnight* on 9 September) as his preferred solution to the so-called 'West Lothian question' – that is, the anomaly of Scottish and Welsh MPs voting at Westminster on English matters, but English MPs being unable to vote on matters devolved to the parliaments of Scotland and Wales. As might be expected, such constitutional matters were extensively discussed on *The Daily Politics*, with its cast of London-based MPs and journalists, but they also were a background to the TV news agenda as a whole.

More pressing perhaps, and interesting for political commentators, were the implications of the referendum debate for traditional political parties. A general point here, which, as we shall see, was flagged up by Nick Robinson in the BBC news on 9 September, was the risk of Westminster party leaders campaigning in Scotland, given the deep distrust of Westminster politics in some sections of the Scottish electorate. On 10 September, Laura Kuenssberg on *Newsnight* questioned the efficacy of such 'controlled visits', which she contrasted with the two-year 'real campaign which belongs to the street'. The same programme concluded with two journalists discussing the consequences of a Yes vote for the Prime Minister, and there was much reference (e.g. *Newsnight*, 16 September) to the decline of the Conservative Party right across Scotland. However, as the debate intensified in its final two weeks, more attention was focused on the Labour Party, particularly in its so-called 'heartlands' in the west of Scotland. On 15 September former Labour cabinet minister John Reid was interviewed on *The Daily Politics* on the question 'is Labour failing in Scotland?'; and on *Newsnight* former Labour spin doctor Alastair Campbell linked the 'anger at Labour in Scotland' to a general point about Scots being 'hacked off with Westminster politics'.

It is in this context that I now want to examine in a bit more detail the contribution to BBC TV news made by Nick Robinson on Tuesday, 9 September. I shall use this as a 'test case' for the 'bias' of which he was accused. First, however, it should be noted that Robinson's role, like that of other senior 'editors' and correspondents, is to reproduce a particular sub-genre of news discourse – a type of commentary that Martin Montgomery characterises as 'doing being interesting'.[3] That is to say, in a brief slot of between one and two minutes, the political editor is permitted not simply to report, but also to analyse and even to speculate (and Montgomery shows how analysis is typically 'hedged' by speculation as it 'rings the changes from moment to moment'). This is evident in Robinson's piece, the evening before the three Westminster party leaders were due to travel to Scotland. Prefacing the whole thing in an exchange with the anchor, Huw Edwards ('As long as you and I live Huw I think we are extraordinarily unlikely to see a day like this one repeated'), he goes on to emphasise the unprecedented constitutional developments of (1) the party leaders abandoning Prime Minister's Question Time in the House of Commons, (2) the critical intervention by the Governor of the Bank of England and (3) the difficult constitutional position of the Queen. All this climaxes, in the first section of his commentary, with a (twice hedged – see italics) repetition of a statement made earlier that day by representatives of the SNP, namely that the British establishment was in a state of 'panic':

> It's a reminder *if you like* of how high the stakes are, it's a reminder of how much anxiety, a wave *if you like* of panic and anxiety has gone through the British establishment.

However, Robinson does not stop there. Following quotation of a statement by Cameron about to appear in the *Daily Mail*, he then goes on to offer some speculative political analysis. Here the SNP reference becomes explicit, but also a claim that the referendum is 'unpredictable' is linked to a point about UK politics:

> Now of course it could all be horribly counter-productive. Alex Salmond we've heard mocking this as panic mocking this as the establishment desperate to stop Scots making their minds up. And why this is so unpredictable I think is to do with the nature of the coalition backing Yes: nationalists who've been nationalists in their blood for years if not decades Yes; people who want more Scottish self-government Yes; but a crucial third group those who are furious

with the political elite, they are people who *even though Alex Salmond is very different from Nigel Farage* are very similar to the people Nigel Farage is appealing to in England as well. And the nature of that anger means that the result is now completely unpredictable.

Where is the bias here? Robinson is not (unlike the BBC's economics editor) repeating substantive points that are problematic for the Yes campaign; indeed he is, at one remove, repeating a point made by Salmond himself. But what he is also clearly doing is linking the Yes campaign to an English political agenda. This may be because he thinks the comparison will help his English viewers understand the populist element in the Yes campaign. But what it also makes, I would suggest, is a very controversial link between that campaign and a right-wing form of English populism that is total anathema to many supporters of Scottish independence. It is not my job in this chapter to make political judgements, but even if there was, in Scotland, a 'hatred' of the Westminster establishment, the argument does not need to be developed in this way, as demonstrated for example by Alastair Campbell (quoted above).

Finally, however, what Robinson's piece also illustrates is the fundamental preoccupation of the TV news coverage. At its most basic level, on a day-to-day basis, this was focused on the *conduct* of the campaign: on what were taken to be the 'primary definers', on their campaign strategies, and on manifestations of public opinion in polls and demonstrations. Here the narrative was in two parts, with the penultimate week dominated by official campaigning, and the days before polling on the campaign on the streets. For example, on 8 September, as Gordon Brown was dispatched to Loanhead, Jo Coburn was speaking in *The Daily Politics* studio of a 'panicked reaction at Westminster'. The following day in the same programme Angus Robertson of the SNP suggested that he could 'smell the panic' as the 'Westminster establishment [was] going into meltdown', which was repeated as 'absolute panic' by Cathy Newman on Channel 4 news, and, as we have seen, as 'panic and anxiety' by Nick Robinson on the BBC. Subsequent discussion of the No campaign was less dramatic, but there was sustained critical interrogation of what exactly was being promised to voters, on the anomaly of making further promises after postal ballots had already been completed, and how Gordon Brown, as a backbench MP, was in any sort of position to 'guarantee' the No campaign's 'vow' to the people of Scotland. The general point here is that, if the TV news agenda included critical points for the Yes campaign, it also interrogated the inconsistencies of No, and here the comments of some journalists echoed observations made by Yes politicians.

In the final week before the ballot, news coverage of the campaign was curiously contradictory. On the one hand, emerging around 13 September, when Channel 4 news reported on the 'largest Orange march in Scotland in many years', there were suggestions that the campaign was becoming overheated and turning nasty. In her interview with Blair Jenkins on 15 September, Jo Coburn asked him about negativity and intimidation in the Yes campaign, and 'hatred in this campaign' was also mentioned by Jon Snow in a Channel 4 news report from Linlithgow. Jackie Long was dispatched to Pitlochry to report on 'families split down the middle' (in this case the family of clan chief Donald MacLaren). Questions about negativity and intimidation were put to invited audiences for successive editions of *Newsnight* (15 and 16 September) but by polling day this seemingly negative tide had turned. On *Newsnight* (18 September) Kirsty Wark conducted a lengthy, consensual interview with Alan Little (BBC special correspondent) on what was characterised as an 'extraordinary national debate' (the turnout of course was exceptional); and this is how Jon Snow signed off that evening's Channel 4 news:

> Before we go it is impossible to exaggerate what a remarkable experience it's been to be present at this exceptional moment. Whoever wins the discourse has been intelligent, the arguments coherent and the enthusiasm of the people remarkable.

'Intelligent discourse and coherent argument' was definitely not a focus for much of the earlier news coverage, either in the political 'panic' of the previous week, or in the politics of the street. However, I also have to say that I wonder what Scottish readers in particular will make of this quotation. It perhaps connects with what I have to say later about this being a 'cross-cultural' event.

To summarise this review of 'deliberative' editorial strategies, what we have, I think, is a mixed assessment. On the one hand there was certainly much critical interrogation of the efficacy of the No campaign, particularly after it became apparent that it might lose. Of course some of this criticism might have reflected an implicit preference for a No victory, but it also extended to an interrogation of what the Westminster leaders were promising, the dubious status of their collective 'vow' and allegations of unsavoury manoeuvring, particularly by David Cameron. Furthermore, by the end of the campaign, and before the result was known, TV presenters (like Snow) were praising its conduct, and there was even a hint of (grudging?) admiration for Salmond, who appeared to have achieved something (in the form of enhanced devolution) of what he wanted to achieve all along. On the other hand, however, in tandem with its criticism of the No campaign, BBC TV news in particular did reflect aspects of the No agenda, and as this analysis has shown, it covered Scottish politics from a UK-wide perspective. This meant that so-called 'uncertainties' were foregrounded, constitutional conundrums were endlessly debated (especially on *The Daily Politics*) and the fate of Westminster parties (Labour in particular) was linked to the Scottish question. Most problematically, dubious comparisons with English politics resulted in some misconceptions of Scottish politics being (arguably) created. In this respect, although the broadcasting institutions themselves are not 'English', English interests were reflected in much of the TV coverage, to the detriment of the case for Scottish independence being widely heard south of the border.

'English' TV News: Presentation and Reporting

Blair Jenkins's complaint on *The Daily Politics* that Scottish journalists were being marginalised by their English counterparts, however, requires some further scrutiny. In terms of a headcount of the personnel involved this was not strictly true, particularly at the BBC. BBC news made extensive use of Scottish journalists who, even when they were London based, might be expected to have knowledge of Scottish politics: such as the presenters Andrew Neil (*The Daily Politics*) and Kirsty Wark (*Newsnight*); correspondents Alan Little (BBC News) and Laura Kuenssberg (*Newsnight*) and the BBC news reporters Lorna Gordon and Adam Fleming. Actually it was on Channel 4 news that the presenters and reporters were exclusively English. Furthermore, in the final two weeks of the campaign, BBC national news also gave a nightly slot to its Scottish political editor, Brian Taylor. So, at least so far as the BBC is concerned, was Blair Jenkins being fair in his charge that Scottish journalists were being 'elbowed aside'?

The critical point here is that this question is not reducible to the employment of Scottish journalists, but is also to do with where they are located in the structure of news discourse. This discourse is presented through a hierarchy of 'anchors', 'editors' and reporters, with evening news bulletins defined as 'flagship' programmes. What was very apparent, even at the BBC (which had the resources to vary things), was that the presenters and 'editors' in these 'flagship' bulletins were not Scottish, but English (or in the case of the BBC anchor Huw Edwards, Welsh) journalists transported to Scotland for the duration. Moreover, in the penultimate week, as far as reporting the referendum was concerned, first the BBC and then Channel 4 abandoned their London studios and decamped to Scotland. There, in both Edinburgh and Glasgow, they generally eschewed the confines of studio presentation in favour of external locations. Thus, for the BBC news, Huw Edwards was mainly situated on Edinburgh's Calton Hill,[4] and for Channel 4 Krishnan Guru-Murthy appeared variously on Calton Hill and in front of Edinburgh Castle. In the final week, Channel 4's chief news anchor Jon Snow broadcast from a building adjacent to the Scott Monument with a high-angle view down Edinburgh's Princes Street.

In addition, the 'editors' were co-present at these locations, and it is important to appreciate the novelty of this. Normally, when he delivers his political commentaries in London, Nick Robinson is situated in a suitable location (Downing Street or the Palace of Westminster) doing a 'piece to camera', in a live two-way, with the anchor in the studio. For the referendum news, however, he was positioned next to Edwards on Calton Hill and their interaction obviously did not take the form of a two-way, but rather was a 'quasi-interview' ('quasi' because there was only one question and Robinson was allowed to proceed uninterrupted). The same situation obtained for the BBC's economics editor (Robert Peston) and Channel 4's political editor (Gary Gibbon). The only Scottish journalist presented live at this location was Brian Taylor, but his contributions were restricted to impressionistic, metaphorical and very brief 'last words'. In short the bulk of the live news discourse was performed by non-Scottish personnel in front of recognisable (to English eyes) Scottish landmarks. What was the effect of this?

As I have previously suggested, I think the intended effect might have been to mark this news as something special, worthy of the significance of the event.[5] It might also have been thought inappropriate to be broadcasting news about Scotland from a studio based in London. But of course the BBC and STV (for ITN) also have studios in Glasgow, so it was not actually necessary to choose as a backdrop the monuments of Edinburgh. This decision seems to have been driven by a level of intuitive, as much as deliberative, editorialising; perhaps as a further visual dimension to 'doing being interesting'. However, what it also achieved, at least in the eyes of this viewer, was an effect that was perhaps not intended. For I think it made the non-Scottish journalists in these unconventional but very familiar locations, look a little bit like *tourists*.

Indeed, on 15 September in Edinburgh, on a somewhat murky evening, Jon Snow invited his Channel 4 viewers to share his 'tourist gaze':[6] 'Just look down Princes Street here where the spires and towers are drifting into the twilight of fog.' However, it was in the 'roving reporting' on both Channel 4 and the BBC that this practice was most prevalent. There are perhaps different levels of controversy here. First, and least controversially, there was the continuous demand for vox pops with voters all around Scotland (and some in England) which involved identifying their locations. Here it was perhaps inevitable that a trip to Inverness should include shots of its castle, or that a series of vox pops with Yes voters in Dundee should conclude with a view of the Firth of Tay rail bridge. Second, there is also the common practice in this kind of reporting of constructing puns and visual metaphors. This might explain why Channel 4 had an item entitled 'bitter together' about a pub in Ayr selling Yes and No brands of beer (6 September) and a visit to Musselburgh racecourse on 15 September had Alan Little of the BBC covering a specially staged two horse race and asking 'is the race really neck and neck?' His conclusion was that 'the stakes couldn't be higher'.

More controversial as far as a 'tourist gaze' is concerned were reports like that undertaken by Inigo Gilmore for Channel 4 news (5 September) which involved him touring the far north, from Bettyhill to Nairn, 'wearing his Englishness on his sleeve'. Around Ullapool ('a scenic fishing port and gateway to the Western Isles') images of the countryside were described as 'breathtaking scenery'. The piece by Jackie Long, also for Channel 4 (15 September), was introduced from the 'incredibly scenic if incredibly wet setting of Pitlochry's festival theatre' and her vox pops were conducted on the banks of the River Tummell. As previously mentioned, she interviewed the Chief of the Clan MacLaren at Balquhidder ('a MacLaren glen for hundreds of years'), the Chief dressed for the occasion in his kilt. When he arrived at Inverness, Inigo Gilmore was also fitted with a kilt, for a spot of Scottish dancing (this piece was entitled 'Highland fling'). On 15 September Alex Thompson conducted his vox pops for Channel 4 news whilst climbing Ben Nevis, and his piece on polling day incorporating shots of Dunfermline Abbey ('resting place of Robert the Bruce') asked 'through what perspective shall we view such places tomorrow?' The critical question here is who are 'we' in this discourse; and who are 'they', as identified by Robert Peston in his report from the Scottish borders on BBC news (9 September): 'in a pub where Robbie Burns had the odd dram [and] they certainly know how to have a good time in the time honoured way'. You have to ask yourself, was it really necessary to conclude such a report in a pub?

At these moments, the reporters were not simply reporting, they were also 'doing being tourists'. What was built into their discourse was an outsider's perspective and even in the case of Gilmore, an explicitly English identity. Furthermore, in their flirtations with 'tartanry' these reporters were arguably reproducing the representation of Scotland that has been subject to detailed critique for over thirty years by academic analysts.[7] But there is also of course another representation of Scotland, the antithesis of the 'Highland fling', but from a similar perspective, and that is the image of urban deprivation represented by parts of the Central Belt. Unsurprisingly, this also found its way into the news reporting, where it was not enough for reporters to interview working class voters – they were also required to sample an alien subculture, particularly in the east end of Glasgow. There were no fewer than three visits to Shettleston, one by Adam Fleming ('with his hard hat on') for *The Daily Politics* (12 September) and two by Jon Snow (16 and 18 September). Fleming's report starts with him eating a Scotch pie ('the problem round here is that people eat too many of these') and concludes with vox pops at a children's football training session, via a job centre and a tattoo parlour. Snow's first visit starts with shots of a block of flats awaiting demolition and takes him to a community centre where bizarrely two boxers are shadow boxing as he conducts his vox pops with a group of local residents and councillors. His tour also takes in a visit to a pub, a nail bar, a café and a tattoo parlour. Again the critical question is from whose perspective are these films constructed, where voters are located in situations that might be perceived as stereotypical?

Conclusions

We are now in a position to return to the question posed in the introduction to this chapter, namely the 'Englishness' of British television's coverage of the referendum. We can also, in passing, review the charge of 'bias' against the BBC. Our conclusions must be that the answers to these questions relate to different levels of journalistic practice. As we have seen, there were certainly aspects of the BBC coverage that gave prominence to the economic and constitutional 'uncertainties' of Scottish independence, and there was some political commentary that might have been highly problematic from the Yes campaign's point of view. On the other hand all the main British news programmes, including the BBC's, critically interrogated the conduct of the No campaign and the promises made by the three Westminster party leaders, so reflecting to some extent Scottish suspicion of, and disillusionment with, the English political establishment. Furthermore the BBC, in particular, gave prominence to some of its Scottish journalists (especially the 'special correspondents' Alan Little and Laura Kuenssberg) which deflected some of the criticism that its news was entirely a non-Scottish/English product.

However, as this analysis has shown, what was also problematic was not what was explicitly reported in the news, and by whom, but how such reports were introduced, presented and constructed. This is another level of the 'discourse' of television news. Here there were critical connotations created by the presentation of 'flagship' news programmes in their iconic, monumental settings, as well as the way non-Scottish personnel occupied key positions in the hierarchy of news presentation (and the way in which the BBC's Scottish political editor was relegated to providing the last word). But arguably most problematic of all was the type of reporting that reproduced an outsider's, even a tourist's, point of view – and in fact it was Channel 4, with its team of English journalists, not the BBC, that was most guilty of this. There was certainly a problem in some of this reporting that it reproduced regressive Scottish stereotypes, hardly conducive to an image of a progressive, independent Scotland. But as Jon Snow's final signing off made clear, even when the intention was to deliver a positive verdict, in his reference to 'a remarkable experience' of being present at 'this exceptional moment', this was still coming from the perspective of a non-Scottish journalist. And so when he went on to talk about 'intelligent discourse' and 'coherent arguments' in the Scottish referendum debate, isn't there a possibility that some viewers might perhaps have found this just a wee bit patronising?

Notes

1. In this context the term 'editor' carries some ambiguity. Currently the term is used by British TV news organisations to refer to senior journalists, such as Nick Robinson, with specialised portfolios (e.g. 'political editor', etc.). Clearly this is different from the broader decisions made by programme directors about editorial policy. So to make the distinction clear, in its first meaning the term 'editor(s)' is used with inverted commas in this chapter.
2. It was relegated to the third item on the BBC news of 12 September (after news of the death of Ian Paisley) and to the second item on 14 September following news of the death of a British hostage in Syria.
3. See Martin Montgomery, *The Discourse of Broadcast News*, p. 128. Montgomery's book is subtitled 'A Linguistic Approach' and he pays close attention to forms of talk in television news.
4. Edwards made an appearance in Glasgow on 15 September with a backdrop of the Kelvingrove Art Gallery.
5. The same type of presentation, from an external location, occurs for instance in reports of major terrorist incidents, such as the terrorist attacks in Paris on 7 January 2015.
6. See John Urry, *The Tourist Gaze*.
7. See Colin McArthur (ed.), *Scotch Reels*. I also cover some of this ground in my book *Mediations: Text and Discourse in Media Studies*: see pp. 165–70 for a relevant example and further references.

Bibliography

McArthur, Colin (ed.), *Scotch Reels: Scotland in Cinema and Television* (London: BFI Publications, 1982).

Montgomery, Martin, *The Discourse of Broadcast News* (London: Routledge, 2007).

Tolson, Andrew, *Mediations: Text and Discourse in Media Studies* (London: Arnold, 1996).

Urry, John, *The Tourist Gaze* (London: Sage, 1990).

10

The English Press and the Referendum

Karen Williamson and Peter Golding

Our concern in this chapter is with the coverage of the Scottish referendum (and that very phrase is indicative of its perception south of the border) in the English press. In any routine assessment of media reporting of a political contest, most commonly in elections, the obvious question to ask is 'so who did they support or favour?' This would be followed by claims and counter-claims about the importance and success of any such support in achieving the desired political result. *The Sun*'s infamous claim in April 1992 (after the UK general election) that it was 'The Sun Wot Won It', a triumphalist verdict regularly disputed afterwards by psephologists, has become a much-trumpeted catchphrase to illustrate the putative impact of the national press on electoral behaviour, but also its self-absorbed over-confidence in its real significance.

Adjudication of such issues becomes difficult in the case of the referendum on Scotland's continued membership of the United Kingdom. First, the No campaign, to oppose separation, was uniformly supported by the English press. Second, the press we will be analysing in this chapter is overwhelmingly read by citizens who had no vote in the referendum.

So, why does what the English press had to say matter? There are at least two reasons. First, it is a commonplace of media research that while the media are unlikely to directly determine what people think, they demonstrably have a huge impact on what they think about. Analysis of other areas of coverage has formulated this distinction as one between evaluative and interpretative dimensions of news. Evaluative coverage assesses, or imputes, the relative merits of policy or party, and directly or indirectly points to a conclusion in favour of one or another. Interpretative coverage unpacks what an issue is about, by highlighting some aspects and ignoring or muting others.[1] While English newspapers will have been read largely by people who did not have a vote in the referendum, their framing of the major issues can be assumed to have had a significant impact on how the merits and problems of separation were construed and addressed by those who did.

The reason for this is that while the UK press is hugely metropolitan, the

London-based press does have a presence in Scotland. As Hutchison[2] summarises: 'The press in Scotland comprises indigenous titles and titles which, with or without Scottish editions, are London newspapers which circulate throughout the UK.' Many of the major titles have a (very) limited circulation in Scotland. Indeed it is reasonable to argue that the presence of the *Daily Record*, not merely the Scottish version of the *Daily Mirror* but a distinct product which reaches a large number of Scottish homes and makes much of its claim to be the paper 'real Scots read', alone confirms the Scottish newspaper market – historically at least – as a separate one (although between 2003 and 2013 sales of the *Record* dropped by half, not least because of the inroads to its circulation made by the Scottish edition of *The Sun*, which now outsells the indigenous title). The Scottish population is about 8.3 per cent of the UK. But while *The Sun* has about 12 per cent of its circulation north of the border, for most papers the figure is much lower. Both *The Times* and *The Guardian*, for example, circulate only 5 per cent of their total in Scotland, whilst the figures for *The Independent* and the *Daily Telegraph* are 4 per cent and 3 per cent respectively. More detail and discussion of this may be found in Chapter 2.

However, the English press has real presence as well as significant influence in Scotland, for, as is pointed out in Chapter 2, Scottish editions of English titles together with non-editionised titles now account for over half of daily sales north of the border. The relative decline of the Scottish indigenous press in the face of both general falls in newspaper readership and the advance of the national (that is London-based) press is a matter of frequent lament among Scottish journalists. A former editor of *The Scotsman* wrote, not long before the referendum, that 'at this seminal political moment . . . [t]he Scottish press appears to be dying on its feet . . . Indigenous newspapers are shrinking, staff are being cut and . . . the [information and informed opinion] are being squeezed to the point of extinction'.[3] More dramatically, he concludes, 'it is hard to see how the indigenous Scottish press can survive'.[4] However this picture is construed, the London ('English') newspapers are clearly of significance in Scottish political communications.

Second, with 84 per cent of the UK population living in England, public opinion in that country is bound to be a significant force in any policy debate within the UK. It is a central theme of this chapter that the referendum was perceived and treated by the English press as a relatively foreign event taking place in another country, and that interest in it was at a level and of a form common to much overseas news. In 2011 a YouGov poll found there to be stronger support for an independent Scotland in England and Wales than there was in Scotland itself. Colin Kidd[5] argued that Scottish unionists have been exposed not only to opposition from Scottish nationalists but also 'the polite, blinkered non-recognition by the English that Britain is a multi-national United Kingdom', arguing that 'this will be a moment of supreme indifference south of the border'.

In general then, the English press mattered, even though, as far as non-editionised titles are concerned, it was unlikely to have had much of an immediate impact on voting behaviour in Scotland. Nonetheless, it has to be acknowledged that this is unlikely to be true of the collective impact of the *Scottish Sun*, the *Scottish Daily Mail*, and the Scottish editions of the *Telegraph* and *Times*, whose coverage is discussed elsewhere in this book.

The 'UK press', despite Scottish editions, where they exist, does, however, remain largely English in tone and rhetoric. As MacInnes et al.[6] point out, what is commonly regarded as the UK or British press is often more correctly described as English or even London-based. Their subtle and detailed assessment of the 'banal nationalism'[7] conveyed by the London press, and used as a descriptive term in analysis of it, goes beyond the central point we argue here, namely that in its coverage of the referendum the press in England was largely describing an event taking place outside the purview of most of its readers (on this issue see also the chapter by Tolson in this volume).

Extent of Coverage[8]

Neither the English press nor its readers were hugely excited by the referendum outside the period immediately before and after the vote. In order to assess the extent and character of this coverage we analysed *The Times*, *The Guardian*, the *Daily Mail* and the *Daily Mirror*. These four titles reflect views on both the left (*Guardian* and *Daily Mirror*) and right (*Times* and *Daily Mail*) of the political spectrum, as well as differences in journalistic discourse between broadsheets (*Times* and *Guardian*) and tabloids (*Daily Mail* and *Daily Mirror*). Our quantitative analysis shows that the topic was more or less invisible during the whole of 2014 prior to the period immediately before the vote. At the end of August there was a monumental spike in coverage, but by the end of September the event had departed the front pages, and had all but disappeared by mid-October. Figure 10.1 shows the number of stories in the titles analysed during this period.

The most immediately obvious aspects of this data are the very limited amounts of coverage of the referendum and the highlighting of it during a very compressed period of time. It is also notable that the *Daily Mirror* gives far less coverage than the other titles in our sample. Whilst there was a peak in coverage as with the others, this reached only 26 articles in the *Mirror*, while *The Times* had 165, *The Guardian* 179, and the *Daily Mail* 163 between 18 August and 12 October 2014.

Immediately before the referendum the increase in coverage in part reflected an eleventh hour panic about the potential implications for 'us' of a Yes vote. As a *Times* story argued, 'It's only 15 days until the Scottish referendum but few in Westminster seem bothered'.[9]

The Guardian was equally, if belatedly, apocalyptic the following day, reporting that

Amid warnings of a 'constitutional meltdown' after a Yes vote, which would place severe personal political pressure on the prime minister, a growing number of Tory MPs are saying they will call for legislation to be introduced to postpone the general election.[10]

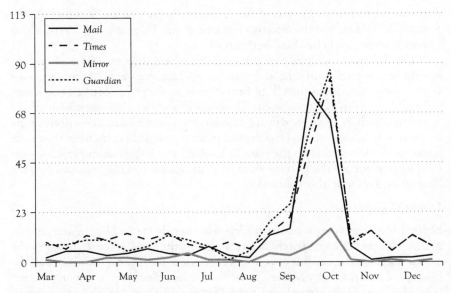

Figure 10.1 Number of stories on the referendum in four English national newspapers, March–December 2014.

The *Daily Mail* reported a 'Battle cry to save Britain',[11] and the *Daily Mirror* reported fears of a constitutional crisis and the possibility that

> MPs could be hauled back to discuss the future of the UK and the vote's effect on the British economy. A Commons source said: 'If Scotland votes Yes, the implications for the UK, the economy and constitution are immense. Parliament will have to be recalled.'

The tone here and elsewhere is of dismay or even resentment about the possible outcome and its implications for the country (construed as 'us', in other words the English). Following the day of the vote on 18 September, coverage of the issue rapidly disappeared, being replaced either by news relating to how the results affect the 'rest of the UK', or as a side-note in coverage of the party conferences. Indeed by 25 September *The Times* was writing of 'the distraction of the Scottish referendum'[12] as an explanation for what it regarded as Labour's lacklustre display at its annual conference.

The Major Themes of News Coverage

We analysed the main themes in all news stories about the referendum in the *Daily Mail*, *The Times*, *The Guardian* and the *Daily Mirror* between 18 August and 12 October 2014. Four such themes were dominant.

Table 10.1 Frequency of major appearances by four political leaders (Brown, Cameron, Miliband, Farage) between 18 August and 12 October 2014.

Title	No. of appearances	% of all stories
Daily Mail	82	50
Times	61	55
Guardian	68	47
Daily Mirror	16	27

Focus on leaders

Reflecting the usual character of electoral news, much of the news coverage was about the senior figures in the 'debate', and not least the English characters in it, namely Gordon Brown (though a Scot, for these purposes a national, i.e. English-based, politician), David Cameron, Ed Miliband and even Nigel Farage, the leader of UKIP. These four featured in 227 of the 445 stories (just over 50 per cent) we analysed between 18 August and 12 October 2014. Table 10.1 gives the details.

Smaller pro-independence organisations such as the Scottish Green Party, the Scottish Socialist Party, Labour for Independence, and several civil society groups, were all but invisible, while headlines portrayed the apparent ubiquity of a small number of leaders. A few examples make the point:

Daily Mail
'Ed tells Scots: no need to vote Yes, Labour will be in power next year!' (4 September)
'I won't resign if Scotland votes to leave says Cameron' (5 September)
'Stay away, No campaign tells Farage' (6 September)
'Farage's visit was a gift to the Yes campaign, says Salmond' (13 September)
Times
'Cameron gives clash of the Scots a miss' (27 August)
'Miliband rallies left-wing voters to save the Union' (4 September)
'The three main party leaders are heading to Scotland in near panic. They may lack the poetry of independence, but they are armed with hard facts' (10 September)
'Dave shuns despair to keep calm and carry on; Panic would be understandable with so much at stake, but the PM is accustomed to adversity' (11 September)
'Cocky Cameron surrenders keys to the Kingdom' (16 September)
'Campaign chaos as Miliband is jostled by jeering Yes activists' (17 September)
Guardian
'Cameron in plea to Scots on UK trade: Prime minister highlights single market's success: Home Secretary says no campaign must try harder' (28 August)
'Cameron met with Yes camp heckles and humour as he tries to avoid the protesters: Prime Minister sets out focused economic case for keeping Scotland in the UK' (29 August)

'Clegg urges greater devolution for all UK: Cat is out of the bag on issue, says deputy PM Give regions more control over finances – report' (12 September)
'Party leaders' power pledge angers MPs in England: Council chiefs warn English cities and counties will demand own devolution' (17 September)
Daily Mirror
'Clash Gordon, Brown rides to rescue: Medics say patients will suffer if UK splits. He blasts Salmond's 'lies' on future of NHS Ex-PM vows to end Nats'grip on Holyrood' (12 September)
'Cam's lack of respect' (20 September)

The 'West Lothian' question

This somewhat technical issue ('why should Scotland-based MPs at Westminster be able to vote on issues affecting only the English if the reverse is not true – English MPs cannot vote on issues within the remit of devolved assemblies?') was not frequently addressed. However, the tacit, if more abrasive, version – 'who needs them?' – did lie behind much commentary and coverage. The first TV debate between Alistair Darling (chair of the Better Together campaign) and Alex Salmond, in which the issue was raised, was not even aired in England. The second was, but as reported by the *Mirror*, 'David Cameron didn't interrupt his holiday to watch the second debate on Scottish independence' (*Daily Mirror*, 27 August).[13]

When the polls began showing signs of the increasing success of the Yes campaign, debates in the English press shifted quite rapidly from questions of Scotland's uncertain future (its ability to cope economically; its status with regard to the UK sterling zone; the value for Scotland of North Sea oil; the relation of Scotland to the EU) towards panic and often (in the case of *The Times* and the *Daily Mail*) anger and resentment that the union was seriously (inexplicably so, for the majority of the English national press) under threat. This resonated with the heightened distress in the days before the referendum as the English press both voiced and reported the belated recognition of the implications of a now suddenly, it was thought, quite possible Yes vote. The tone now was of a self-righteous expression of responsible circumspection by a press dismayed at the short-sightedness of the politicians:

'David Cameron is focused on his tussle with his own backbenchers. Ed Miliband is worried that the result could derail his party conference speech the next day. Nick Clegg is absorbed in pushing his free school dinners. The polls, however, are narrowing. *The Times* YouGov poll yesterday showed the Better Together lead has shrunk to six points.' (*Times*, 3 September)[14]
'Our country could soon be finished. And yet I don't detect much sense of panic. Life goes on in an unruffled way.' (*Daily Mail*, 4 September)[15]
'Unless pro-union big guns can hit the panic button more effectively, a post-imperial upset of historic proportions could be about to fracture the British

state. The spectacle of a former Scottish Secretary, Labour's Jim Murphy, saying publicly 'I am confident we can win' merely reflects growing doubts in the once-dominant no camp.' (*Guardian*, 5 September)[16]

'With only 10 days to go, the rest of Britain finally awoke yesterday to the enormity of what is happening in Scotland. For years, the rise of Scottish national feeling has been underestimated and misunderstood. The possibility that the United Kingdom might be heading for the history books has been complacently dismissed as unthinkable. But there can be no excuse for any ignorance or complacency now.' (*Guardian*, 8 September)[17]

'With panic growing in Westminster over a surge in support for independence, Mr Cameron, Labour's Ed Miliband and Lib Dem leader Nick Clegg have taken the extraordinary step of agreeing to abandon Prime Minister's Questions today. Instead, they will make unscheduled trips to Scotland to try to rally the faltering No campaign . . . The message of this extraordinary, last-minute reaction is that the Westminster elite are in a state of absolute panic as the ground in Scotland shifts under their feet.' (*Daily Mail*, 10 September)[18]

As Kumar has noted,

> taken vaguely for granted, unexamined and untheorised, it is only when Britain is faced by threats from within and without, only when there is talk of 'the break-up of Britain', that serious attention has turned to the character of the United Kingdom.[19]

Whether or not the news coverage of the potential fragmentation of the union in September 2014 can be described as 'serious attention', plainly the likelihood of such an outcome was a focus of news for only a short, if intense, period.

The implications for business

Economic matters formed the main focus of coverage of the Scottish referendum in the English press both throughout the period under study as well as across the whole of 2014. As in coverage of economic matters more generally, and as is often observed, especially in periods of political contestation, business and more generally economic matters are presented in news as 'good' or 'bad' by subjecting them to the judgement and comment of business leaders. Indeed the reactions of 'the City', 'business', or 'industry', reified as disinterested voices offering objective assessment of the benefits or folly of specified initiatives, frequently become the basis for the news item.

As *Times* business editor Ian King reflected, 'saying nothing during the Scottish referendum was *not* an option for business leaders. Many were prepared to speak out, especially after the publication of a YouGov poll for *The Sunday Times* that put the Yes campaign ahead' (*Times*, 22 September[20] [emphasis added]).

Representatives and spokespersons of the British and international capitalist class stood behind the three unionist parties, and stories regularly reported the threats of many businesses (banks, phone companies, etc.) to re-locate their headquarters if the Scots voted for separation. Their views became a focus of reportage following the 11 September Downing Street reception for business leaders.

The salutary warnings of captains of industry formed a recurrent refrain in the English press. For example, 'John Menzies snubs independence vote' (*Times*, 20 August), 'HSBC chair tells Scots to vote No' (*Daily Mail*, 23 August), 'CBI chief warns of Scots' Yes threat' (*Daily Mail*, 29 August), 'Goldman warns of economic crisis after Yes vote' (*Times*, 4 September), 'Blue-chip companies step up to warn of dangers of independence' (*Times*, 11 September), and so on.

The economic consequences both for Scotland and for the wider UK of a vote for Scottish independence were a constant and dominant feature of the coverage. The stories rarely, if ever, sounded an encouraging tone, and some-times even managed an apocalyptic one, as in 'Nobel economist warns Scots of financial meltdown' (*Times*, 9 September). The complexities of currency and oil were not widely explored, other than to sustain a tone of unease and caution about the consequences of a reckless vote for independence. Such stories took their lead from the admonitory statements of those counselling against such a vote. So in the *Daily Mail* headlines warned that the 'Pound falls on support for Scottish Yes vote' (3 September), and, reporting the consequences of anticipa-tory fears, 'Oil plummets as fears grow over Scots vote' (9 September) and that 'Jitters hit shares and sterling's on the slide' (9 September). The fears of the CBI and 'the banks' were widely and repeatedly reported as the date of the referen-dum approached.

The horse race

The bulk of coverage (in the period under study) focused on the campaigns, their tactics, strategies and performances. This 'horse race' aspect of campaign cover-age is a commonly observed feature of elections.[21] Polling formed the basis for the bulk of coverage across the titles under investigation. This largely reported polls relating to decisions of voters in Scotland, but described them largely in terms of the effects of Scottish independence on the rest of the UK. Polls relating to English attitudes were also much used. Much of the coverage used polls on the anticipated outcome as a peg to hang stories on; in other words familiar reversion to 'horse race' coverage.

As the referendum day approached, the likely outcome as predicted by polls became *the* story, not least in the drama manufactured by apparent rises in the Yes vote or the narrowness of the expected outcome, with the implications for, or views of, the majority of readers or the implications for business confidence never far from the lead. Typical examples were:

'Pollsters claim real shift in opinion as Yes vote rises' (*Times*, 18 August)
'English voters take harder line on Scots' (*Times*, 20 August)

'Pound slumps to 5-month low as Scottish poll rocks markets' (*Daily Mail*, 3 September)

'Shock poll forces the Treasury to prepare for independence turmoil' (*Times*, 3 September)

'Now polls could rock markets' (*Daily Mail*, 8 September)

'Oil plummets as fears grow over Scots vote' (*Daily Mail*, 9 September)

'No campaign holds on to lead with less than a week to go' (*Guardian*, 12 September)

'Seven in 10 English want Scots to remain part of the UK' (*Daily Mail*, 13 September)

'ICM poll: possibility of separation from Scotland stirs feelings of sadness in England and Wales' (*Guardian*, 16 September)

Notable in our analysis is the relative paucity of coverage of many other aspects of the referendum debate and the various issues surrounding it. For example, the implications for membership of the European Union (would Scotland wish to join if independent?, would it automatically be a member?, and so on), though raised and reported, were seldom aired at any length in the English press, though occasional and unexpected international ramifications did surface – two stories in *The Times* were 'North Korea comes out for Scotland' (12 September) and 'a vote for Scottish independence could be as damaging for Europe as the assassination of Archduke Franz Ferdinand of Austria, a former Italian prime minister warned yesterday' (17 September).[22]

Interestingly, in the lament for the indigenous press by Linklater referred to earlier, he notes sadly that 'on defence, energy costs, entry to Europe, welfare and pension costs – the building blocks of the nation's future – we rely on reports and opinions from elsewhere',[23] listing almost exactly those issues which we find were, in fact, not that well represented in English press coverage of the matter either.

Conclusion

In this chapter we have been concerned with the preoccupations and priorities of the English press in reporting the Scottish referendum. The referendum was an event of huge significance for the structure and future of the British state, with constitutional ramifications on a scale beyond the experience of any current citizens. Yet our first observation is the sheer paucity of coverage, and its narrow concentration in the period immediately before the actual vote. As our data show, there was little coverage until relatively close to the date of the referendum, and what there was coalesced around a small number of issues with many of the wider or more complex implications of a possible vote for independence rarely reported.

Thus, beyond the dearth and transience of coverage, is the limited range of issues and events portrayed about the referendum in the English press. Two aspects of this are prominent. First, the people dominating the news were a few major political actors. Second, the range of issues featured in news stories was itself limited. First and foremost was the economy, and the prospects for business activity, frequently presented as adjudged by the 'business community', and featuring stories reporting the Olympian warnings and injunctions of captains of industry on the risks (most often) or benefits (rarely) of a vote for separation.

Polls predicting the outcome provided a second significant peg for coverage, as in any election trying to inject the excitement of the 'horse race' into what might otherwise have been a difficult story with which to attract readers (increasingly warned by columnists as the referendum day approached of what Matthew Paris in *The Spectator* described as 'the collective shrug of English shoulders',[24] or Andrew Rawnsley in *The Observer* had presciently described in 2012 as 'blissful indifference'[25]). Far less frequently covered in stories were such ostensibly important dimensions of the issue as the future of Britain's (or Scotland's) membership of the European Union, defence, or the future of currency in the countries if separated.

In many respects, to read the English press on the referendum is to be struck by its similarity in tone and range to foreign news as a broad category. For many readers of the English press the referendum will have seemed a far-away event in another country. Its coverage shared three characteristics often noted in research on foreign news.[26] First, it was written for non-participants, who were being told about an event, whether significant or not, being endured or enjoyed by people living somewhere else. Second, it shared the features (as we have noted, a focus on a small number of elite actors and so on) common to foreign news. Third, it was often framed for its readers as 'home news abroad', in other words of interest because of its potential indirect impact on the reader. While never as blatant as archetypical formulations of this type – '*Stanford Dingley man among 200 killed in airplane crash in Peru*' – the English interest, whether in its politically technical form as the West Lothian question or more generally, was a major driver of coverage, surfacing also in a 'who needs them?' vexation often expressed by columnists voicing impatience and irritation at the whole issue and what they regarded as its attendant tartanry.

While the irritating distraction of the referendum campaign was boring readers who did not have a vote in the matter, some tabloid newspapers were more concerned with their more usual priorities. An exclusive front page revelation of a 'Bus Driver's 26 Kids with 9 Women' had preoccupied *The Sun* the day before the referendum and, like most papers, it had outraged prominently about the 'pure evil' of 'Jihadi John' (14 September), the following day using its front page to challenge him to 'Show Us Your Face, Coward'. The *Mail on Sunday* front page lead before the referendum was 'Co-Op Chief's Affair with his "Head of Talent"' (14 September), while the *Star* led with 'Corrie Jack in Dog Fire Outrage' (14 September). Two murder stories preoccupying the popular press were first, the murders of two British tourists in Thailand ('Bloodbath in Paradise', *Daily Mirror*, 16 September; 'Brit Couple Beaten to Death in Thailand', *Daily Star*, 16 September), sensation quickly turning to front page indignation ('Smearing of Britons Murdered in Paradise', *Daily Mail*, 18 September), and second, gathering revelations about the murdered teenager Alice Gross ('Missing Alice Suspect is a Murderer', *Daily Mirror*, 19 September, the same story predictably constructed as 'Suspect is Killer Migrant' in the *Daily Express*, 19 September). More immediately worrying, the day before the referendum was the headline news that we could expect an 'Invasion of the Giant Spiders', followed the next day with the even more disheartening 'Now It's Killer Mutant Mosquitoes' (*Daily Star*, 17 September to 18 September).

The coverage of the referendum by the English press may not have been significant in the final outcome, but the very fact of there being such a topic and of its self-evident separateness from the broader concerns of this volume speaks loudly about the metropolitan and national character of the British press.

Notes

1. Golding, 'Political communication and citizenship'; Deacon and Golding, *Taxation and Representation*, p. 19.
2. Hutchison, 'The media and the referendum', p. 4.
3. Linklater, 'Emphatically not their finest hour', p. 26.
4. Ibid., p. 27.
5. Kidd, 'Brown v. Salmond: Colin Kidd on the State of the Union', p. 8.
6. MacInnes et al., 'Where is the British national press?'
7. Billig, *Banal Nationalism*.
8. All articles throughout 2014 relating to the Scottish referendum were collected in order to quantify coverage, revealing heightened coverage between 18 August and 12 October 2014. Articles during this six-week period were then subject to a qualitative analysis focusing on uncovering themes and patterns relating to coverage of the Scottish referendum.
9. *The Times* (3 September 2014), 'Wake up unionists you really could lose this', p. 25.
10. *The Guardian* (4 September 2014), 'PM is urged to delay 2015 election if Scotland says yes to independence: Warning of constitutional crisis after referendum', p. 4.
11. The *Daily Mail* (9 September 2014), 'Battle cry to save Britain'.
12. *The Times* (25 September 2014), 'Miliband inner circle in line of fire as hope gives way to doubt', pp. 12–13.
13. The *Daily Mirror* (27 August 2014), 'Cameron snubs Scots TV debate', p. 2.
14. *The Times* (3 September 2014), 'Wake up unionists you really could lose this', p. 25.
15. The *Daily Mail* (4 September 2014), 'Just two weeks left to save Britain'.
16. *The Guardian* (5 September 2014), 'Sweat, swing and swither: why "no" lead may just be Scotch mist: A unionist win has long seemed assured, but as decision day nears the yes bandwagon is gathering pace', p. 14.
17. *The Guardian* (8 September 2014), 'Nothing else now matters in British politics', p. 1.
18. The *Daily Mail* (10 September 2014), 'Don't rip our family apart'.
19. Kumar, *Nation and Empire*, p. 575.
20. *The Times* (22 September 2014), 'Striking the Right Business Balance', p. 47.
21. Cappella and Jamieson, *Spiral of Cynicism*.
22. *The Times* (17 September 2014), 'Independence would harm Europe', p. 11.
23. Linklater, 'Emphatically not their finest hour', p. 28.
24. *The Spectator* (18 December 2010), 'With a shrug of the shoulders, England is becoming a nation once again', p. 28.
25. *The Observer* (29 January 2012), 'Who most wants independence for Scotland? The English . . . If the Union referendum were held south of the border, Alex Salmond would be more likely to get his way', p. 39.

26. Galtung and Ruge, 'The structure of foreign news'; Chang et al., 'Determinants of international news coverage in the US media'; Harcup and O'Neill, 'What is news? Galtung and Ruge revisited'.

Bibliography

Billig, M., *Banal Nationalism* (London: Sage, 1995).

Cappella, J. N. and K. Jamieson, *Spiral of Cynicism: The Press and the Public Good* (New York: Oxford University Press, 1997).

Chang, T.-K., P. J. Shoemaker and N. Brendlinger, 'Determinants of international news coverage in the US media', *Communication Research*, 14(4) (1987), pp. 396–414.

Deacon, D. and P. Golding, *Taxation and Representation: The Media, Political Communication and the Poll Tax* (London: John Libbey, 1994).

Galtung, J. and M. H. Ruge, 'The structure of foreign news: the presentation of the Congo, Cuba and Cyprus Crises in four Norwegian newspapers', *Journal of Peace Research*, 2(1) (1965), pp. 64–90.

Golding, P., 'Political communication and citizenship: the media and democracy in an inegalitarian social order', in M. Ferguson (ed.), *Public Communication: The New Imperatives* (London: Sage, 1990), pp. 84–100.

Harcup, T. and D. O'Neill, 'What is news? Galtung and Ruge revisited'. *Journalism Studies*, 2(2) (2001), pp. 261–80.

Hutchison, D., 'The media and the referendum: uncharted waters, perilous seas?', in Klaus Peter Müller (ed.), *Scotland 2014 and Beyond – Coming of Age and Loss of Innocence?* (Frankfurt am Main: Peter Lang, 2015).

Kidd, C., 'Brown v. Salmond: Colin Kidd on the state of the union', *London Review of Books*, 29(8) (2007), pp. 6–8.

Kumar, K., 'Nation and Empire: English and British national identity in comparative perspective', *Theory and Society*, 29(5) (2000), pp. 575–608.

Linklater, M., 'Emphatically not their finest hour', *British Journalism Review*, 25(2) (2014), pp. 26–28.

MacInnes, J, M. Rosie, P. Petersoo, S. Condor and J. Kennedy, 'Where is the British national press?', *British Journal of Sociology*, 58(2) (2007), pp. 185–206.

11

Wales, Devolution and the Scottish Independence Debate

Sian Powell

If there was one nation within the United Kingdom watching the Scottish independence referendum with great interest it was Wales. Historically, Wales has followed Scotland's political lead, albeit a little more tentatively and less enthusiastically.[1] Independence for Wales, however, has never been as popular with the Welsh electorate as with their Scottish counterparts. A YouGov poll held in April 2014, prior to Scotland's independence referendum, showed that only 12 per cent[2] of the principality's electorate would support Welsh independence if Scotland became an independent nation. Nevertheless, given that the referendum, regardless of the result, would potentially have an effect on Wales's constitutional future, it was certainly worthy of news coverage within Wales. This chapter examines that coverage.

First, the chapter will examine the Welsh media landscape, including the historical weaknesses of the Welsh media and the lack of engagement with Welsh politics. Second, the chapter will discuss the contrasting political trajectories between Scotland and Wales – Wales historically has always looked towards Scotland as a more powerful and autonomous nation – and consider the possible effect of the result on Wales's constitutional and political make-up. Then the chapter will examine the coverage of the referendum both in the press and in broadcasting and will also look at the coverage of previous referendums in Wales. Finally, the chapter will suggest some conclusions about the coverage of the Scottish referendum within Wales and discuss whether that coverage had an effect on people's understanding of Welsh politics and Welsh identity.

The Media Landscape in Wales

Wales's weak media and press industry has been widely discussed[3] and is often compared unfavourably to the Scottish media industry. While Scotland has three national daily newspapers (*The Scotsman*, *The Herald* and the *Daily Record*) and two strong regional dailies, based respectively in Aberdeen and Dundee, Wales only has the *Western Mail*, whose circulation has fallen since the beginning of devolution in 1997 from around 55,000 to under 24,000 in mid-2014,[4] and the

Daily Post, which has a circulation of around 28,000. There are differences too between the readers in north and south Wales; for example, the *Western Mail* is not largely read in the north of the country and the *Daily Post* is not sold in the south.[5]

Scotland, on the other hand, has benefited from a stronger media industry. In addition to the titles mentioned above, many British newspapers offer Scottish versions of their titles, for example, the *Scottish Sun* and *Scottish Daily Mail*. These include a few pages specific to Scottish news, including Scottish politics and devolution. Welsh versions of these newspapers are not available; therefore most people in Wales buy newspapers which are produced in London and often present stories through the prism of England, with very little information being offered about Wales and its devolved government.

Welsh voters rely heavily on the media to receive information about politics and democracy in Wales. However, as has just been noted, the press industry in Wales is weak and the readership of newspapers produced in Wales is very low, with the majority of the population reading British newspapers with their limited coverage of Welsh affairs. But it is still the responsibility of the media in Wales – press and broadcasting – to ensure that they reflect and communicate information about politics in Wales to the electorate.

A study conducted by Geraint Talfan Davies and Nick Morris for the Institute of Welsh Affairs in 2008 found that on average 260,000 people watch BBC Wales's *Wales Today* programme, while 121,000 watch ITV Wales's *Wales Tonight*. The same study found that only 23,000 watch S4C's *Newyddion* programme.[6] Comparing these with the low circulation figures of the daily newspapers in Wales, it is evident that a significant responsibility is placed on television news in Wales, particularly the BBC.

Although in Wales the responsibility for serving the public sphere via broadcasting is shared between the BBC, ITV, Channel 4 and S4C, because many more viewers in Wales choose the BBC it is mainly for the Corporation to communicate stories about politics and, in particular, decisions made by the National Assembly for Wales. The most popular news programmes in Wales remain those produced by the BBC's UK network which include British and international stories; however, following devolution, these broadcasts do include some stories on the Scottish Parliament, the Welsh Assembly and the Northern Ireland Assembly.

In addition to a higher number of viewers, BBC Wales also has more resources compared to ITV Wales, including, crucially, journalists, so there is more opportunity for it to give attention to political stories than for ITV Wales.

Many observers hoped that devolution would strengthen the Welsh media landscape, but these hopes have not been realised, as demonstrated by the lower readership figures fifteen years after devolution. This follows the UK trend of falling readership figures, but is acutely felt in Wales due to the lack of national newspapers and the lack of engagement with current affairs.

Lack of Engagement in Wales

McAllister and Cole[7] state that the weakness of the media has an effect on political coverage within Wales and on how informed the Welsh electorate are. This deficiency is particularly detrimental during elections as voters are unclear which are the contentious issues under discussion. The Scottish referendum may not have had a direct effect on Wales, but the result would certainly have repercussions in Wales, and a different set of repercussions for Wales than for voters in England, who have not experienced devolution at all. However, due to the lack of indigenous Welsh media, the Welsh public could well have lacked the information to judge the effect that the referendum would have had upon their lives.

The weakness of indigenous media could certainly go some way towards explaining the low level of engagement in Welsh politics. The lack of scrutiny and knowledge surrounding the Welsh public sphere could also have led to low levels of support for devolution in Wales. Following the 2011 National Assembly for Wales election, the Electoral Commission noted the scarcity of the coverage: 'the prominence of the Assembly elections in the media continues to be an issue'.[8]

Rosemary Butler, the National Assembly for Wales's Presiding Officer, has called this a democratic deficit, where there is a gap between the news that the Welsh electorate receives about how the country is run and their actual knowledge and understanding of devolution. Denver [9] notes how the differing media landscapes between Scotland and Wales may have led to different levels of understanding of the issues at stake within the 1997 referendums which preceded the establishment of devolved governments in both countries:

> The fact that coverage of the referendum in the British-wide press was low-key was irrelevant to the great majority of Scots, but not to the Welsh, which may account for the lower turnout in Wales . . . the coverage of the referendum in the Scottish press was very extensive, prominent and heavily skewed in favour of a Yes vote. As with the signals sent by the parties, voters in general had no difficulty in picking up the message. By the end of the campaign, there were very few voters who were not aware that a referendum was taking place and what it was about.

This lack of coverage has led to a low level of awareness and understanding of which government, Westminster or Cardiff, has the power to set policies in which areas. A recent BBC poll underlined this by finding that only 48 per cent of the Welsh electorate were aware that the Welsh government was in control of the NHS in Wales.[10]

This lack of awareness and understanding fifteen years after devolution highlights the poor attention the British press and other media give to the reality of devolution in Wales. Given the possible constitutional changes that could take place as a result of Scotland's independence referendum, the lack of awareness surrounding Welsh politics and the possible implications for Wales raises serious concerns. Following the Scottish referendum result more powers could be transferred to the National Assembly for Wales, including tax varying powers, but without any diminution of the democratic deficit.

Scottish Distinctiveness

Scotland's long-standing history of distinctiveness within the UK has led the country on a differing path of devolution from Wales. Wales's incorporation with England during the sixteenth century made it much harder for Wales to maintain a sense of distinctiveness. As Bogdanor comments: 'the Welsh people did not find it easy to maintain their identity. For governmental purposes, indeed, Wales came to be treated as if it were part of England'.[11]

Scotland's legal and educational systems have always differed from those in England and Wales and helped lead Scotland on a differing path of devolution compared to the one pursued in Wales. A more powerful Parliament was set up in Edinburgh following the 1997 referendum compared with the Assembly in Cardiff, in part because of these national institutions, which helped maintain a feeling of distinctiveness within Scotland: 'For Wales, unlike Scotland, did not enjoy those independent institutions which not only ensured separate treatment, but, more crucially, preserved the memory of independent statehood'.[12]

The 1997 referendum results within both nations also underlined the differing opinions held by the electorates: 74 per cent of Scotland's electorate voted in favour of devolution, while only 50.3 per cent of Wales's electorate supported the devolved settlement and on a very low turnout.[13] In 2011 another referendum was held in Wales to ratify the granting of further powers for the Assembly but even then its total powers remained fewer than those of Holyrood. The low turnout in the 2011 referendum was also blamed, in part, on the lack of media coverage. Very few people in Wales were engaged with the debate.[14]

Implications for Wales

Regardless of the result, the Scottish independence referendum could have an effect on Wales's devolved settlement and the future constitutional arrangements across the UK. In the event of a Yes vote, the political make-up of the United Kingdom would have been altered, with 92 per cent, rather than 85 per cent, of the population living in England. This would have led to questions being raised about the balance of power within the successor state. In addition, the Barnett formula, which is central to the calculation of how much money should be transferred from Westminster to the devolved governments, would have been void, as one nation would no longer need to be funded by the UK government. In the wake of a No vote, any further powers offered to Scotland would widen the divergence of power between the Scottish Parliament and the Welsh Assembly.

How Much Coverage?

So it was clear that the result of the vote in Scotland could have a profound effect on Wales's constitution and political system. But how much attention should the referendum debate have received in Wales? How much would have been proportional? In practice, how much opportunity was given to the Welsh electorate to scrutinise the possible effects of the vote? And should the referendum have taken precedence over indigenous Welsh political issues?

A year to go . . .

A year before the vote, in September 2013, there was plenty of coverage of the referendum and its possible effects on Wales and Wales's constitution. Most of that coverage was within the Welsh press and on BBC Wales and concentrated on the politicians' views on reforming Wales's devolved settlement. Some of the reforms that were discussed included securing a reserved powers model similar to the one already seen in Scotland, and devolving further powers, for example tax varying powers. The Silk Commission[15] was also underway, reviewing the financial and constitutional arrangements of Wales, and most of the coverage of its work concentrated on technical and constitutional aspects of the devolution settlement.

In September 2013, a year before the vote, the UK's Changing Union project[16] held an event in Cardiff Bay at which the First Minister, Carwyn Jones, discussed the implications of the Scottish referendum on Wales at this time.[17] The First Minister called for the full implementation of the Silk Commission's proposals, including devolving some taxes and legislating to allow the Assembly to call for a referendum on whether income tax should also be devolved.

The First Minister went on to call for a constitutional convention across all parts of the UK and a new UK-wide constitution in the wake of the Scottish referendum. He outlined three key principles which should be followed when reforming the UK constitution: first, respect for devolved legislatures; second, parity of structure between the nations of the UK; and third, a presumption in favour of devolution of legislative and executive competence.

While Carwyn Jones's calls for a constitutional convention were widely covered in the Welsh press, in the broadcast news and online, the story was not covered widely in the UK press. Ed Miliband also called for a constitutional convention[18] within the same week and that call was covered by the UK-wide press. However, Miliband mainly concentrated on the future constitutional arrangements for Scotland and England following the referendum vote and made no specific mention as to how Wales's political make-up might change substantially.

These discussions about the constitutional arrangements of the UK and the devolved settlement in Wales failed to encourage much debate within the Welsh public about their national identity. The coverage did not seem to engage the public on the question of how these proposed changes would impact on their day-to-day lives.[19]

Reaction to the closing poll results

Twelve days before the 18 September vote YouGov released a poll which showed that the Yes side could win. Prior to this close poll result, the coverage in Wales had been limited to discussions within policy elites and the political class on the future constitutional model in the principality.[20] These discussions rarely engaged the public with the contentious issues at stake for Wales following the Scottish referendum.

Up until the possibility of a Yes majority, the mainstream media within Wales were subdued and mention of the referendum was made in passing, as if to signal that it was happening, but not much about its possible impact on Wales was discussed. This lack of attention may also have been linked to the heightened media coverage surrounding the NATO Summit, which was being held in Newport during the first week of September.

From the week beginning 8 September 2014, and once the polls tightened and signalled a possible Yes vote and upheaval to the status quo, the coverage heightened, with daily accounts on Wales Today and on BBC radio programmes about the possible impact upon Wales. Welsh politicians also travelled to Scotland to campaign on opposing sides and this gave journalists from Wales an opportunity to interview them and question them as to how the referendum would impact at home.

That in itself posed a problem for the journalists within Wales. Those working on programmes or newspapers specifically for Welsh audiences were faced with trying to find a way of highlighting how the referendum would affect Wales differently each day, in order to justify including the story. This was particularly challenging for Wales Today on BBC 1 Wales, which was confronted with the difficulty of finding a Welsh angle that was different to the coverage already offered by the BBC network's News at 6 programmes.

For example, on 9 September 2014 both the BBC network's News at 6 programme and BBC Wales's Wales Today programme covered many of the same stories. They both outlined the panic within the Better Together campaign and the Prime Minister's decision to abandon Prime Minister's Questions the following day to travel to Scotland to campaign for a No vote. Both programmes also noted that the Scottish flag was flying above 10 Downing Street and how the three main UK parties were trying to show a united front against independence.

BBC Wales also produce S4C's nightly news programme, Newyddion 9, which is a mixed news programme, with international, British and Welsh content (it is rather similar to the news bulletins transmitted in Scotland by the Gaelic television service, BBC Alba.) On the same day as News at 6 and Wales Today offered many of the same stories in their coverage of the referendum, Newyddion 9 dealt with what the referendum meant for the whole of the UK, with the fact that the leaders of the three main UK parties travelled to Scotland, and what the implications would be for Wales.

Arguably the Welsh language news coverage offered a more succinct picture of what the implications would be for Scotland, for the UK and for Wales. More time was also offered to discuss the issues with political commentators and guests in the studio. This disparity between coverage in Welsh and English highlights the challenges facing the journalists following devolution, that is, how to make the news coverage relevant to a UK-wide audience when powers are devolved asymmetrically to the differing nations within the UK.

Voters trust the BBC to reflect events accurately, but the King Report of 2008, which was commissioned by the Corporation, detailed some of the stories which were inaccurate, for example a story in October 2007 which focused on the 'English votes for English Laws' proposal but only discussed the policy from the perspective of English MPs and failed to mention what effect this would have on MPs from Wales and Northern Ireland.[21] Inaccurate stories, containing mistakes or misinterpreted facts, are confusing to the electorate and ultimately could have an effect on Welsh democracy or election results.

The idea of a 'Scottish Six' – a bulletin produced by BBC Scotland but containing UK and international news as well as domestic material – was discussed during the emergence of devolution but was swiftly quashed by the political establishment. The question of a 'Welsh Six' was never discussed as widely. However, during the Scottish independence referendum the need for a separate mixed English language news programme for Wales, along the same lines as *Newyddion 9*, re-emerged. It was very difficult for a single UK news programme to explain the implications for the constituent nations of the Britain correctly and without causing confusion. Having a separate news programme would have made it easier for the viewers to fully comprehend the implications.

The answer may be to establish a Welsh Six. If that happened, the question 'how is this likely to affect Wales?' would not need to be asked in order to justify the inclusion of a story. The story would simply be covered on its own merit. The inconsistencies and inaccuracies highlighted by the King Report would also be avoided, by ensuring that all political stories concerning devolved matters would be handled by journalists possessing the necessary expertise.

Following the result

Following the close No result, the political establishment were quick to announce the need for constitutional reform across the UK. However, much of the UK media coverage concentrated on the implications for England, leaving the Welsh electorate in the dark as to how they would be affected.

During the aftermath of the referendum David Cameron called for income tax to be devolved across the UK, but the media coverage mainly concentrated on the possible differences between England and Scotland and failed to tackle how the variations could mean differing levels of income tax elsewhere. The coverage also failed to highlight that the Silk Commission had already called for income tax to be devolved to Wales.

Another popular story following the referendum was David Cameron's plans for 'English votes for English laws'. As this was, in a way, signalling devolution for England for the first time, the story received a lot of coverage. The stories about Wales's place within the UK's new constitutional framework were very sparing and left the Welsh public uncertain as to how this historical event would impact on their lives. This in part was due to the democratic deficit in Wales and in part to the UK news programmes concentrating on England, where most viewers live.

What about Welsh Politics?

The democratic deficit in Wales caused by the lack of media outlets and lack of daily national newspapers has already been discussed. During the Scottish referendum period the opportunities available to discuss indigenous Welsh political stories were limited even further by the coverage of the Scottish referendum. The referendum was almost covered as a story about Welsh politics and squeezed out stories specifically about Welsh politics and current affairs.

The lack of plurality and in particular the lack of journalists working within Wales was emphasised during the campaign as many were sent to Scotland to cover the event and what it could mean for Wales, especially following the close polling results a couple of weeks before the referendum. Therefore, the referendum highlighted a particular problem within Wales, which is, with so few journalists and news outlets based in the country, when a big story is covered outside Wales, there is very little opportunity available to scrutinise indigenous events within the same period.

In order to highlight Wales's case for a new model of devolution, the First Minister, Carwyn Jones, asked all political party leaders in Wales to join him to call on the UK government for further powers. This emphasised how weakness within the Welsh media can have an effect on the way politicians make the case for further devolution within Wales. In order to ensure as much coverage as possible, the First Minister felt obliged to call upon the four main party leaders to agree on the way forward.

Political party press officers have often noted the low number of journalists attending press conferences and briefings at the National Assembly for Wales. This suggests that stories about indigenous Welsh politics could frequently have failed to reach the Welsh public and again underlines the fundamental issue facing Wales that with so few journalists and news outlets, if journalists are sent to another country to cover a particular story, very few are left covering stories within Wales.

In comparison, in the London press there is a momentum generated by the large number of journalists and outlets that ensures that political stories from Westminster are heard and scrutinised by the electorate.

The high level of coverage given to the Scottish referendum by the Welsh-based media during the last few weeks of the campaign also raises questions about the level of coverage that past and future referendums receive in Wales. It could have been plausibly argued that the further powers agreed for the National Assembly for Wales after the referendum in 2011 will have a greater impact on the lives of the people of Wales than a No vote in Scotland would have had for the Scots. However, that referendum did not receive the attention it deserved in the press, and the low turnout suggests that accounts on the broadcast news programmes engaged very few people with the debate. Of course a referendum on independence is also heavily connected to the question of national identity, which perhaps resonates rather more with people than the issue of increasing the competence of a legislature.

Further referendums are currently being discussed in the UK, for example on membership of the EU and specifically in Wales, on transferring power over income tax to the Welsh government. The level of coverage given to the Scottish referendum does set a useful precedent. In the final weeks of the campaign the Scottish referendum received a lot of attention in the Welsh media and press; however, it is difficult to feel confident that a subsequent income tax referendum would gain the same level of coverage, especially as this certainly would not be discussed widely outside the weak Welsh media. Yet, the result of such a referendum could have a greater impact upon Wales.

Conclusions

Although the Scottish independence referendum could have effects upon Wales's constitutional future and was well worthy of media coverage and scrutiny, the weakness of indigenous media meant that there was less opportunity to scrutinise these effects. Furthermore, as the opinion polls became closer nearer 18 September and more attention was given to the referendum, less time was given to examining and highlighting indigenous Welsh political developments.

Questions must also be raised as to how UK network news programmes and the London-based press cover stories about the devolved governments and whether they give enough attention to all the nations and regions. The disparity in the Welsh and English language coverage discussed above highlights how a separate mixed news programme for each nation would offer more appropriate coverage to devolved politics as well as to other matters. Such a development is perhaps fifteen years overdue. It would go some way to ensuring that Wales is given the opportunity to scrutinise the policies that truly have an impact upon day-to-day lives and would perhaps also encourage greater engagement with Welsh politics.

Notes

1. Bogdanor, *Devolution in the United Kingdom.*
2. Available at <http://www.walesonline.co.uk/news/wales-news/wales-says-no-scottish-independence-7007185> (last accessed 16 December 2014). Historically this figure has been lower. It was suggested that the wording of the question meant that this figure was higher than usual.
3. Mackay and Powell, 'Wales and its media'; Williams, *Shadows and Substance;* Allan and O'Malley, 'The media in Wales'; Talfan Davies, *Not By Bread Alone.*
4. Available at <www.mediawales.co.uk/info-base/circulation-distribution-figures/> (last accessed 18 January 2015).
5. Available at <http://www.clickonwales.org/2013/09/changing-consumption-patterns-of-welsh-news/> (last accessed 18 January 2015).
6. Talfan Davies and Morris, *Media in Wales,* p. 51.
7. McAllister and Cole, 'The 2011 Welsh general election'.

8. Electoral Commission Report, 'Report on the National Assembly for Wales general election 5 May 2011', p. 3.
9. Denver, 'Voting in the 1997 Scottish and Welsh devolution referendums', p. 831.
10. Available at <http://www.bbc.co.uk/news/uk-wales-politics-27739205> (last accessed 16 December 2014).
11. Bogdanor, *Devolution in the United Kingdom*, p. 144.
12. Ibid., p. 144.
13. Taylor and Thomson, *Scotland and Wales: Nations Again?*.
14. Wyn Jones and Scully, *Wales Says Yes*.
15. The Silk Commission was launched by the former Welsh Secretary Cheryl Gillan on the 11 October 2011. It was chaired by Paul Silk, and the commission had eight members drawn from Welsh business, academia, the four main political parties and civic society. Its role was to review the financial and constitutional arrangements in Wales and the work was carried out in two parts; the first looked at the fiscal powers and the second looked at the wider powers of the National Assembly for Wales.
16. The UK's Changing Union project began in 2011 and was a collaboration between the Wales Governance Centre at Cardiff University, the Institute of Welsh Affairs and Tomorrow's Wales. The project's aim was to attempt to consolidate the debates on constitutional matters in the four countries of the UK.
17. Available at <http://www.clickonwales.org/2013/09/uks-changing-union-one-year-until-the-referendum/> (last accessed 16 December 2014).
18. Available at <http://www.theguardian.com/politics/2014/sep/19/labour-ed-miliband-constitutional-convention> (last accessed 16 December 2014).
19. Available at <www.bbc.co.uk/news/uk-28852584> (last accessed 18 January 2015).
20. Available at <https://yougov.co.uk/news/2014/09/06/latest-scottish-referendum-poll-yes-lead/> (last accessed 16 December 2014).
21. King, *The BBC Trust Impartiality Report*, pp. 39, 43.

Bibliography

Allan, S. and T. O'Malley, 'The media in Wales', in D. Dunkerley and A. Thompson (eds), *Wales Today* (Cardiff: University of Wales Press, 1999).
BBC Online, 'Fewer than half the population know who runs the Welsh NHS, says poll', *BBC*, 9 June 2014, <http://www.bbc.co.uk/news/uk-wales-politics-27739205> (last accessed 16 December 2014).
BBC Trust, 2008, 'Trust impartiality report: network news and current affairs coverage of the four UK nations', <http://www.bbc.co.uk/bbctrust/our_work/editorial_standards/impartiality/network_news.html> (last accessed 18 January 2015).
Bogdanor, V., *Devolution in the United Kingdom* (Oxford: Oxford University Press, 2001).
Dahlgreen, Will, 'Yes campaign lead at 2 in Scottish referendum', *YouGov*, 6 September 2014, <https://yougov.co.uk/news/2014/09/06/latest-scottish-referendum-poll-yes-lead/> (last accessed 16 December 2014).
Denver, D., 'Voting in the 1997 Scottish and Welsh devolution referendums: information, interests and opinions', *European Journal of Political Research*, 41 (2002), pp. 827–84.
Electoral Commission Report, 'Report on the National Assembly for Wales general election 5 May 2011', <http://www.electoralcommission.org.uk/elections/past-elections2/?a=141330> (last accessed 18 January 2015).
Henry, Graham, 'Wales says no to Scottish independence: our exclusive YouGov poll', *Wales Online*, 19 April 2014, <http://www.walesonline.co.uk/news/wales-news/wales-says-no-scottish-independence-7007185> (last accessed 16 December 2014).

Jones, Carwyn, 'UK's changing union – one year until the referendum', *Click on Wales*, 18 September 2013, <http://www.clickonwales.org/2013/09/uks-changing-union-one-year-until-the-referendum/> (last accessed 16 December 2014).

King, Anthony, *The BBC Trust Impartiality Report: BBC Network News And Current Affairs Coverage Of The Four UK Nations* (King Report) (June 2008), <http://downloads.bbc.co.uk/bbctrust/assets/files/pdf/review_report_research/impartiality/uk_nations_impartiality.pdf> (last accessed 15 September 2015).

McAllister, L. and M. Cole, 'The 2011 Welsh General Election: an analysis of the latest staging post in the maturing of Welsh politics', *Parliamentary Affairs*, 67(1) (2014), pp. 711–30.

Mackay, H. and T. Powell, 'Wales and its media: production, consuption and regulation', *Contemporary Wales*, 9 (1996), pp. 8–39.

Talfan Davies, G., *Not By Bread Alone: Information, Media and the National Assembly* (Cardiff: Wales Media Forum, 1999).

Talfan Davies, G. and N. Morris, *Media in Wales: Serving Public Values* (Cardiff: Institute of Welsh Affairs, 2008).

Taylor, B. and K. Thomson (eds), *Scotland and Wales: Nations Again?* (Cardiff: University of Wales Press, 1999).

Williams, K., *Shadows and Substance: The Development of a Media Policy for Wales* (Llandysul, Ceredigion: Gomer, 1997).

Wintour, Patrick, 'Labour proposes devolution settlement to "shape own futures"', *Guardian*, 19 September 2014, <http://www.theguardian.com/politics/2014/sep/19/labour-ed-miliband-constitutional-convention> (last accessed 16 December 2014).

Wyn Jones, Richard and Roger Scully, *Wales Says Yes* (Cardiff: University of Wales Press, 2012).

12

Our Friends Across the Water: Northern Ireland Media Coverage of the Scottish Independence Referendum

Anthea Irwin

Background

The resonance of the referendum for the people of Northern Ireland

Galtung and Ruge[1] talk of news values that tend to construct the news, and one of these is 'proximity'. Events tend to be more likely to make the news if they are geographically close, so it is no surprise that we saw significant coverage of the Scottish independence referendum in Northern Ireland. Perhaps more importantly, however, 'proximity' refers also to political closeness, and there is no doubt that this aspect made the referendum all the more newsworthy for the Northern Irish media, to differing extents for different media providers.

Independence, nationhood, self-determination and identity are highly resonant and contested concepts for the people of Northern Ireland. There are few incidences these days of these issues being contested by violent means, which was the lens through which the world's media largely knew and understood us in the past. The issues might be more symbolic now, but they are based on very real shifts in power over the years. The potential for another shift in power, albeit one that would affect us indirectly rather than directly, took these issues beyond the symbolic realm for a time, and legitimised explicit discussion of potential changes in our own situation, which unsurprisingly were welcomed and scorned, depending on who you were speaking to, or what you were reading or watching.

Given the extent of the coverage, choices of focus have been necessary. This chapter will discuss in detail the press coverage of the referendum, and provide a broad outline of the tone of broadcast coverage, along with responses to the result from key Northern Ireland politicians.

Some historical and political context

The Irish Republic secured its independence from Britain in 1921 after a bloody conflict. The six counties in the north remained part of the UK, but opinion was divided on whether this was an acceptable settlement, and some continued the struggle for the 'six counties' to reunite with the Irish Republic. It is widely accepted that Catholics were discriminated against under the devolved Parliament of Northern Ireland in terms of both representation and parliamentary practices. In the 1960s a civil rights movement (of both Catholics and Protestants) formed which fashioned itself on the US civil rights movement. There was disagreement about how to resolve the situation, however, and the Irish Republican movement moved to armed conflict in an attempt to achieve a United Ireland.

'The Troubles' in Northern Ireland saw paramilitary activity from both republicans and loyalists. In 1972 the Parliament of Northern Ireland was suspended, and Direct Rule from Westminster was re-established. The Troubles continued until 1998, when the Good Friday Agreement effectively symbolised their end. The agreement recognised that the majority of the people of Northern Ireland wished to remain part of the UK and that a significant minority of the people of Northern Ireland, and a majority of the people on the island of Ireland as a whole wished there to be a United Ireland. It stated that Northern Ireland would remain part of the United Kingdom until majorities in both Northern Ireland and the Republic of Ireland wished it to become part of a United Ireland, but that if this happened the two governments must grant it. The agreement also recognised the right of the citizens of Northern Ireland to categorise themselves as Irish, or British, or both.

Furthermore, it set up a new 'power sharing' devolved assembly in Northern Ireland in which the positions of the First Minister and Deputy First Minster must be from each of the two political persuasions, unionist and nationalist, the executive (cabinet) must be balanced, and agreements on bills must gain not just an overall majority, but a proportion of both unionist and nationalist support. The two biggest parties in the Stormont Assembly are currently the Democratic Unionist Party (DUP), which is strongly unionist, and Sinn Fein (translates into English as 'We Ourselves'), which is strongly republican. The three other main parties are the Ulster Unionist Party (UUP), which is moderately unionist, the Social Democratic and Labour Party (SDLP), which is moderately nationalist, and the Alliance Party, which is now neutral on the union.

The media context

The main press titles in Northern Ireland are as follows: the *Belfast Telegraph* is a compact daily owned by the Dublin-based Independent News and Media with a circulation of 48,014.[2] It claims to have a neutral editorial stance, and has a cross-community readership, though it is generally considered to lean towards unionism. The *Irish News* is a compact daily independently owned by the locally based Fitzpatrick family with a circulation of 39,935.[3] Its editorial stance is broadly nationalist. The *News Letter* is a compact daily owned by the Scottish Johnston Press, with a circulation of 19,314.[4] Its editorial stance is unionist. The broadcasters in Northern Ireland are BBC Northern Ireland, one of the national regions of the BBC, and UTV (Ulster Television), then an independent company but part of the ITV network. Both BBC and UTV have radio stations (BBC Radio Ulster and U105, respectively), and a number of commercial radio stations also broadcast.

Key Methods and Concepts for Analysis

Content analysis[5] was carried out on the press coverage. This method of analysis codes texts and quantifies patterns and trends, which is useful when considering similarities and differences between coverage in different titles.

Fairclough[6] points out that absence can be as significant as presence in texts; it is important to consider what is not included and why, in addition to analysing what is included.

Several theoretical concepts are drawn on in the following analysis of both the press and broadcast coverage. 'Framing'[7] considers which aspects of an individual, group or event are drawn out and highlighted, which is by extension at the expense of other aspects. A simple way to think about this is the question of whether a glass is half full or half empty; in one case the situation is framed positively and in the other it is framed negatively.

'Discourses'[8] are the different ways we talk (or write) about the same thing. For example, asylum can be talked about with a discourse of threat ('they're taking our jobs') or a discourse of humanitarianism ('we should welcome people fleeing persecution').[9]

'Intertextuality'[10] refers to the ways in which one text can, explicitly or implicitly, draw on other texts to tell its story. This can be an economical way to make a point because with an echo or image from another time or place can come ready-made connotations. Intertextuality, then, is often emotive or ideological in nature.

Press Coverage

What are we looking at? Data

Searches were carried out of the online archives of the *Belfast Telegraph*, the *Irish News* and the *News Letter* using the keywords 'Scottish Independence'. Each piece was coded in several ways. First, the pieces were categorised according to when they appeared, by year until 2012–14, by month in 2014, and by date in September. Second, they were categorised by type, for example news, feature, opinion, reader's letter. Third, they were categorised according to where the main focus of the piece lay, whether on Scotland, on Northern Ireland, on the United Kingdom, on the Republic of Ireland or beyond. Fourth, they were categorised with regard to whether they appeared to be pro-Scottish independence, anti-Scottish independence or neutral. This categorisation is of course sometimes rather more nuanced than a blatant pro or anti stance, and aspects of this will be discussed more fully. Finally, a key theme of each piece was identified. There were significant differences between the three titles in all of these aspects.

How much? Volume of coverage

By far the highest volume of coverage appeared in the *Belfast Telegraph*, which ran 284 pieces in total. The *News Letter* ran 89 pieces, and the *Irish News* ran just 40. This would suggest that the outcome was considered to have significantly less impact on those of a nationalist political persuasion than those of a unionist political persuasion. Some 67 per cent of the pieces in the *News Letter* and 60 per cent of the pieces in the *Irish News* appeared in September 2014, suggesting a relatively focused approach, with not much broader discussion preceding or following the referendum. The proportion of the *Belfast Telegraph*'s coverage that ran in September 2014 was around half that of the other titles, at 33 per cent, which suggests a broader and more lengthy discussion.

There was also a clear peak in the *News Letter*'s coverage in 2012, when 23 per cent of the coverage appeared, and a smaller, but still notable, peak in the *Belfast Telegraph*, at 14 per cent. The centenary of the Ulster Covenant, which half a million unionists signed in 1912 to protest about the then British government's Irish home rule proposals, occurred in this year and, whilst only a minority of the 2012 pieces have that explicit theme, it is clear that this event encouraged increased focus on the Ulster Scots identity and the historical relationship between Northern Ireland and Scotland.

Fact or opinion? Type of article

The breakdown of coverage by type of article is very similar in the *Belfast Telegraph* and the *News Letter*. Both were heavily weighted towards news pieces (74 per cent and 73 per cent respectively). There was a notable trend in *News Letter* news pieces towards starting from the comments of politicians (overwhelmingly unionist) as well as news events per se, so it is clear that the unionist parties were proactively producing press releases about the referendum, and referring to it in speeches at party conferences and other events. Such pieces somewhat blur the boundary between fact and opinion.

In the *Irish News* the majority of the pieces (55 per cent) were also news pieces. It is notable in this title, however, that the total of opinion pieces (30 per cent) and readers' letters (12.5 per cent) is almost 80 per cent of the total of news pieces. This suggests that, whilst the referendum gained a lot less coverage in the *Irish News* than in the other two titles, in this title it was treated as an area for civic discussion and reflection, more so than in the other titles.

Who are we talking about? Focus

All three titles had around a quarter of pieces focused on Northern Ireland (25 per cent in the *Irish News* and the *Belfast Telegraph* and 23 per cent in the *News Letter*). A significant majority (57.5 per cent) of the pieces in the *Irish News* were focused on Scotland itself, with just 12.5 per cent focusing on the UK. The *Belfast Telegraph* also had Scotland as the main focus, though less significantly (46 per cent), and its focus on the UK (27 per cent) was on a par with its focus on

Northern Ireland. The *News Letter* placed similar focus on the UK (40 per cent) and Scotland (37 per cent). The Republic of Ireland was the focus of 5 per cent of the *Irish News* coverage, 3 per cent of the *Belfast Telegraph*, and did not feature in the *News Letter*. If we consider the NI focused pieces and the UK focused pieces together, it is fair to say that the *News Letter* constructed the referendum as a UK issue, the *Irish News* constructed it as a Scottish issue, and the *Belfast Telegraph* gave equal weight to both.

What do we think about it? Position

In terms of the extent to which the coverage was for or against Scottish independence, unsurprisingly none of the titles had a majority of supportive coverage, but the *Irish News* had 20 per cent supportive coverage which, considered along with its neutral coverage (75 per cent), shows very little negativity. There were only two negative pieces, one of which was a reader's letter, which would seem to display the paper's openness to giving voice to diverse opinion in its civic discussion, and one was an opinion piece about the economy that was written very much from a UK business perspective.

The *Belfast Telegraph*, like the *Irish News*, was overwhelmingly neutral (78 per cent). It is important to point out, however, that, whilst these pieces were balanced in terms of quotes and so on, the overall topic of the pieces and/or the way in which they were headlined was overwhelmingly negative rather than supportive, so this 'neutrality' is nuanced; indeed, the paper did at various points in its editorials state that it was of the opinion that remaining in the union was the preferable outcome of the referendum, albeit it respected that this was a matter for the people of Scotland. The positive and negative proportions of the *Belfast Telegraph* were opposite to those of the *Irish News*. The *Belfast Telegraph* had 18 per cent negative pieces and just 4 per cent supportive pieces. The supportive pieces, similarly to the *Irish News*'s negative ones, suggest a degree of openness to presenting a rounded debate: four were readers' letters, two were invited pieces by Scottish supporters of the Yes campaign, one journalist and one celebrity, and one was an invited piece from the Sinn Fein chair.

The *News Letter* took a much more explicit position than the other two titles. Whilst it had 55 per cent neutral coverage, 40 per cent of its coverage was negative, and only four pieces (5 per cent) were supportive. One of these was a reader's letter, suggesting that this title too has a commitment, at least in its letters page, to diversity of opinion.

What are we talking about? Themes

In keeping with its weight of focus on Scotland, the most popular theme for pieces in the *Irish News* was the referendum itself (23 per cent). And in keeping with its weight of focus on the UK, the most popular theme for pieces in the *News Letter* was maintenance of the union (20 per cent). In both titles, the four most popular themes together made up 70 per cent of the coverage, and there was, perhaps surprisingly, some overlap between these. In the *Irish News* the next most popular themes were the democratic and participatory nature of Scottish politics (18 per cent), devolved powers (15 per cent) and the economy (15 per cent). In the *News Letter* the next most popular themes were devolved powers (20 per cent), the referendum itself (16 per cent) and the democratic and participatory nature of Scottish politics (8 per cent). Like the *Irish News*, the *Belfast Telegraph* had the referendum itself as its most popular theme; at 29 per cent it was by far the most popular. The economy was next at a much lower 17 per cent. Thereafter, there was a cluster of six minor themes with around 5 per cent coverage each: celebrity opinion, maintenance of the union, devolved powers, corporation tax, a potential border poll and more general impact on Northern Ireland.

It is notable that the theme of 'the democratic and participatory nature of Scotland's politics' appeared significantly in both the *Irish News* and the *News Letter*; we might not expect that in the latter, given its anti-Scottish independence stance and its proactive focus on the maintenance of the UK. (This theme appeared in the *Belfast Telegraph* as well, but only amounted to 2 per cent of the coverage so is not worthy of discussion in relation to this title.) To a greater or lesser extent, both the *Irish News* and the *News Letter* recognised Scotland as a country whose politics are more developed, more fluid, more nuanced and, perhaps most significantly, as having dealt with perceived disempowerment by Westminster by non-violent means, hugely more successfully than Northern Ireland ever did. Employment of this theme, however, was as much about reinforcing the editorial/party political position of these titles as it was about speaking highly of Scotland. It sets the *News Letter* explicitly, and the *Irish News* implicitly, against Sinn Fein and their history of support for armed struggle in Northern Ireland.

The Sinn Fein factor can also account for a significant absence in the press coverage. Only 5 per cent of pieces in each of the *News Letter* and the *Irish News* had the theme of a potential border poll. This might seem surprising because there was significant political debate about this, some of which was covered in broadcast news, news review and political debate programmes. There are two points to make here, however. First, whilst the *Irish News* has a nationalist position, it is more akin to the politics of the SDLP than those of Sinn Fein, and it is the latter who are largely calling for a border poll. Second, whilst one might expect negative coverage of a potential border poll in the *News Letter*, it seems the title (or perhaps more specifically the unionist parties' press offices, given the proportion of its news pieces that appear to arise from parties' press releases) decided that an absence of this aspect was more empowering to their position than reactive coverage of it.

What else are we talking about? Echoes of other events and texts
THE TROUBLES
The spike in coverage in the *News Letter* and the *Belfast Telegraph* in 2012 contained several explicit comparisons between the potential fallout from an independent Scotland and the Troubles in Northern Ireland. It is important to

say that all of these references drew on direct quotes from unionist politicians and were not positions explicitly taken by the papers. In a couple of cases the comparison was blatant and negative: 'Mr Elliott accused SNP leader Alex Salmond of appearing to pose "a greater threat to the Union than the violence of the IRA"' (*Belfast Telegraph*); 'Empey: Scottish split "may reignite Troubles"' (*News Letter*).

In other cases the link was more implicit, whilst still clearly drawing intertextually on stories about the Troubles. For example, in the following quote the 'violence' is symbolic: 'Lord Trimble said that every Scot had a "British component" in their national identity, and that to "separate that is to do violence to people's own sense of identity"' (*Belfast Telegraph*). Peter Robinson took a different, and somewhat contradictory, approach: an opinion piece in the *News Letter* discussed the First Minister, suggesting Alex Salmond 'puts a new twist on the republican slogan "Armalite and the ballot box" when he said Scottish Independence "can be defeated with a Saltire in one hand and a Union Flag in the other"'. This piece, unlike the preceding ones, appeared not to liken Scottish Nationalists to Irish Republicans, but to compare the former favourably to the latter.

In January 2014 the blatant approach from some unionists was still in evidence: 'Take Ian Paisley Jnr's comments this week. "A Yes vote in Scotland would, the North Antrim MP said, be a spur for dissident republican violence, destabilising Northern Ireland and unravelling the gains of the Good Friday Agreement"' (*Belfast Telegraph*). This came from an opinion piece which saw the paper explicitly criticise Paisley's approach, something that was not seen in the 2012 coverage:

> It is unclear how a democratic referendum in another part of the United Kingdom could give succour to gunmen who have minimal support even within their own communities. If anything, the SNP's success proves beyond a reasonable doubt the supremacy of constitutional means. Regardless of the result in September, Alex Salmond and his party have shown that it is the ballot box – not the Armalite – that works.

Whilst the force of these references varied, they served a common purpose of implicitly critiquing Irish republicanism in general and Sinn Fein in particular, for inferring that a Yes vote would lead to calls for a border poll in Ireland which would lead to unrest, and of highlighting the failure of the relatively recent (republican) violence.

THE SECOND WORLD WAR

The *News Letter* also used some war terminology, for example '*D Day* for Union as polls open in Scotland for referendum vote' and 'BREAKING NEWS: A VICTORY FOR NO IN SCOTLAND' [my emphasis].

The discourse of war is rather common in news reporting of anything that can be constructed as having two 'sides'. Its use constructs the conflict element as relatively more extreme. In this case, however, the use of *D Day* echoes the Second World War, probably the most key point in history for the notion of the unity of nations being a strength. It thus provides an emotional appeal to maintain the union. Indeed, a proactive emotional appeal (without the battle metaphors) appeared in an opinion piece on the same day: 'Vote No, Scotland, and stay with your friends in the UK'.

SCOTTISH AND IRISH LITERATURE

The *Irish News* provided a couple of pertinent nods to literature that painted a rich picture of the approach of the journalists (both are opinion pieces).

The following is an extract from 'Mileage in vision of a distinctive Scotland', which appeared in December 2013:

> Even with repeated contemplation of the alternatives, where independence brings insoluble problems and little compensation, it is *no mean prospect* to see a people weighing their chances in a future they have changed for themselves. There is clearly mileage in the vision of a socially progressive, distinctive Scotland, clear and free from the assaults of a welfare-bashing Tory-led coalition . . . [my emphasis]

The use of the words 'no mean prospect' are unlikely to be a coincidence here, and they echo the title of the 1935 book *No Mean City*, about life in the Gorbals area of Glasgow, co-written by a journalist and an unemployed worker.[11] The book provides an account of life from the perspective of the working class, a perspective rarely taken in literature of the time, so it would seem there is a point being made here about the fact that the referendum, and the discussion and debate around it, have been a truly participatory process for all sections of the community, something this writer, and the *Irish News* in general, praised.

A piece entitled '*Changed utterly* – no matter the result' [my emphasis] appeared on 13 September 2014. The following is an extract:

> DEAR People of Scotland, Congratulations. Whatever the outcome of Thursday's referendum, you will have significantly changed the structures and systems of the United Kingdom for the first time since Irish partition. Most importantly, you will have achieved it without as much as having thrown a stone. (We killed over 3,600 people in the past half-century and are bound within the UK by an international treaty, while governed by an Assembly which does not work.)
>
> After all, what have the Scots ever done for us? Oh all right, they invented porridge, haggis and deep-fried Mars bars (I think). But apart from that, what have they ever done for us?
>
> Well, they avoided sectarian politics. In doing so, they challenged the concept of unionism, not through the intellectual laziness of branding unionists as British, but by accepting them as Scottish and debating social, economic, cultural and constitutional issues with them along non-sectarian lines.
>
> That's what the Scots did for us. For that, they deserve our thanks and our envy.

The first part of the headline, 'Changed utterly', is, again, no coincidence, and this is further supported by the reference to the partition of Ireland. Intertextually, it echoes W. B. Yeats's poem 'Easter, 1916' about the Easter Rising in Ireland, in particular the line 'All changed, changed utterly: A terrible beauty is born'. Yeats, who previously had been disengaged from politics, was inspired by the events of the Easter Rising, but also of course devastated by the loss of life that followed it. This piece, then, recognises the huge significance of the independence referendum, and the surrounding history of politics in Scotland, as the disempowered challenging the empowered, but doing it through reasoned argument rather than the violence that occurred in Ireland in 1916 and in Northern Ireland during the Troubles of the latter part of the twentieth century. It also references the often stereotypical way in which Scotland is represented and dismisses it, replacing it with a respectful construction that recognises Scotland as a politically developed nation.

Broadcast News

What are we looking at? Data

There was much of interest in the political comment included in Northern Ireland broadcast news coverage of the Scottish independence referendum. Given space limitations, however, this chapter will consider the reactions to the result from the leaders of the main parties and other key politicians during the Stormont Assembly business, which were picked out by both BBC and UTV News as representative of the parties' positions, and contributed to the overall 'framing' of the result in terms of how news programmes/pieces are introduced.

What are they saying? Key NI politicians' reactions

Mike Nesbitt, UUP party leader: 'Obviously as unionists we rejoice and are delighted with the result. The case for Scottish independence was never made, and common sense has prevailed.' Political commentators picked up on the use of the word 'rejoice' by Nesbitt and previously by the DUP's Ian Paisley Jnr. There are two significant aspects to this. First, the word echoes Margaret Thatcher's reaction to the UK's victory in the Falklands War, so using it in the context of the Scottish independence referendum is a significant claim of power and position by unionists. Second, the word draws on Christian discourse and as such makes a claim that the result is inherently right. This inherent rightness is supported by the claim that 'the case for Scottish independence was never made'.

Sammy Wilson, DUP: 'I congratulate the people of Scotland in recognising the benefits of the union despite the tartan terror tactics of the SNP during what was a very contentious referendum campaign.' The word 'recognise' is referred to linguistically as a 'factive verb', in other words one that suggests that what follows it is fact. Politicians often use these to present opinion as fact, and in this sense Sammy Wilson adopted a similar stance to Mike Nesbitt in presenting the result as inherently right. In addition, the use of 'congratulate' is somewhat patronising;

the result was the right thing, but the people of Scotland came to this 'recognition' after the rest of the UK. The words of strongest import in Sammy Wilson's contribution are 'tartan terror tactics'. 'Tartan' paints the Scottish in a stereotypical and objectified light. 'Terror tactics' is another example of the ongoing equating by some unionists of the SNP and the IRA.

Daithi McKay, Sinn Fein:

> We should have the same debate. It was a healthy exercise in Scotland, there has been some scaremongering about that but I think that across the world Scotland has been held up as a shining light of how to hold a mature debate about its future governance.

Unsurprisingly, Daithi McKay's contribution opposes Sammy Wilson's by constructing the negative 'scaremongering' as being on the side of the unionists. Given the result, the focus is on the health of the debate and the potential for other countries to follow suit. Whilst Daithi McKay does hold Scotland up as 'a shining light', a somewhat mythical, perhaps almost religious image (with a rather different force than Mike Nesbitt's), he also said 'we should have the same debate', which constructs Northern Ireland as being ready and able to do so (in relation to a border poll about a potential United Ireland), something that would be contested even by the nationalist SDLP.

Alex Attwood, SDLP: 'The people of Scotland demonstrated the power of the democratic approach, what Alex Salmond referred to as the democratic and consent process.' This contribution is short but it does three key things. It constructs the Scottish debate and political process as positive, though rather less dramatically than Daithi McKay's contribution. It could also be interpreted as differentiating between 'the democratic process' in Scotland and the violent process in Northern Ireland, though unlike Sammy Wilson's contribution, this could only be interpreted from Attwood's comment by inference. Finally, by absence rather than presence, it makes no suggestion that Northern Ireland is ready to embark on a similar process, so, again, by inference, implies that it is not.

David Ford, Alliance Party: 'We are currently running through a crisis because of our inabilities and our immaturities, so how could we possibly make a case for suggesting that we should be looking for additional powers until we seek to resolve those problems?' This contribution states clearly what Alex Attwood's implies. Using the metaphor of maturity to differentiate between Scotland and Northern Ireland, it places Northern Ireland even further away from being able to have the same debate as Scotland by claiming we should not even have 'additional powers' (further devolution), never mind any larger constitutional change.

How is it framed? Reporting the result

There was significant contrast between how the referendum result was 'framed' by BBC News and UTV News. The BBC's coverage highlighted the maintenance of the status quo, whereas UTV's coverage highlighted the significance of the Yes vote and the changes that would come as a consequence.

Some quotes from BBC news bulletins on 19 September: 'Scotland has rejected independence'; 'The SNP has accepted defeat in the referendum on Scotland's independence'; 'speaking at Downing Street the prime minister David Cameron said the debate had been settled for a generation'; 'Scotland's first minister Alex Salmond thanked those who had voted for independence. He said the campaign had touched sections of the community who had never before been touched by politics.'

The word 'rejected', whilst it is a point of fact, constructs the result as rather more clear-cut than the figures imply, and suggests the country deciding as one. 'Accepted defeat' has echoes of war reporting and perhaps suggests that the result was clear some time before it was accepted, which is at best arguable. The selected quote from David Cameron reinforces the status quo, and the selected quote from Alex Salmond highlights the emotive impact rather than recognising the level of political impact.

Some quotes from UTV news bulletins on 18 and 19 September: 'The polls have closed, with millions of voters having their say on the nation's continued membership of the UK'; 'A staggering 97 per cent of people have registered to vote. 4.2 million people will put their mark on a referendum paper today, making it potentially the biggest turnout the UK has ever seen'; 'Whatever the outcome Scottish politics has been galvanised. This is history in the making, and people know it'; 'Reaction is still coming in tonight after Scotland's first minister Alex Salmond became the first casualty of the referendum result. The Prime Minster says more powers could now be devolved to politicians in Northern Ireland, England and Wales.'

Whilst the first quote focuses on the potential maintenance of the status quo with 'membership of the UK', it refers to Scotland as a 'nation'. Furthermore, the quotes that follow highlight the political impact of the process, regardless of the result, and the selected material from David Cameron's input highlights the potential for increased devolved powers. Alex Salmond's stepping down is arguably constructed sympathetically by the word 'casualty', and this use of the discourse of war seems dynamic in comparison to the BBC's focus on the status quo.

Conclusions

The Scottish independence referendum proved significant for the media in Northern Ireland. It was variously framed as a Scottish concern by the nationalist leaning press and as a concern for the union by the unionist leaning press. Unionist politicians took an 'agenda setting' approach to the referendum from years before in an attempt to maintain the union and their position within it, and the unionist leaning press gave voice to this. The nationalist leaning press was more time limited but also more discursive in its approach. Notably, whilst the voice of Sinn Fein was key (along with that of the DUP) in broadcast coverage, it was very much backgrounded by the press coverage, unsurprising given the party political leanings of the press titles.

The *News Letter* constructed the potential for Scottish independence negatively, and the *Irish News* constructed it neutrally to positively. The *Belfast Telegraph* was balanced, but with much more space given to critical voices. The referendum was viewed through the lens of Northern Irish history a significant minority of the time, and a minor but significant trend overall was to pay respect to the people of Scotland for the democratic and participatory nature of the process and to compare that favourably to paramilitary activity during the Troubles.

The broadcast coverage gave voice to all Northern Ireland parties. The framing of the BBC and UTV coverage differed significantly, with the maintenance of the status quo and strength of the union highlighted by the BBC and the extent of the shift and gains of the independence movement highlighted by UTV. Whilst space restraints did not allow for analysis of it here, this trend was replicated in news review and political debate programmes across the two channels, something well worthy of further examination.

Notes

1. Galtung and Ruge, 'The structure of foreign news'.
2. ABC Island of Ireland Report January – June 2014.
3. Ibid.
4. Ibid.
5. See, for example, Riffe and Lacy, *Analyzing Media Messages*.
6. Fairclough, *Analyzing Discourse*.
7. See, for example, Goffman, *Frame Analysis*; Lakoff, *The All New Don't Think of an Elephant!*.
8. See, for example, Mills, *Discourse*.
9. Irwin, 'Race and ethnicity in the media'.
10. Kristeva, *Desire in Language*.
11. McArthur and Kingsley-Long, *No Mean City*.

Bibliography

ABC Island of Ireland Report January – June 2014.
Fairclough, N., *Analyzing Discourse: Textual Analysis for Social Research* (London: Routledge, 2003).
Galtung, J. and M. Ruge, 'The structure of foreign news', *Journal of Peace Research* 2(1) (1965), pp. 64–91.
Goffman, E., *Frame Analysis: An Essay on the Organization of Experience*, 2nd edn (Lebanon, NH: Northeastern University Press, 1986).
Irwin, A., 'Race and ethnicity in the media', in N. Blain and D. Hutchison (eds), *The Media in Scotland* (Edinburgh: Edinburgh University Press, 2008).
Kristeva, J., *Desire in Language: A Semiotic Approach to Literature and Art* (New York: Columbia University Press, 1980).
Lakoff, G., *The All New Don't Think of an Elephant!*, 2nd edn (White River Junction, VT: Chelsea Green Publishing Company, 2014).
McArthur, A. and H. Kingsley-Long [1935], *No Mean City* (London: Corgi, 1978).

Mills, S., *Discourse* (London: Routledge, 2004).
Riffe, D. and S. Lacy, *Analyzing Media Messages: Using Quantitative Content Analysis in Research* (London: Routledge, 2013).
www.bbc.co.uk/ni
www.irishnews.com
www.newsletter.co.uk
www.thebelfasttelegraph.co.uk
www.u.tv
Yeats, W. B., *The Collected Poems of W. B. Yeats* (Ware: Wordsworth Editions, 2000).

PART THREE

International Perspectives

13

'Knock-on Consequences': Irish Media Coverage of the Scottish Referendum

Kevin Rafter

Introduction

The focus on recent relations between Scotland and the Irish Republic has been on economic matters, notwithstanding historical ties including common membership of the United Kingdom until the passing of the Anglo-Irish Treaty in 1922. The strong performance of the Irish economy from the mid-1990s until 2008 attracted considerable interest in Scotland and, in particular, from the Scottish National Party (SNP).

At the outset of Tony Blair's premiership in 1997, and New Labour's election promise to offer Scottish voters a choice on devolution, SNP leader Alex Salmond took encouragement from Ireland's nascent boom.[1] Writing in the *Irish Times* in May 1997, Salmond made explicit reference to economic matters in building his case, not just for a Scottish Parliament under the Blair proposals but also for independence: 'Looking across from Scotland we see what a small nation, mobilising its own resources, can achieve, and we reflect on our own indifferent economic performance'.[2]

The SNP leader articulated an argument that would become a familiar refrain over the following decade as Ireland's economic performance continued to dazzle national and international observers:

> In Scotland, we can only envy Ireland's access to Europe's top table, just as we can only envy Ireland's international visibility and all the advantages in tourism and investment – not to mention self respect – which go with it.

The Irish success story was a regular reference point for newspaper headline writers who sought to capture what Ireland's economic boom could, apparently, teach the Scots. Examples included: 'The Celtic Tiger has a playmate, a Caledonian cub;[3] and 'After the Celtic Tiger, is the Scottish Tiger far behind?'.[4] Moreover, as the boom times continued – we were told – the politicians at Holyrood were still 'casting an envious eye to the Celtic Tiger'.[5]

Ireland's economic growth was, in part, facilitated by low interest rates that followed entry into the eurozone and domestic banks having increased access to less expensive credit. Investment decisions, especially from 2002 onwards, were heavily motivated by a belief that local property demand would remain strong and values would continue to increase. Foreign banks were also enticed into the booming Irish market, among them high street leaders from Edinburgh including Royal Bank of Scotland (RBS) and Halifax/Bank of Scotland. An independent report on the collapse of the Irish economy later noted that profit margins were cut and new riskier products promoted as 'foreign-owned institutions competed aggressively with the domestic players for market share'.[6]

During this period business interests in Ireland also looked internationally in pursuit of profit. The Scottish market was on the radar of Irish property developers, as a 2001 newspaper article reported: 'A large influx of Irish investors has been targeting the office sector and finds Edinburgh offering good returns'.[7] The then Taoiseach (Prime Minister), Bertie Ahern, spoke about the 'boom times getting even more boomier'.[8] There were, however, some signs that the Irish economy was slowing and that financial institutions had engaged in far too much risky lending. Yet, there was little currency for these warnings, when Salmond visited Dublin in February 2008.

By this time Scotland's First Minister Salmond's message was not that dissimilar to the one contained in the newspaper article he had penned eleven years previously. He said Scotland would borrow from the Irish model of social partnership – involving employers and trade unions – in order to build a 'Celtic Lion economy' that would match the Irish Celtic Tiger.[9] In a lecture at Trinity College, Dublin, Salmond claimed there was an 'arc of prosperity' surrounding Scotland that included Ireland, Iceland, Norway, Finland and Denmark. He identified similar features in these five countries. They were all small and independent, stable, secure and prosperous. While he may have been pandering to his local audience, the First Minister singled out Ireland from the list: 'of all these nations, no example is more impressive and inspiring than Ireland'.

It would probably be one of the last glowing associations Salmond, or for that matter any Scottish politician, would seek to make between Scotland and Ireland. The Irish banking system effectively collapsed in late 2008, with the Dublin government having to guarantee €440bn in liabilities. Two years of tax increases and significant reductions in public expenditure – which had been not been controlled adequately in the 2002–8 period – could not prevent Ireland seeking a €67.5bn external assistance facility from the International Monetary Fund and the European Union in late 2010. Arriving in Dublin in November 2010, author Michael Lewis recorded that, 'the entire Irish economy has almost dutifully collapsed'.[10]

In its heyday, as noted, 'Celtic Tiger' Ireland was central to the Scottish independence debate. By 2014 Ireland as a role model – and, in turn, as a justification for independence – no longer featured prominently in Irish media coverage.[11] Economic matters were still a preoccupation, albeit a minor one, in referendum reporting in Ireland but only in so far as an independent Scotland might offer stronger competition for direct foreign investment. In this chapter, two specific aspects in referendum coverage throughout 2014 in the main national media outlets in Ireland are identified. First, the application of traditional journalistic news values in determining coverage, with the referendum very much treated as a normal news story. Second, a focus on what constitutional change might mean for Ireland in terms of the UK's relationship with the EU, and, in particular, the future of Northern Ireland. In the discussion that follows these two features of Irish media coverage will be explored in greater detail.

Foreign Coverage

For many years after independence in 1921 a lack of resources limited the ability of Irish media organisations to appoint their own foreign correspondents. Syndicated material from international agency services such as Reuters and the Press Association filled the pages of local domestic newspapers in Ireland, along with occasionally 'parachuting' their own reporters into short-term foreign assignments.[12]

Coverage from the United Kingdom was always treated differently owing to the historical connection between Dublin and London and the ongoing close trade and political links between the two jurisdictions. Long before having their own correspondents in various international centres, the leading national newspapers and the state owned public service broadcast service had offices in London. In a sense, British coverage was akin to a domestic story for the Irish media. Reportage was, however, London-centric, with coverage beyond the British capital, including from Scotland, more likely to be taken from syndicated press agency reports or local freelance journalists.

The main newspapers and RTÉ, the national broadcaster, had by the mid-1970s added Brussels to their permanent office in London, a decision driven by Irish membership of the then European Economic Community (EEC), now European Union (EU).[13] The political and economic importance of London and Brussels for Ireland – and their role as sources of regular news – necessitated these foreign bureaus. Further investment in foreign correspondents during the 1980s and 1990s was driven largely by the *Irish Times*, and to a lesser extent by RTÉ, with bureaus opening – and later closing – in cities such as Washington, Beijing, Johannesburg and Moscow. Despite the post-2008 economic downturn the *Irish Times* maintained staff reporters in locations including Brussels, Washington, Paris and London. Financial pressures, however, led RTÉ to close its office in Beijing and, more controversially, in London in 2012. The latter decision – which was heavily criticised – was estimated at saving €800,000 annually as a component of a wider €25m cost reduction plan.[14] Compared to the *Irish Times* and RTÉ, other Irish media outlets have shown a much stronger preference for relying on wire copy and international news services. The second national television service, TV3 – a privately owned commercial broadcaster – has no correspondents based outside Ireland. The station rarely sends staff abroad to cover foreign news stories. The main national daily newspaper, the *Irish Independent*, had a full-time London editor until late 2006 when the position was allowed to lapse as part of a financial restructuring process (its Brussels office also closed, in 2007). The newspaper now takes its foreign news primarily from syndicated press agencies and several British newspapers, including the *Telegraph* and the London *Independent* – which, like the *Irish Independent*, was also owned by Dublin-based Independent News and Media until its sale in 2010.

These recent industry changes meant that when it came to reporting on the Scottish referendum in 2014, the *Irish Times* was the only Irish media outlet with a full-time staff journalist based in the UK. The other national newspapers and RTÉ were reliant on press and broadcast news services, although they did send their own staff on short-term reporting assignments prior to 18 September 2014 (polling day).

Determining Irish Referendum Coverage

News selection

Coverage of the referendum followed a similar pattern in the main media organisations in Ireland. There was limited reporting in the first half of 2014 with increasing attention from July 2014 onwards, with a peak in coverage immediately before 18 September, and with attention declining significantly once the result was known. This pattern of coverage is not surprising when considered against the news value of the referendum story from an Irish editorial perspective. The literature on news selection shows that editors attach stronger value to stories that directly affect their audience, that are 'closer to home', and that involve conflict and novelty.[15]

In the early months of 2014 the referendum story received attention based on its apparent newsworthiness for an Irish audience. In general, most media outlets in Ireland covered the early stages of the campaign sporadically, as would be expected from the news selection literature. The twists and turns of the campaign were at that point far away from decision day, so referendum developments would have been perceived to have less immediate interest for, and impact on, an Irish audience. Even the *Irish Times*, which covered the campaign in most detail as a running news story in this initial period, stressed in its coverage the impact of the result for Ireland – in keeping with news selection requirement that stories are more likely to be considered 'news' where they are relevant to the local audience.[16]

The 'unexpectedness' of the YouGov opinion poll result on 6 September heightened Irish media interest in the referendum campaign. The gap between the two sides had narrowed throughout 2014 although the No side had maintained a comfortable lead. The 6 September poll put the pro-independence side ahead by 51 per cent to 49 per cent (when undecided voters were excluded).[17] Strong media response to this type of unexpected development is in keeping with predictions in the literature that rare events 'have the greatest chance of being selected as news'.[18] Moreover, the 'entertainment' value of events associated with the referendum also attracted media interest in Ireland. For example, comments by Scottish actor and comedian Billy Connolly were widely covered: 'I don't want to influence Scottish vote, says Connolly' (*Irish Independent*, 18 February 2014). In addition to judging coverage based on an evaluation of the referendum as a news event or for its 'newsworthiness', Irish editorial decision makers also looked for a 'local angle' in the story, an issue to which we now turn.

Irish self-interest in the outcome

The government in Dublin adopted a policy of neutrality on the referendum decision. In a parliamentary reply in April 2014 the then Minister for State at the Department of Foreign Affairs, Paschal Donohoe, noted that the question was 'one which the people of Scotland, and they alone, should decide. I do not believe it would be appropriate for the [Irish] Government to comment, there-fore, on issues which at this stage are hypothetical, especially where comment might be perceived as an intervention in the debate.'[19]

The 'politics of silence' dominated the stance of the main parties in Dáil Éireann (national parliament) – Fine Gael and Labour, who formed the incumbent coalition administration, and the two main opposition parties, Fianna Fáil and Sinn Féin. These parties all offered variations of Donohoe's parliamentary reply in response to media queries. The positioning was most surprising, however, in the case of Sinn Féin, which has political representation on both sides of the Irish border and a strong Irish unity platform. A re-writing of the constitutional settlement in the UK involving a loosening of regional linkages would clearly assist with Sinn Féin's long-term political aspirations. But a party spokesperson explained that 'Sinn Féin believes in the right to national self-determination free from external interference. Therefore our position on the Scottish referendum is that it is a matter for the Scottish people alone'.[20]

Ahead of the vote, Martin McGuinness, Sinn Féin's Deputy Leader and Northern Ireland's Deputy First Minister, predicted 'a profound impact' in Northern Ireland arising from a changed constitutional arrangement in Scotland but he declined to express a preference for the outcome.[21] The non-interventionist stance may well be explained by a Sinn Féin assessment that either outcome would ultimately bring UK constitutional change to the benefit of its specific goals on the island of Ireland, and its relationship with London.

The most senior national political figure to explicitly intervene in the campaign was a former Foreign Affairs Minister, Gerry Collins, who told the pro-independence Scottish-based website National Collective that he favoured a 'yes' vote.[22] His comments were reported in the *Irish Times* but Collins had little contemporary resonance in Ireland, having last held ministerial office in 1992.

The silence of the main political players in Dublin did not go unnoticed in media coverage: as one correspondent wrote, 'the Government has gone to extraordinary lengths to say as little as it can about the matter'[23] An official position of neutrality should not, however, be equated with a policy of indifference to the outcome. The public was informed that the Department of Foreign Affairs in Dublin was assessing 'the policy implications for Ireland on an ongoing basis', while the Irish Embassy in London and the Consulate General in Edinburgh had an active watching brief.[24]

There was official recognition that the vote had implications for Ireland in a way that a similar referendum in another state, with less immediate economic or political ties to Ireland, would not. As Minister Donohoe admitted in April 2014: 'A decision in favour of independence would of course have both political and policy implications for Ireland, reshaping our relations with Scotland as well as relations within the United Kingdom and the European Union.' Paul Gillespie, an *Irish Times* leader writer and a well-informed writer on foreign policy matters, captured private official unease in the early part of 2014. Writing in a think tank publication, Gillespie observed that 'Irish policy-makers have been watching the UK's intensifying debate on membership of the European Union and Scottish independence with growing fascination and alarm'.[25]

This focus on the referendum from a national self-interest vantage point was a dominant theme in Irish media coverage. As one newspaper editorial, under the headline 'A consequential referendum', observed: 'Ireland cannot be indifferent to Scotland's forthcoming vote on independence, even if diplomatic caution and prudence prevent Government and diplomatic leaders from voicing their preferences on it' (*Irish Times*, 21 July 2014).

Media coverage that focused on the consequences of the referendum outcome for Ireland identified three strands to Irish interest: first, the impact on the United Kingdom's relationship with the European Union; second, the impact on Northern Ireland; third, but to a much lesser extent in coverage, the impact on the Irish economy. Writing in the *Irish Independent* in April 2014, political journalist Fionnan Sheahan observed that 'If passed, the vote will have knock-on consequences for Ireland in terms of the status of Northern Ireland, Scotland's individual membership of the EU and Dublin's relations with London'.[26]

In posing questions about the future of the United Kingdom, the referendum outcome was in turn opening up vital national interest questions for Ireland. In an editorial in April 2014 the *Irish Times* noted that 'A great deal is at stake in this debate for the UK's internal and external futures. Scottish independence would throw the remaining union into doubt, particularly for unionists in the North' (*Irish Times*, April 2014). The same newspaper's Foreign Editor, Paddy Smyth, returned to this issue in July 2014, noting that the political fallout from the break-up of the UK was of as much concern in Dublin as the prospect of greater competition from an independent Scotland for foreign direct investment:

Already nervous about the possibility of a British break from the EU, there is a strong sense that a Scottish go-it-alone would accelerate the process, first by changing the Westminster political maths, making an anti-referendum Labour government less likely. And then, by eroding what has been seen until recent times as a pro-EU majority in the UK.[27]

The Irish Republic's complicated post-independence relationship with the United Kingdom had reached an advanced stage during the period of the Northern Ireland peace process. The passing of the Belfast Agreement in 1998 was a significant constitutional milestone in normalising relations. Former Irish minister Martin Mansergh, one of the peace process architects, explicitly addressed the impact of the Scottish referendum on Northern Ireland in an opinion article.[28] Mansergh argued that while 'official Ireland' had little enthusiasm for an independent Scotland, Ireland could adapt to either referendum outcome. The real importance, he claimed, was not in Scotland's future but what impact the outcome might have on British–Irish relations.[29]

In the *Irish Examiner*, another former political advisor, Gerard Howlin, speculated that this Dublin–London relationship, and its consequences for Northern Ireland, 'was now on the verge of being tipped into the melting pot again'.[30] Martin Devlin in the *Irish Independent* argued that the main repercussion for Northern Ireland if the referendum proposition was passed would be acceptance of a weakened unionism:

> It seems inevitable that England will become less inclined to maintain the link – the province is an expensive UK add-on. This is an uncertain period for unionists and it might be timely for the Republic to reach out with guarantees about respect for their traditions within a united Ireland.[31]

Another perspective was advanced in the *Irish Times* by Peter Geoghegan, who recalled that in 2012 the then Ulster Unionist Party leader had described the SNP as 'a greater threat to the union than the violence of the IRA'.[32]

The third local interest element, the economic threat posed by post-referendum Scotland, received less attention but was still a running reference point in many opinion articles and editorials. This viewpoint was clearly articulated in an editorial in the *Irish Examiner* on 18 September 2014: 'Whatever the result, it is beyond doubt that the Scots will either assert or be given increased powers to set their own taxes, including corporation tax. This could lead to direct competition between Scotland and Ireland for multinational investment' (*Irish Examiner*, 18 September 2014).

Extent of coverage

As discussed in the previous section, viewing the referendum through 'local eyes' and with attention on its 'local impact' was a dominant theme in Irish media coverage. This emphasis on the local was maintained right up to decision day. Database searches with the words 'Scottish' and 'referendum' in the two main 'quality' daily newspapers and the national broadcaster produced 219 articles in the *Irish Times*, 61 in the *Irish Independent* and 46 stories on RTÉ (radio and television news and current affairs programmes).[33]

Figure 13.1 shows the pattern of *Irish Times* coverage from January to October 2014. Interestingly, having a London-based correspondent – who also travelled to Scotland to report on the campaign – would appear to have had a positive

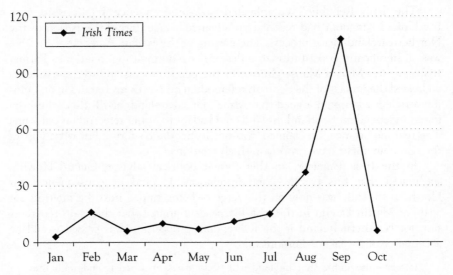

Figure 13.1 *Irish Times* referendum coverage, 1 January to 31 October 2014.

influence on *Irish Times* coverage levels. Moreover, the *Irish Times* devoted considerably more attention to the referendum in the first seven months of 2014 than the other media outlets considered here, although in all three cases overall coverage was heavily skewed towards the months of August and September.

News coverage increased when the televised debates were broadcast in August 2014. In keeping with the general assessment in the British media, the judgement in the Irish newspapers was that Salmond 'lost' the first debate (5 August 2014) but came back strongly to 'win' the second (25 September 2014). As Mark Hennessy concluded in the *Irish Times* after the second debate: 'Mr Salmond was not only the better performer, more agile and quick-witted than the earnest Mr Darling, but the First Minister also appeared to have the better arguments and a surer grasp of which issues resonate with voters' (Hennessy, *Irish Times*, 28 August 2014).

Interestingly, despite this assessment of the second debate outcome, Hennessy still concluded that Darling, and not Salmond, would be on the winning side: 'The betting must still be on Scotland rejecting independence next month but a buoyant Yes campaign could yet ensure that it will be a close run thing' (Hennessy, *Irish Times*, 28 August 2014). This analysis was proven to be highly accurate, given the direction the campaign took in the following three weeks.

RTÉ sent reporters to Scotland before the main campaign period, for example for its flagship morning radio show, *Morning Ireland*, in July 2014, although the station's coverage peaked in the days immediately prior to 18 September. Radio news programmes generally included 'down-the-line' interviews with British-based journalists and academics. The issues covered were also not dissimilar to those in the print media. For example, the station's radio business programme discussed the impact of Scottish independence (13 September 2014), while its European Editor summarised reaction from across Europe to the campaign (17 September 2014). Some of RTÉ's own staff also reported from Scotland as the campaign entered its final phase. For example, on 9 September 2014 reporter Robert Shortt – who was in Edinburgh – blogged on the station's online service that:

> if three hundred years of history is potentially unraveled in a single vote, the repercussions will be seismic and not just for UK politics. Its echoes could be felt in Northern Ireland. Its echoes could reach and influence the emerging debates about self-determination in Spain, Belgium and beyond.[34]

Throughout the campaign, stories in newspapers, including both the *Irish Times* and the *Irish Independent*, were generally positioned on inside foreign or world news pages. The referendum moved to page one on 18 September. The polling day edition of the *Irish Independent* included as its main page one photograph, a colourful image of pro-independence campaigners, alongside the headline 'Is this the last day of the United Kingdom?' A two-page spread inside the same edition was dominated by a syndicated article with the headline 'Let's make history, Salmond urges Scots'. Accompanying this wire copy piece was a colour feature by one of the newspaper's own staff sent to Edinburgh to cover the result. The *Irish Times* opted not to include a front-page image on 18 September 2014 but the referendum was its main news story: 'Scotland decides as UK's future in balance' (18 September 2014). RTÉ also gave extensive news coverage to the campaign on radio, television and online. Reporter Robert Shortt had returned to Edinburgh, blogging that:

> Down at the Holyrood parliament building, the world's media is gathering. There are TV crews from the four corners of the globe. And it seems there are supporters of Scottish independence from far away too. I saw people draped with Catalan flags, Corsican flags, Basque flags and Welsh flags.[35]

Conclusion

This analysis of Irish media coverage of the Scottish referendum – with a particular focus on the two main daily 'quality' newspapers and the national broadcast station – found little, if any, evidence of explicit preference for either side in the campaign. This neutrality is best illustrated by the *Irish Examiner*'s 18 September 2014 edition. As voters went to the polls in Scotland, the *Irish Examiner* reported on the referendum on its front page: 'Scots got to the polls as historic days dawns'. The article was accompanied by a photographic image dominated by the words 'yes' and 'no'.

The referendum story was primarily presented to the local audience in terms of its editorial value as a news story and also in the context of any possible impact on Ireland. More coverage appeared in the *Irish Times*, at that point unique in still having its own staff correspondent in the UK and possibly influenced by that title's 'newspaper of record' ethos. In truth, however, Scottish politics was only considered sufficiently interesting, or relevant for an Irish audience, when news values influenced editors to immediate, controversial and colourful stories associated with the referendum campaign.

A great deal of the post-results coverage was captured in a headline to an article published in the *Irish Independent* on 20 September 2014: 'Bravehearts vanquished by silent foe in clinical rout'. The Irish media moved on fairly rapidly. News coverage of Scottish politics effectively collapsed, although the *Irish Times* reported extensively on the election of Nicola Sturgeon as SNP leader. The Irish government maintained its watching brief. The Foreign Affairs Minister, Charlie Flanagan, told Parliament on 24 September 2014: 'The further devolution of powers to Scotland and the political changes outlined by Prime Minister Cameron do of course have political and policy implications for Ireland, North and South. It will take time to tease out these political and policy implications with all stakeholders, on these islands and within the European Union'.[36]

Notes

1. The current author was a radio presenter with RTÉ News in Dublin at that time and visited Scotland to report on the devolution referendum (1997) and also the subsequent election to the new Scottish Parliament (1999).
2. Salmond, 'Irish show Scots road to success'.
3. Fraser, 'Caledonian cub looks to Celtic Tiger for stimulus'.
4. Cooney, 'After the Celtic Tiger, is the Scottish Tiger far behind?'.
5. Bell. 'Union ponders the prospect of a messy divorce'.
6. Nyberg, *Misjudging Risk*, p. 37.
7. *Irish Times*, 'Investors find good returns in Edinburgh'.
8. Coleman, 'Economic growth shows little sign of letting up'.
9. McGee, 'Salmond praises Ireland's "global standard" social partnership model'.
10. Lewis, *Boomerang The Biggest Bust*, p. 85.
11. The debate about what currency an independent Scotland would use – and the challenges of having national fiscal independence in a common currency zone – did not feature strongly in Irish media coverage. Without specifically referencing Ireland, but mentioning the travails of the EU, economist Paul Krugman in his syndicated *New York Times* column argued that it would be 'mind-boggling that Scotland would consider going down this path after all that has happened [in the EU] in the last few years' (7 September 2014). The column was reproduced in the *Irish Times*. When economic matters were referenced it was generally to increased competition for direct foreign investment.
12. Rafter, 'Get there and stay for two or three weeks, or until the money runs out'.
13. The *Irish Times* had appointed a part-time correspondent in Washington in the late 1960s and alongside Brussels opened an office in Paris in the 1970s.
14. RTÉ, 'RTÉ to cut top presenter pay and close London office'; this decision was reversed in November 2014 when RTÉ appointed a new London correspondent.
15. Sheridan Burns, *Understanding Journalism*, p. 52.
16. Harcup and O'Neil, 'What is news? Galtung and Ruge revisited'.
17. BBC, 'Scottish independence vote will "go down to the wire"'.

18. Harcup and O'Neill, 'What is news? Galtung and Ruge revisited', p. 263.
19. Dáil Debates, 3 April 2014.
20. O'Connell, 'Where do the political parties stand on the Scottish independence?'.
21. Ryan, 'Martin McGuinness: Scottish independence referendum would have a "profound impact" on Northern Ireland'.
22. Hennessy, 'Former Irish foreign minister backs Scottish vote for independence'.
23. Beesley, 'Dublin silence not optional if Scotland goes independent'.
24. Dáil Debates, 2014.
25. Gillespie, Scotland's Vote On Independence: Implications for Ireland, p. 11.
26. Sheahan, How a changed political landscape laid the seeds'.
27. Smyth, 'Irish seem lost for words on Scottish independence'.
28. Rafter, Martin Mansergh: A Biography.
29. Mansergh, 'Ireland can adapt to either Scottish referendum result'.
30. Howlin, 'Scottish yes vote would pose major risk for Northern Ireland'.
31. Devlin, 'Scare tactics in Scotland can't detract from the glory of democracy in action'.
32. Geoghegan, 'Unionists in North faced with a Scottish problem'.
33. Results derived from searches on irishtimes.com (Irish Times), rte.ie (RTÉ) and Irish Newspaper Archive (Irish Independent) from 1 January 2014 to 31 October 2014.
34. Shortt, 'Prime Time. The Scottish Referendum', 9 September.
35. Shortt, 'Prime Time. The Scottish Referendum', 18 September.
36. Dáil Debates, 24 September 2014.

Bibliography

BBC, 'Scottish independence vote will "go down to the wire"', 7 September 2014, <http://www.bbc.com/news/uk-scotland-29096458> (last accessed 19 November 2014).

Beesley, Arthur, 'Dublin silence not optional if Scotland goes independent', Irish Times, 6 September 2014.

Bell, Alex, 'Union ponders the prospect of a messy divorce', Irish Times, 20 January 2007.

Coleman, Marc, 'Economic growth shows little sign of letting up', Irish Times, 14 July 2006.

Cooney, John, 'After the Celtic Tiger, is the Scottish Tiger far behind?', Irish Times, 30 November 1999.

Dáil Debates, 3 April 2014, <http://oireachtasdebates.oireachtas.ie/debates per cent20authoring/DebatesWebPack.nsf/takes/dail2014040300050?opendocument&highlight=scottish per cent20referendum#WRA04550> (last accessed 17 November 2014).

Dáil Debates, 24 September 2014, <http://oireachtasdebates.oireachtas.ie/debates per cent20authoring/DebatesWebPack.nsf/takes/dail2014092400091?opendocument&highlight=scottish per cent20referendum#WRX00350> (last accessed 1 December 2014).

Devlin, Martin, 'Scare tactics in Scotland can't detract from the glory of democracy in action', Irish Independent, 18 September 2014.

Fraser, Douglas, 'Caledonian cub looks to Celtic Tiger for stimulus', Irish Times, 28 November 1998.

Geoghegan, Peter, 'Unionists in North faced with a Scottish problem', Irish Times, 9 September 2014.

Gillespie, Paul, Scotland's Vote On Independence: Implications for Ireland (Dublin: Institute of International and European Affairs, 2014).

Harcup, Tony and Deirdre O'Neil, 'What is news? Galtung and Ruge revisited', Journalism Studies, 2(2) (2001), pp. 261–80.

Hennessy, Mark, 'Former Irish foreign minister backs Scottish vote for independence', *Irish Times*, 30 May 2014.

Hennessy, Mark, 'Salmond bounces back', *Irish Times*, 28 August 2104.

Howlin, Gerard, 'Scottish yes vote would pose major risk for Northern Ireland', *Irish Examiner*, 10 September 2014.

Irish Examiner, 'Scottish referendum – a Kingdom that is far from United', 18 September 2014.

Irish Times, 'Investors find good returns in Edinburgh', 2 May 2001.

Irish Times, 'Scotland's uncertain vote', 22 April 2014.

Irish Times, 'A consequential referendum', 21 July 2014.

Lewis, Michael, *Boomerang The Biggest Bust* (London: Penguin Books, 2011).

McGee, Harry, 'Salmond praises Ireland's "global standard" social partnership model', *Irish Times*, 14 February 2008.

Mansergh, Martin, 'Ireland can adapt to either Scottish referendum result', *Irish Times*, 16 July 2014.

Nyberg, Peter, *Misjudging Risk: Causes of the Systemic Banking Crisis in Ireland* (Nyberg Report) (March 2011), <http://137.191.228.14/documents/publications/reports/2011/nybergreport.pdf> (last accessed 15 September 2015).

O'Connell, Hugh, 'Where do the political parties stand on the Scottish independence?' journal.ie, 30 August 2014, <http://www.thejournal.ie/scottish-independence-political-parties-1643099-Aug2014/> (last accessed 17 November 2014).

Rafter, Kevin, *Martin Mansergh: A Biography* (Dublin: New Island, 2001).

Rafter, Kevin, 'Get there and stay for two or three weeks, or until the money runs out': the Irish media's engagement with foreign news reporting', in A. Stepinska (ed.), *News in Europe. Europe on News* (Berlin: Logos Verlag, 2010), pp. 159–70.

RTÉ, 'RTÉ to cut top presenter pay and close London office in €25m cost reduction plan', 30 March 2012, <http://www.rte.ie/news/2012/0329/315501-rte-london-office-to-go-as-part-of-25m-cut-plan/> (last accessed 17 November 2014).

Ryan, Philip, 'Martin McGuinness: Scottish independence referendum would have a "profound impact" on Northern Ireland', *Irish Independent*, 11 September 2014.

Salmond, Alex, 'Irish show Scots road to success', *Irish Times*, 1 May 1997.

Sheahan, Fionnan, 'How a changed political landscape laid the seeds', *Irish Independent*, 3 April 2014.

Sheridan Burns, Lynette, *Understanding Journalism*, 2nd edn (London: Sage, 2013).

Shortt, Robert, 'Prime Time The Scottish Referendum', RTÉ, 9 September 2014, <http://www.rte.ie/news/primetime/2014/0909/642563-prime-time-the-scottish-referendum/> (last accessed 18 November 2014).

Shortt, Robert, 'Prime Time The Scottish Referendum', RTÉ, 18 September 2014, <http://www.rte.ie/news/primetime/2014/0918/644751-prime-time-the-scottish-referendum/> (last accessed 20 November 2014).

Smyth, Paddy, 'Irish seem lost for words on Scottish independence', *Irish Times*, 18 July 2014.

14

Spain, Catalonia and the Scottish Referendum: A Study in Multiple Realities

Enric Castelló, Fernando León-Solís and Hugh O'Donnell

Introduction

It is no exaggeration to say that the Scottish referendum on independence was presented in the Spanish media as a top-priority domestic issue throughout the whole campaign, reaching a climax of expectation and, in some quarters, even trepidation towards the end. Given the territorial tensions in Spain at the time, this is hardly surprising and, as we will see, coverage of the Scottish referendum acted primarily as a proxy for position-taking in relation to those tensions.

Spain consists of seventeen Autonomous Communities, of which Catalonia is one, each with its own Parliament. Following the Catalan elections of 2012,[1] Catalan First Minister Artur Mas of *Convergència i Unió*[2] (CiU) repeatedly asked the Madrid government for a referendum on Catalan independence along the lines of the one to be held in Scotland. This request was met with steadfast refusals from the Spanish Prime Minister, Mariano Rajoy of the ruling conservative *Partido Popular* (PP), on the grounds that it was not compatible with the 1978 Spanish constitution which enshrined the unity of the Spanish nation. The main Madrid opposition party, the centre-left *Partido Socialista Obrero Español* (PSOE), supported Rajoy's stance while at the same time arguing for political dialogue with the Catalan nationalists and for a federal reform of the constitution (the so-called 'third way'). In the face of these refusals, Mas then proposed a non-binding popular 'consultation' to be held on 9 November 2014.[3] Rajoy refused to recognise this, arguing that it was simply a referendum by another name. In protest, a demonstration was called in Barcelona on 11 September 2014, Catalonia's national day (the *Diada*). An estimated (though the figures are of course disputed) 1.8 million people took part, forming a giant 'V' along the *Gran Via* and the *Diagonal* in the centre of the city.[4] In defiance of Madrid, the Catalan Parliament (the *Generalitat*) approved the consultation by 106 votes to 28 one week later on 19 September, the day after the Scottish vote.[5] As can be seen, political and territorial tensions in Spain were running extremely high both before and after the Scottish referendum.

In this chapter we examine the ways in which the referendum was covered in the media based in two different parts of Spain, with a primary focus on the period between 25 August and 25 September 2014: Madrid, whose Spanish-language print and broadcast media are available throughout Spain, and which we will therefore refer to as 'Spanish'; and Barcelona, whose Spanish and Catalan-language media are consumed primarily (though not exclusively) within Catalonia, and which we will refer to as 'Catalan'. The media outlets analysed are:

Madrid:

- the main all-Spain public service television channel *La1*, belonging to TVE (*Televisión Española*), historically always close to the party in power in Madrid (the PP in this case)
- the leading centre-left daily *El País*, historically close to the PSOE (a closeness which has not prevented it from being very critical of the party at times)[6]
- *El Mundo*, a daily newspaper historically close to the more right-wing sectors inside the PP and a champion of Spanish centralism.

Barcelona:

- the main Catalan-language public service television channel TV3, funded by the Catalan Parliament and historically sympathetic to it
- the Spanish-language daily *La Vanguardia*,[7] one of the oldest newspapers in Spain (founded in 1881), moderately conservative in outlook, and the leading Catalan newspaper in terms of readership
- the Catalan-language daily *Ara*, the 'newest' of the outlets examined (launched in 2010).

The amount of coverage offered by both the Madrid and Barcelona press titles was impressive in quantitative terms. As the referendum drew closer all papers invested significant resources in 'mapping' Scotland for their readers. There were numerous reports from many different parts of the country, interviewing individuals from a wide range of walks of life who supported, opposed or were even indifferent to independence. On the day of the referendum itself *La Vanguardia* dedicated fourteen articles to the topic, including a lengthy editorial titled 'A perfect exercise in democracy', while *Ara* dedicated seventeen, including an equally lengthy editorial titled 'A free country called Scotland'. *El País* had fifteen pieces as well as a vlog by deputy editor Francesc Valls and 'minute-by-minute' updates in its online edition. *El Mundo* offered ten feature articles and op-ed columns on 18 September and thirteen the following day.

As regards television, TV3 broadcast both Darling–Salmond debates in their entirety, simultaneously translated into Catalan by conference interpreters, and on eight separate occasions between 25 August and 25 September the referendum appeared in the opening headlines of its midday news bulletin. There were, however, perceptible differences in the resources invested by TVE and TV3: TVE did not send a correspondent to Edinburgh until 17 September, the eve of the referendum, with earlier reports coming from London, while TV3 had a correspondent in the Scottish capital as early as 2 September and also prepared a special report from there for its *30 minuts* current affairs series.

From 16 September it had two correspondents in Edinburgh and on 18 September the main news bulletin was, in an unprecedented operation, broadcast live in its entirety from that city. From this complex coverage a range of different Scotlands, and indeed UKs, emerge, none of which would necessarily be immediately recognisable to a Scottish/UK reader/viewer. In generating these competing realities, both journalistic and political rhetoric made widespread use of metaphors,[8] the two most frequently deployed being Scotland as a 'mirror' and as a source of 'lessons'.

The Mirror and its Effects

It is difficult to pinpoint the origin of any political metaphor, but perhaps the earliest reference to the 'Scottish mirror' in Spain was the Catalan book of that title, *El Mirall Escocès*, written by the then Catalan advisor to the SNP Xavier Solano in 2007,[9] and presenting Scotland as a mirror for the aspirations of (at least some) Catalans. The mirror referred to by Spanish journalists covering the referendum is not to be understood in any literal sense, of course, since what it 'reflected' was not a perfect image of what was happening, but the particular Scotland/UK required by the media institutions in question to legitimise their own interpretation of events in both Scotland and Spain, and to delegitimise others. As Castelló et al. argue regarding such media 'mirror effects': 'The mirrored image of the external community is, in a sense, always distorted or framed in a particular way to reinforce a discourse that is deeply grounded in the ideological construction of national identity'.[10]

The Catalan press wholeheartedly embraced the mirror metaphor. Thus an article in *La Vanguardia* of 18 September was titled 'Scottish mirror' (*Espejo escocés*), presenting Scotland as a model of the 'third way'. *Ara*, which subtitled a section of one of its reports on 9 September 'The mirror of Scotland' (*El mirall d'Escòcia*), contrasting the attitudes of the British and Spanish governments to their respective independence questions, returned to the idea ten days later when the focus had moved formally to the upcoming unofficial 'consultation', and argued very much the same point:

> Now that we are moving towards the 9 November consultation, the Scottish mirror has shown [Spanish] unionism that a referendum can be won, but you have to be willing to play the game. And in the mirror the saddest and most distorted image which comes to us from the Spanish state[11] is the fact that it won't turn up for the match. (Carles Capdevila, *Ara*, 19 September 2014)

Scotland therefore functions simultaneously as both a reflecting and a distorting mirror, and the resulting 'mirror effects' produce a series of corresponding 'mirror images'. For those who supported the Catalan request for a referendum, Scotland 'reflected' the way forward, while the PP's position 'distorted' the democratic example given by the UK. For those opposed to it – keen to prevent any type of Scottish 'contagion' (a frequently used metaphor, along with its corollary 'vaccination') – the main aim was to show that Scotland was not in any sense a usable mirror for Catalonia. As El País put it in its 15 September editorial, 'Scotland is unique'.

Mirror image (1): the past versus the future

For those opposing the Scottish mirror concept, Scotland's historic pedigree as a formerly independent country was constantly contrasted with what was presented as Catalonia's lack of anything similar.[12] This was offered as the explanation for the almost complete absence of history as a topic in the Scottish debate and its generally rational, forward-looking nature, in contrast with, as El País (editorial, 15 September 2014) saw it, an obsession with historical grievances in Catalonia. This argument was in turn paralleled by strong assertions from the pro-Catalan independence side that their project was not about the past but was entirely future-oriented. This was the central theme of *Ara*'s editorial on 11 September – the *Diada* and tercentenary of the fall of Barcelona in 1714 during the War of Spanish Succession – a moment when irredentist fantasies, had they been truly central, could have been reasonably expected to come to the fore:

> The National Day, and 300th anniversary of 1714, which Catalan society is cel-
> ebrating today has not, thankfully, arrived marked by nostalgic remembrances of
> the past, but of hope for the future, a future which we all want to write together,
> without naivety but also without giving up . . . This is a historic moment, not
> so much for emphasising where we come from, but above all for making clear
> where we want to go.

For this camp it was the PP that was immobilised by the past, slave to an outdated constitution written over thirty-five years earlier: what was needed by contrast was a (Madrid) government with the political *nous* of its UK equivalent, able to respond flexibly to the demands of the present. As Antoni Bassas put it in *Ara* on 18 September, stressing (and praising) the UK's ability to make the past work for the present:

> Today's referendum in Scotland honours Great Britain, which is no longer the
> Empire it once was, but which today is giving an imperial demonstration of why
> it is not necessary to adore a written Constitution to be a model of democracy.

Mirror image (2): popular versus constitutional democracy

As Carmen del Riego reported in *La Vanguardia* on 9 September, 'Rajoy does not view Scotland as a mirror in which to look, mainly because the referendum there is legal and in the case of Catalonia it is not'. For both the PP and supporters of the 'third way', the Scottish referendum is to be accepted (though not necessarily welcomed) on the grounds of its legality, repeatedly presented as made possible by the absence of a written constitution and a process of consensus and agreement. Consequently, Scotland and the UK emerge as champions of constitutional correctness (though not necessarily of political acumen), as opposed to 'certain leaders of the Catalan independence movement who are lining up to break the law' (editorial, *El País*, 15 September 2014). It is the consensual nature of the Scottish process which is seen as guaranteeing its civility:

> Despite the importance of what is at stake [in the referendum], which is both agreed and constitutional, Great Britain does not see itself as standing at the edge of the abyss: respect for your opponent is an accepted principle in Scotland. (Francisco G. Basterra, *El País*, 12 September 2014)

At times the debate centred on the referendum question itself, seen as 'clear' in contrast to the 'ambiguity' of the Catalan two-question process (Basterra, *El País*, 12 September 2014), but as 'unintelligible' for the bullish Arcadi Espada in *El Mundo*:

> Do you want Scotland to be an independent state? is an unintelligible question. Nobody knows what it means. No-one can answer in full knowledge of the facts. How can this question be answered without knowing if Scotland will have the pound or the euro, if it will be in Europe or not, and even if it will still have the queen? . . . A referendum cannot ask unanswerable questions. (Arcadi Espada in *El Mundo*, 19 September 2014)

As can be seen, *El Mundo*'s columnists at times adopted an extremely aggressive rhetoric which went some way beyond the PP's more strictly legalistic position. In incendiary and even insulting mode, Espada called the Scottish referendum 'stupid', and the same intemperance was extended to David Cameron in person. While the newspaper limited itself to reproaching him for creating 'dangerous uncertainty' and not doing enough to 'correct the strategy' of the Yes campaign (editorial, 17 September 2014), its columnists portrayed him as an 'Eton-educated simpleton' (Jorge de Esteban, 18 August 2014) and 'dim witted' (Espada, 19 September 2014) and accused him of a string of political blunders: allowing the referendum when under no obligation to do so (de Esteban, 18 September 2014); granting sixteen-year-olds the right to vote (Felipe Sahagún, 18 September 2014); 'blindingly' assuming that unionism would win (Casimiro García-Abadillo, 21 September 2014); ignoring the extremely low level of support for the Tories in Scotland, 'perverting the course of the referendum during the final sprint of the campaign' with the 'vow' to Scottish voters, thus opening up the door to the 'third way' and 'presenting the vote as the solution to a problem' (Javier Redondo, 21 September 2014).

Even so, the unionist camp was given some minimal credit in *El Mundo* which, in a clear warning to Spanish political parties, commended the 'united action of the [UK's] parties and leaders [which] was key in convincing the majority of voters that Union is always better than division' (19 September 2014), thus ignoring the bad press suffered by the last-minute vow of the No campaign, critically interpreted as 'improvised' by *El País*'s London correspondent Walter Oppenheimer (9 September 2014).

For its part, TVE's 'Scotland, Better Together' (*Escocia, Mejor Juntos*) report,[13] broadcast on 20 September, presented the (now completed) referendum process as a 'secessionist adventure' – a phrase used by many Madrid politicians to refer to the Catalan process – indeed as 'yet another of those dangerous adventures of which Cameron is so fond'. This unremittingly negative approach to the referendum merely continued that established over a year earlier in the same organisation's June 2013 documentary *El dilema de Alba* ('Alba's Dilemma'),[14] which had depicted the entire process as stressful and worrisome for the Scottish population, a presentation which can be contrasted with TV3's May 2014 documentary *Homenatge a Escòcia* ('Homage to Scotland'),[15] which made a much more sustained attempt to capture the complexity of the situation and to explore views from all sides of the argument.

For those in favour of the Catalan referendum, on the other hand, it was not Cameron's but Rajoy's behaviour which was reprehensible, revealing 'the antidemocratic nature of a state [Spain] which will not allow a community [Catalonia], which constitutes an electoral unit and has a representative body such as the [Catalan] parliament, to express itself' (David Miró, *Ara*, 4 September). Reversing the PP position ('Scotland is not Catalonia'), the negative comparison here is 'Spain is not the UK':

> CiU will stick to its position that 'prohibiting democracy makes no sense' and it will maintain its strategy of comparing the Spanish attitude – vetoing 9-N – to that of the United Kingdom, which has agreed the Scottish referendum of 18 September with the Scottish government. (Roger Tugas/Oriol March, *Ara*, 27 August).

Within this frame, issues of constitutional legality are less important than questions of popular democracy (responding to the clear wishes of the people as shown on the *Diada*), and Scotland and the UK have shown the way forward. Westminster's offer of greater devolved powers to Scotland as the polls narrowed attracted widespread admiration when compared to the continuing threats emanating from Madrid in relation to 9-N: 'The difference with Scotland isn't just that there they can debate publicly without fear of reprisals or of being called a Nazi, but that the United Kingdom has opted for a strategy of seduction by promising improvements' (Salvador Cardús, *La Vanguardia*, 4 September 2014). Such a strategy is seen as reflecting a true understanding of how to 'do politics', again in implicit contrast to the behaviour of Rajoy: 'Far from arousing fear, Cameron's government has expressed its appreciation [of Scotland]' (Màrius Carol, *La Vanguardia*, 8 September 2014).

However unlikely an idea for at least some Scots, David Cameron emerges, for *Ara*, as 'the hero of the Catalans' (Toni Vall, 20 September 2014).

The Lesson(s)

Each side of the debate on the Catalan 'referendum' was keen to use the Scottish process as a source of lessons and 'examples' with which to lecture and 'warn' the other, who in each case is chastised and urged to 'take note' (these lessons overlap with some of the themes explored above, and also reproduce the associated mirror images). Examples from *La Vanguardia* include headlines such as 'The Scottish lesson' (19 September 2014), 'Lessons from the Scottish vote'/'A lesson, a great lesson' (both 20 September 2014), while *Ara* offered no fewer than 'Seven Scottish lessons' in an op-ed piece of that title published on 24 September.

Lesson (1): an exercise in democracy

For the pro-referendum group, Scotland – and above all the UK in the figure of David Cameron – provided an exemplary lesson in democracy, the latter by allowing the Scots to vote. For example, the day after the referendum Mas congratulated 'the British people and the Scottish people and the institutions of the United Kingdom for this strong and powerful lesson in democracy which they have given Europe and the world',[16] and according to an editorial in *Ara* on 20 September 2014, 'The democratic lesson offered by Scotland and the United Kingdom is the way ahead: Spain should take note'. An article by David González in *La Vanguardia* on 23 September argued that 'This is the great lesson from the Scottish referendum: Re-United Kingdom' (the last two words in English). Its last paragraph makes it clear what is meant: 'The British State, whatever its configuration going forward, agreed to submit itself to a stress test without any limits in terms of sovereignty . . . and has passed with flying colours because this is what the Scots have freely decided.'

From its 'third way' standpoint, *El País* likewise saw lessons for Rajoy in the Scottish process. In its attack on his steadfast refusal to engage with the 'Catalan question' the consensual and compromising nature of the British political system was praised: the whole process was presented as an 'impeccable democratic exercise' and regarded as a model for both Mas and Rajoy (editorial, 19 September 2014). However, the final lessons taken from the process were not seen as generally edifying: as *El País* put it in its 20 September editorial, 'secession is debilitating'.

Not unexpectedly, views expressed in *El Mundo* were much more hostile, with the Scottish referendum being seen as a lesson in anti-democracy. Thus for Espada (19 September 2014) it was the product of a:

> frivolous democracy [which], following frenzied orgies of emotion, while all the television-consuming citizens are still oozing anthems, flags and Bravehearts [in English], agrees to open the polling stations and ask them if they wouldn't like a future based on the good old times. Bizarre government by melancholy.

In the same article he saw the Scottish referendum process not as 'doing politics' but as:

the opposite of politics as law-making for the real world. The ultimate example of politics as invention and artefact and not as the patient and humble bringer of light to human conflicts. The Scottish referendum is an example of intolerable frivolity when we think of Palestine, Syria, Cuba: a piece of petit bourgeois nonsense of the kind that, once in a century, has disastrous consequences.

Commentators in *El Mundo* also ridiculed the so-called 'exemplary' nature of the British system (praised in the Catalan press and also in *El País*) by highlighting the fact that London had sent its army to Northern Ireland and suspended its devolved assembly (García-Abadillo, 21 September 2014; Iñaki Gil, 21 September 2014; editorial, 19 September 2014). In the same paper Federico Jiménez Losantos argued that far from being 'an exercise in democracy', the referendum 'had brought the greatest discredit to the democratic system in the EU . . . in Scotland and the United Kingdom nobody knows what they have voted for or why they have not been able to vote' and that the process had not been democratic because other parts of Britain had not been allowed to vote (21 September 2014).

Lesson (2): living in (dis)harmony

Both *La Vanguardia* and *Ara* consistently presented Scotland as an example of democratic harmony,[17] here referring to the ability of the Scots to carry out an at times intense and passionate political debate calmly and in a spirit of 'exquisite civility' (Rafael Ramos, *La Vanguardia*, 14 September 2014), a debate which had been 'calm and very civilised' (Oriol Gracià, *Ara*, 18 September 2014). References to this abound, and take visual as well as linguistic form, with many (at times entertaining) photographs in both newspapers showing members of the Yes and No campaigns chatting and joking with each other, or friends who have voted different ways entering or leaving polling stations side by side. The coverage offered by *El País* also generally insisted on the moderate and civilised tone of the debate, or the predominant 'elegance and sense of fair play'.[18]

For those opposed to the Catalan referendum, however, the Scottish debate was presented – occasionally even by *El País* – as turning increasingly bitter (Tubella, *El País*, 10 September 2014), as becoming a form of 'hand to hand fighting with Salmond under fire' (Oppenheimer, *El País*, 11 September 2014). In its editorial of 17 September *El Mundo* argued that there had been a 'polarisation of Scotland' (17 September 2014), which had become a 'fatally divided society' (editorial, 19 September 2014), 'split in two' (Fernando Sánchez Dragó, 21 September 2014), all of this providing an object lesson for Catalonia on the consequences of a yes–no consultation.

In its 'Scotland, Better Together' report TVE complimented the Scots post-referendum on having given a 'lesson in respect and harmony' (again *convivencia*), not in this case by having a civilised debate but by having voted 'no' – in other words they had shown respect for the union and agreed to continue to live in harmony with the other parts of the United Kingdom (and indeed with the

EU more generally). In a remarkable display of linguistic nonchalance, a news report shown on its twenty-four hour channel included the (mis)translation of the last part of David Cameron's comment 'The people of Scotland have spoken. And it is a clear result. They have kept our country of four nations together' as 'They want to keep our nation united' (TVE voiced over the original statements, rendering them inaudible, whereas TV3 used subtitles). Subsequent protest on the web led to this mistranslation being eventually corrected.[19]

Lesson (3): the winners (do not) take it all

Unsurprisingly – and despite their clear internal differences – the victory of the No campaign in Scotland was received with a marked sense of relief by the PP and its supporters and by those supporting the 'third way', with Rajoy, for example, congratulating Scottish voters on having 'avoided the serious economic, social, institutional and political consequences which separation from the United Kingdom and Europe would have meant' (*Ara*, 20 September 2014). For several writers in *El País* the debate had been between the 'poetry' of the Yes camp and 'prose' of the No campaign (for example, Iñaki Gabilondo, 9 September), or a tussle between 'mind and heart' (José I. Torreblanca, 11 September 2014; Basterra, 12 September 2014), ending with the 'triumph of common sense' (e.g. Tortella, 15 November 2014), an idea echoed in *El Mundo* (Espada, 19 September 2014). It was seen as a victory for 'reality' – a clear placeholder for 'economic rationality' – following 'a battle between today's reality and the idealism of tomorrow in which realism appears to be gaining the upper hand' (Oppenheimer, *El País*, 27 August 2014).

El País left no doubt as to its own views on the subject in its editorial on 10 September: while the Yes camp's visions of a future independent Scotland were described as 'idyllic and fanciful, bogusly inspirational, flourishing thanks to exaggerated projections of the North Sea oil at its disposal, and exhibiting an enormously nonchalant attitude towards the country's continued EU membership and plans for sharing the pound', the No camp's arguments were seen as based on 'solid academic and economic grounds'. The verdict after the referendum and the lessons for Catalonia were clear: 'the defeat of the Scottish National Party's dreams signals the end of the cycle of secessionist fantasies in western democracies', lessons that Catalan nationalists 'are not taking note of' (editorial, 20 September 2014).

Along the same lines, but in a typically more critical tone, *El Mundo* also denounced in an editorial the 'neo-romantic' discourse of nationalism, its selfish attempts to appropriate common assets such as North Sea oil and its 'soothing utopias' (19 September 2014), while commentators in the same newspaper referred to it as an 'emotional apotheosis' (Gil, 14 September 2014) or yet another example of 'emotional democracy' (Manuel Arias Maldonado, 22 July 2014). Unashamedly toeing the line set out by the PP, TVE's 'Scotland, Better Together' report, aired two days after the referendum, opened with 'The No victory has swept away the worst fears of what could have been a traumatic divorce. The break-up of the family of nations', and went on to argue that a Yes victory would have meant 'for most Scots the loss of the pound as their currency, an immediate exit from the European Union, the flight of the major banks and rejection by the markets', all in all 'too high a price to pay in exchange for promises'. The result was also presented as a clear defeat for Alex Salmond – seen as a 'political victim' of the entire process – and an extremely close shave for David Cameron, accused of putting the union at risk unnecessarily. These (at least debatable) claims were offered as simple statements of taken-for-granted fact, while another report on TVE's main news bulletin finished with a Scottish interviewee saying 'Thankfully it's all over now'.

The No vote was equally seen as a triumph of and for Europe. The day before the referendum, Rajoy, speaking in the Spanish Parliament, had described what he saw as 'secessionist' processes such as the Scottish referendum as 'bad' and (using a bizarrely mixed metaphor) as a 'torpedo aimed along the water line of the spirit of the EU'. News bulletins in both TVE and TVC reproduced these statements to again articulate polarised views on the matter, a metaphor circulated widely amongst anti-referendum commentators and opinion-makers, with Catalan mainstream media presenting it as proof of continuing Madrid intransigence. El País – in both editorials and opinion pieces – consistently lectured readers throughout the campaign, again with clear nods in the direction of Catalonia, on the negative effects of Scottish secession whose 'impact threatens to go beyond British borders, exacerbate other irredentist movements and damage the whole of the EU just when Europeans are struggling to overcome the third recession since the fateful year of 2008' (editorial, 10 September 2014); in the same paper Pérez Royo rather dramatically stated – reversing Basterra's view on the consequence of the referendum for the UK quoted earlier – that 'the Scottish referendum has brought Europe to the edge of the cliff' (19 September 2014) and (like the Catalan 'consultation') had been called at the wrong time, when Europe needs 'to become stronger' economically and politically on the global stage. A Yes result, El País argued in its editorial, would have brought to a halt the process of European integration and even put world security at risk if Britain had had to redefine its role as nuclear power.

The allegedly untimely nature of the referendum for the whole of Europe was also argued in El Mundo: 'Europe isn't ready for this' (Antonio Gala, 22 September 2014). According to another El País editorial, the final lesson 'for all Europeans' was: 'In societies which are committed to developing openness, prosperity and integration, segregations, however peaceful and civilised they might seem, are always bad news. And we all pay for the consequences' (19 September 2014).

As far as the Catalan titles were concerned, Ara's support for a Yes victory was never in any doubt, while La Vanguardia was rather more guarded, clearly supporting the process but avoiding a clear position, beyond advocating 'third-way' solutions. Despite this, for both newspapers the referendum itself was always/already a victory irrespective of the result, so that one way or another Alex

Salmond and Scotland were always going to emerge as the winners. Statements to this effect were extremely numerous. Perhaps the most entertaining was the following:

> If football – as they say – is a game of eleven against eleven where in the end Germany always wins, the Scottish referendum has been a game of one against one where in the end, no matter what happens now, Scotland was always going to come out winning in terms of greater autonomy and control over its own destiny. (Ramos, *La Vanguardia*, 20 September 2014)

Continuing the 'mirror effect', an editorial in *Ara* presented this win-win situation as also relating to the Catalan situation itself:

> If this [a Yes victory] happens its impact on the Catalan process could not be more direct, because among other things it will establish the debate over Scotland remaining with the European Union as something normal to be carried out through a process of dialogue and negotiation (and as a result likewise for a hypothetically independent Catalonia). But if the No camp wins, this will also take the heat out of the Catalan consultation planned for 9 November, and it will show that the ballot box is the way ahead in an advanced democracy and that it should not be seen as traumatic. (11 September 2014)

Statements such as these clearly reveal the different logics at play in Catalonia and Scotland: Alex Salmond did not of course view the eventual result as any kind of 'win', and would surely not have resigned had he done so.

Conclusion: Domesticating the News, or Taming the Shrew?

The 'domestication of news' – interpreting events in other countries in a specifically 'national' frame which makes them meaningful to domestic audiences[20] – is a now long-standing feature of journalism, and indeed may be as old as journalism itself, as the early seventeenth-century English *corantos* whose royal letters patent authorised them to cover 'all matters of History of newes of any foraine place or kingdom'[21] suggest. What our study makes clear is that (1) a 'domestic' purview does not necessarily imply a homogeneous 'nation-state' one, since a plurinational or otherwise 'polycentric' polity can house two or more 'domestic' audiences for whom quite different coverages are needed; (2) the differences in coverage are not merely differences in interpretation but can consist of entirely incompatible constructions of the country being covered – a striking example of Schutz's 'multiple realities', those 'finite provinces of meaning upon which we bestow the accent of reality';[22] and (3) the country being covered can, and in the current case does, act as a proxy for what is fundamentally an internal debate.

Beyond any interest in the Scottish case for its own sake – which we cannot of course rule out – it is abundantly clear reading/viewing the outputs analysed here that the Scottish referendum process, and with it both Scotland and the UK, are being instrumentalised as weapons in the battle between Mas and Rajoy and more widely between centre and periphery (a battle which does not align cleanly with a traditional left-wing–right-wing divide). 'Domestication' is therefore not just taking place in the sense outlined above (though this is clear) but also in the other meaning of the term, in other words as a mechanism for 'taming' the opposition. Both Scotland and the UK (Alex Salmond and David Cameron) are used to make either Mariano Rajoy or Artur Mas – whichever happens to be the target – look inept, out of touch, obdurate, belligerent, lacking in political skill, undemocratic, even silly.

And so we end where we began: Scotland counts because it is a useful resource in handling the ongoing territorial tensions inside Spain. A tamed Scotland – with few exceptions, little sense of the day-to-day stresses and strains of the campaign filters through, squeezed out by the competing grand narratives of the 'bumper feast of democracy' on one side (Pilar Rahola, *La Vanguardia*, 19 September 2014) and of doom and gloom on the other (TVE and *El Mundo*, *passim*), and there is constant reference to the sense of 'fair play' shown by all (the actual English term is used, and the process is even described at one point as 'very *British*', this last word also in English) – and an equally tamed David Cameron (mere adventurer or champion of democracy according to taste) are moved around by both parties in an attempt to tame the domestic opposition. The results are fascinating but the phenomenon itself is hardly surprising.

Postscript

In its edition of 19 September, printed before the final count for the Scottish referendum was known, Florencio Domingo wrote the following in *La Vanguardia*:

> When these lines are published the results of the Scottish referendum will be available and we will know the outcome of one of the most intense political processes to have taken place in Europe in recent years, a process which has aroused passions well beyond Great Britain's borders, especially in Spain, where we have experienced the campaign as if it were an internal matter, aware that, whatever happens, it will have repercussions.

An article published in *Ara* the following day was even titled 'Us Scots' (*Nosaltres, els escocesos*).[23] There is no doubt a great deal of truth in these lines. However, it would be misleading to think that the Scottish referendum either routinely dominated the news, or to suggest that the entire Spanish population was gripped by (Scottish) referendum fever. In fact the referendum constantly competed for space with a number of probably more pressing issues – the continuing economic crisis, youth unemployment, changes in the education system, the Catalan referendum process and so on, not to mention meaty sports sections – and though coverage of the referendum both on 18 and 19 September was impressive, in Catalonia at least it was completely dwarfed quantitatively by coverage of the *Diada* demonstrations on 11 September.

As regards readerships, both the political and intellectual classes – not to mention the various media establishments – were undoubtedly gripped by the Scottish referendum, but these fields are by no means coextensive with Spanish society as a whole. The point was made amusingly by Joan de Sagarra in a lengthy article entitled 'I have a drink'[24] (in English) published in *La Vanguardia* on 21 September 2014, one of whose paragraphs reads as follows:

> As I said, no-one in my district had ever heard of Robert Burns, or of the Edinburgh makar and, to be honest, they couldn't give a toss about what might happen in Scotland – only one guy, guffawing with laughter, asked me, at the bar of the Oller pub, if I knew, or could guess, how the Loch Ness monster was going to vote.

Politics may move on, but stereotypes never die.

Acknowledgements

This chapter builds on the work of two research projects: 'The media construction of political and territorial conflicts in Spain. Studying discourses and narratives' (CSO-2010-20047) and 'The role of metaphor in the definition and social perception of conflict. Institutions, media and citizens' (CSO2013-41661-P), both supported by the Spanish Department of Economic Affairs and Competitiveness.

Notes

1. These were presented as a single-issue vote for or against a referendum on self-determination as stated in the various parties' manifestos. They produced a comfortable majority for the pro-referendum parties, though none won an overall majority.
2. *Convergència i Unió* is a more or less permanent electoral coalition of two Catalanist parties, *Convergència Democràtica de Catalunya* and *Unió Democràtica de Catalunya*.
3. Following a now long-established Spanish/Catalan convention, this event is referred to as 9-N.
4. V for 'votarem', 'we will vote'. The following day the newspaper *Ara* dubbed the city 'Varcelona' ('v' and 'b' are pronounced identically in Catalan).
5. Two questions were to be asked: 'Do you want Catalonia to become a State?' and 'If so, do you want this State to be independent?'
6. *El País* has special editions in six Autonomous Communities, including Catalonia (since 5 October 2014 its online version can also be read in Catalan).
7. *La Vanguardia* has produced a Catalan-language edition since May 2011. It is to all intents and purposes a translation of the Spanish-language original.
8. Musolff, *Metaphor and Political Discourse*.
9. Xavier Solano first came to Scotland in 2004 to work for former Labour leader Wendy Alexander. He went on to work for the Labour/Lib Dem Scottish Executive before switching to assisting Nicola Sturgeon when she became leader of the SNP in Holyrood and deputy to Alex Salmond. He recently led the *Generalitat*'s London delegation for three years.
10. Castelló et al., 'The mirror effect. Spanish and Belgian press coverage of political conflicts in Flanders and Catalonia', p. 1625.
11. In pro-independence Catalan news outlets Spain is commonly referred to as 'the Spanish state'.
12. For example Javier Cercas, *El País*, 14 September 2014; Gabriel Tortella, *El Mundo*, 15 November 2014.

13. Available at <http://www.rtve.es/alacarta/videos/informe-semanal/informe-semanal-escocia-dice-no/2770654/> (last accessed 16 September 2015).
14. Available at <http://www.rtve.es/alacarta/videos/en-portada/portada-dilema-alba/1658659/> (last accessed 16 September 2015).
15. Available at <http://www.tv3.cat/videos/5099851/Homenatge-a-Escocia>. Unfortunately this site cannot be accessed outside Spain.
16. The news conference in question can be found at <http://premsa.gencat.cat/pres_fsvp/AppJava/multimedia/detall.do?idMedia=70a83cff10057149f1f1> (last accessed 16 September 2015).
17. The Spanish term is 'convivencia', which means literally 'living together'.
18. Patricia Tubella, 10 September 2014.
19. The mistranslation can be experienced first hand at <http://youtu.be/W0YmuKGekQI>, minute 0:56 (last accessed 16 September 2015).
20. Gurevitch et al., 'The Global Newsroom'.
21. Hart, *The Developing Editorial Syndrome*, p. 24.
22. Schutz, *On Phenomenology and Social Relations*, p. 252.
23. This was in fact a translation of an article by *New York Times* columnist Frank Cohen titled 'We the people of Scotland'. The Catalan translation of the title is 'free', but telling: it contains a clear reference to Valencian writer Joan Fuster's influential book *Nosaltres, els valencians* (Us Valencians), seen by many as marking the birth of Valencian nationalism in its modern form.
24. An ironic reference to 'I have a dream': the verb 'to dream' was much in use in Catalan reporting at the time to refer to Catalans' visions of their future.

Bibliography

Castelló, E., A. Dhoest and S. Bastiaensens, 'The mirror effect. Spanish and Belgian press coverage of political conflicts in Flanders and Catalonia', *International Journal of Communication*, 17(7) (2013), pp. 1622–40.

Gurevitch, M., M. R. Levy and I. Roeh, 'The global newsroom: convergences and diversities in the globalization of television news', in P. Dahlgrén and C. Sparks (eds), *Communication and Citizenship: Journalism and the Public Sphere in the New Media Age* (London: Routledge, 1991), pp. 195–216.

Hart, J. A., *The Developing Editorial Syndrome: Views on the News 1500–1800* (Carbondale: Southern Illinois University Press, 1970).

Musolff, A., *Metaphor and Political Discourse: Analogical Reasoning in Debates about Europe* (New York: Palgrave Macmillan, 2004).

Schutz, A., *On Phenomenology and Social Relations*, ed. Helmut R. Wagner (Chicago: Chicago University Press, 1970).

Solano, X., *El Mirall Escocès: Una visió catalana del procés obert cap a la independència* (Barcelona: Dèria Editors, 2007).

15

The French View

Didier Revest

Highs and lows

Humble beginnings

On the day (21 March 2013) First Minister Alex Salmond announced that the long-awaited referendum on Scottish independence would take place on 18 September 2014, few French dailies or news websites took up the story. The *Figaro* newspaper dedicated just two and a half lines to the issue while another right-wing media site, *Atlantico.fr*, merely had two short paragraphs in the news-in-brief section, inspired in part by what RTBF, Belgium's main radio and TV channel, had said about it earlier that day. *Les Echos*, the daily that specialises in financial and economic news, and *Le Parisien*, France's biggest daily in terms of copies sold (some 500,000 a day), were apparently uninterested, while *Le Monde*, surprisingly, preferred to publish an article on David Beckham. Only in *Libération*, the well-known left-wing daily, did the Scottish referendum make the headlines, with an Agence France Presse (AFP) 650-word contribution on the announcement itself and its possible implications.

Any Scotland-loving reader, or anyone simply interested in international politics, would have been disappointed again on the following day as none of the above-mentioned papers actually took up the subject. True, the French press had plenty on their plate at that time, with Obama's visit to both Israel and Palestine and the announcement that former President Nicolas Sarkozy had been indicted in the Bettencourt case (he was alleged to have taken illegal donations from France's richest woman in the run-up to his 2007 election victory). In the following weeks, it seems the Scottish referendum was dealt with at least once; GEO, France's equivalent to the *National Geographic*, adopted a pan-EU perspective, the emphasis being on those regions – such as Flanders or Catalonia – that (so the story ran) insist upon no longer sharing their valuable assets with their respective centres.[1]

The summer of 2013 saw little change. The economic going was getting tougher, with both the national deficit and unemployment increasing despite an array of policies designed by the Hollande government to curb them, and so any in-depth article or radio/TV programme about the Scottish referendum was bound to go more or less unnoticed. Characteristically, on 26 November 2013, the day the Scottish government launched its *Scotland's Future – Your Guide to an Independent Scotland*, the momentous event did not get a mention on *Le Nouvel Observateur*'s Internet site, nor on *Atlantico.fr*, two of France's most reactive news sites. Yet, arguably, a pattern was emerging behind this wall of apparent indifference.

The French media hitting their stride

While in the very early stages of the coverage of the Scottish referendum the focus had been on party politics (such as David Cameron and Alex Salmond bickering over the exact nature of the question to be put before the Scottish electorate) and on getting down to the detail of who would be allowed to vote and when exactly the poll would take place, now journalists seemed to have a far greater interest in the impact of the referendum on bread-and-butter issues and also on questions such as the current state of the economy, its possible future, and so on. The change in focus, of course, mirrored what the Scottish and British media were saying about the referendum.

By late November, *lefigaro.fr* and *LeMonde.fr* had published two articles each, and in particular two news stories dealing in some depth with the questions of oil, public debt and the currency.[2] By early 2014, two questions in particular drew part of the French media's attention. First, there were at least two reports (on 12 and 13 February respectively) about the categorical refusal by the Cameron government to enter into a monetary union with Scotland, should the Yes camp win the day; one was by *lefigaro.fr*, in the 'Flash Actu' section (in association with AFP) and the other appeared in *LeMonde.fr*.[3] Then, a few days later, there was some interest in the EU Commission's rather cool response to the Yes campaign's claim that, post-independence, Scotland would automatically be allowed to join; the same issue was raised on 16 February by France Info, one of France's most popular radio channels, and by *LeMonde.fr* (in association with AFP and Reuters).[4]

By then, the referendum was tending to hit the news much more regularly; one of France Info's headlines, on 12 April 2014, had to do with the fact that Yes support was catching up and that, as a result, the campaign might well be going their way. Both this and, more generally, the debate itself were also sometimes summarily dealt with on other radio and television channels; a good illustration was Frédéric Taddéï's 'Ce soir (ou jamais!)' programme, broadcast by France Télévision on 21 March 2014.

Be that as it may, the nature of news and news consumption are naturally two different things. Indeed for most of the campaign it seemed that, on the whole, French people showed little interest in what was going on in Scotland.

The rest of us

The Scottish referendum campaign must have been one of the most protracted in political history (UK or otherwise), and yet I cannot remember anyone who knows me well, except for a tiny handful of people (more often than not, academic colleagues interested like myself in Scottish/British politics), engaging me in conversation about it. Even members of my own family, including my children (who incidentally live in the UK), did not seem interested. I did naturally bring up the subject whenever I was given a chance, and they would listen, but they soon lost interest. True, they do not specialise in UK politics, nor in international relations, nor for that matter in constitutional affairs. One would nevertheless have expected young mobile professionals with a solid background in history, economics, philosophy and modern languages to, at the very least, ask themselves what repercussions Scotland's independence was going to have not just on the UK but more generally on the EU and (possibly) its future make-up.

One of my neighbours did ask me one day about the ins and outs of the referendum, but the enquiry came out of the blue and his interest was short-lived in that, while he genuinely wanted to understand what was going on and why, he had little time for whatever I said in terms of the possible implications, as if the Scottish debate, however exciting in itself, had been happening in a parallel universe.

Likewise, although many specialise in English studies, which includes lectures about British society *and politics*, few of my own students (from year 1 to year 4) knew about the referendum, at least before it entered its final weeks (see below). And even fewer would have asked, unprompted, for information. I would suggest that by early September 2014, between one third and one half of all the students attending my tutorial classes and lectures (that is, around 200 people all told) had at least a vague idea of what was going on in Scotland. In mid-November, when our two Scotland-born tutors gave a talk about their referendum experience, just eight turned up, although all my colleagues and all of our students had been invited (that is, some 400 people in all).

Those of my fellow countrymen and women who strongly supported independence for Scotland were of course probably far more eager for information and debate than most, but it is likely that they remained thin on the ground; on Facebook's '*Les Français pour l'indépendance de l'Écosse*' page, an ardent advocate of Scottish independence had by early November 2014 only managed to get 403 'likes'.[5]

If I am not mistaken then, the average French person may have shown an interest in what was going on in Scotland, but essentially on account of the uncertainty of the result and depending on whether or not the media reported it. The crucial issues raised by the debate – (among others) questions of identity, solidarity, mutuality, along with strictly economic and constitutional questions, many of which should have had resonance in France – were apparently lost on a huge majority of people, or, up until the last minute, seen as not sensational enough. Tellingly, when the campaign hit the home stretch, there was (somehow) renewed interest.

Excitation (of a sort)

With the now famous *Sunday Times* poll of 7 September 2014 putting the Yes camp in front (on 51 per cent) just a few days before polling day, coverage of the referendum reached its peak, as if the notion that the result had always been a foregone conclusion had somehow taken the interest out of the debate for most French people from the very beginning.

For example, some three weeks before the referendum itself, *Télérama* (the French TV guide which caters to a rather highbrow readership) did publish an article about the referendum,[6] though its focus was on what pro and anti thought and how they reacted to the sort of arguments used by both sides. In other words, not only did readers have to make do with the gist of interviews involving just a handful of people chosen more or less at random, but also there was little food for thought in terms of what independence for Scotland would mean in a broader sense: to begin with, from a European perspective. In short, it echoed the other haphazard attempts to give French readers a sense of what was happening on the ground by merely focusing on what this or that Scot, more often than not during a chance encounter, had to say.

Rather unexpectedly, on 9 September 2014, the 8 p.m. news bulletin on TV channel France 2 dealt with the possible repercussions of Scottish independence within the EU, and in particular the fact it might trigger other referendums in Northern Italy ('Padania'), Catalonia and Flanders. At least five of my most expert colleagues, including a senior lecturer and a professor, who have written books about the referendum,[7] were also called upon by France Culture, France Info and France Inter (that is, the three public radio channels that are the backbone of Radio France) to provide a clear, balanced and informative reading grid. And I am happy to say they made a thoroughly good job of it as they delved into both the technical and institutional questions.

One could jump to the conclusion that, all of a sudden, many of my fellow citizens were at long last on board. But, alas, their renewed interest was brief: a huge majority remained uninterested or merely ignorant while the masks of those working in newsrooms were soon to come off.

Over and out

The result of the vote, of course, was all over the news on this side of the Channel in the small hours of 19 September 2014, but the interest and excitement lasted only up until (exactly) 4.14 p.m., which was when former President Nicolas Sarkozy officially announced he was making his political comeback. It then looked very much as if the momentous event of the previous day was now almost forgotten. By 8 p.m., indeed, the most watched TV channels, from France 2 to TF1 and BFM, devoted most of their airtime to the return of one of the big beasts of French politics.

Over 18–19 September, *LeMonde.fr* published around thirty articles about Scotland. But there were only five of them between 20 September and mid-October, dealing first and foremost with the constitutional question. However that may be, readers had by then clearly moved on to pastures new. On 26 September 2014, for instance, an article by *Le Monde*'s London correspondent, Eric Albert,[8] elicited no feedback at all and was recommended by just four people. On the previous day, a contribution dealing with the fragility of Britishness and the constitutional headache to come, and published in the same daily[9] by leading journalist Alain Frachon, had equally fallen on deaf ears.

Moreover, while the *Nouvel Observateur*'s Internet site posted some twenty articles about the referendum on 18 and 19 September, these only aroused the interest of three or four readers on average, except for an article on 19 September entitled 'L'Ecosse dit "non" à son indépendance', which led to the sending of thirty-four posts. By 25 September, the referendum was apparently no longer worthy of a mention.

It would seem, then, that, as far as France is concerned, the idea that 'The eyes of the world are upon Scotland', as emphasised by Alex Salmond just one week before the vote, was a little far-fetched, or only at times, and only up until 19 September or thereabouts. The referendum had come and gone, and was now, like so many other things, very much yesterday's news, despite the upbeat reaction of the Yes camp after the initial feeling of dejection following defeat; not to mention, naturally, the fact that a whole new chapter was going to be written in the history of a country that is one of France's closest allies and neighbours.

Patterns and (Possible) Meanings

A nation-based vision

France has her own pro-autonomy/independence parties, prominent among them those in the Basque country, in Brittany, and in Corsica, where people who favour Corsican home rule or complete independence managed to secure some 36 per cent of the vote in the 2010 regional elections. Their reaction to the campaign for autonomy in Scotland may have been dictated by the desire to capitalise upon it for publicity and political gain, but it nevertheless remains quite instructive too, in that it highlights how the referendum was perceived in political circles and by many a politically minded person throughout the land.

In an online article published by *leparisien.fr* on 11 September 2014 and 'recommended' by no fewer than some 2000 readers,[10] all of France's regional nationalists seemed to sing the praises of the Scottish referendum. For example, this was the line taken by the three left-wing, pro-independence Basque parties (*Aberzaleen Batasuna, Euska Alkartasuna* and *Sortu*), which believe the EU should be a federation of sovereign peoples. Similarly, Yves Pelle, chairman of the right-of-centre, euro-federalist Parti Breton, was very excited about the notion that the UK government had allowed Scotland to organise a referendum and deplored the fact that the French government's approach to the regional question was far from being so liberal minded. Herri Gourmelen, of the left-wing and pro-autonomy *Union Démocratique Bretonne*, was very much on the same wavelength as he extolled the principle of letting the people speak and denounced the conservative and 'retrograde' attitude of Paris towards the country's minorities. Last but not least, the Corsican nationalists of *Corsica Libera* and of the more moderate *Femu a Corsica* hailed the referendum as epoch making since, to them, it signalled the end of the large nation states created at the expense of small stateless nations such as Scotland and Corsica.

Likewise, an article about the referendum on *Libération.fr* may have led to the sending of ninety-five posts on 18 September and during the early hours of 19 September, but, whether they attacked the nationalists or stood up for their cause, more often than not the protagonists approached the problem from a Franco-French perspective, the former insisting the Yes campaign was downright selfish and the latter denouncing, on behalf of their own respective peoples, the tricks used by centralisation-minded governments.

This attitude, naturally, is part of the essence of nationalism, and is typical of pro-independence sympathisers; they tend to jealously guard their distinctiveness, which they see as their birthright; this, in turn, inevitably means they can only show utmost respect for other national groups' integrity and decisions. Hence, at the end of the day, their marked tendency to see the question of Scottish independence as, by and large, *Scotland's* problem.

Only politicians and business, it seems, resolutely approached the question from the perspective of 'what it means for us' (regardless of how contextual, too, their own declarations may have been).

The referendum as seen by the powerful (or not so powerful) few

Writing on 17 September 2014, Matthieu Courtecuisse, chairman of SIA Partners (a top management consulting firm), was adamant that, although some looked forward to the demise of the UK (as this might mean a weaker England and therefore a stronger France), independence for Scotland would be a disaster: Scotland's economy would be made fragile and the EU would be immediately threatened by other secessionist movements. Importantly, he went on to lament the fact that France's political and economic elites were remaining practically silent on the issue.[11] This last point, however, remains only partially true.

In an articulate bilingual official statement, dated 10 September 2014, Julien Bayou, national spokesperson for *Europe Écologie Les Verts*, the French equivalent of the Green Party, wrote: '"Yes" to Scottish independence: for a greener and more democratic Scotland'. The reasons for this were as follows:

> What is at stake for the people of Scotland is primarily the opportunity to move public services and decision making closer to the people.
>   The subsidiarity principle is a fundamental principle for all ecologists.
>   . . . Saying 'Yes' to Independence is a means to reclaim control of public policies . . . Independent, Scotland will be able to protect its public health

services and higher education system against the privatisations carried out by the London government. An Independent Scotland will have the powers to further develop their action against climate change: Scotland is already amongst the best at the European level thanks to its ambitious program of carbon emission targets and its Climate Justice Fund.[12]

Nevertheless, the huge majority of French politicians reacted in typical Jacobin fashion. On the day the referendum took place, President François Hollande expressed serious misgivings about the possible implications of a Yes vote; he said he saw the move as adding to the centrifugal forces weighing heavily against the European project, insisting that the outcome might impact upon the very future of the EU in that it might not only lead to its unravelling, but also to that of its member states.[13]

High-profile members of the opposition expressed the same fears: for example, Matthieu Labbé, national secretary of the UMP party (the political formation whose leadership has recently been won by Nicolas Sarkozy and which changed its name to 'The Republicans' in early 2015), pointed out that independence would result in a profound crisis not just in Britain, but throughout Europe as numerous pro-independence movements were pinning their hopes on Scotland paving the way for other regions/nations to follow (to begin with, Catalonia and Flanders).[14]

Conversely, speaking on an RTL radio programme on 12 September 2014, Jean-Luc Mélenchon, the charismatic left-wing politician, leader of the Parti de Gauche, a party to the left of François Hollande's Socialist party, said that he 'of course' supported Scottish independence, justifying his standpoint by laying responsibility for the fragmentation of the UK at the monarchy's door. Meanwhile, many leading Parti de Gauche figures came out in favour of the union, denouncing 'national selfishness' and expressing their worries that wealthy EU regions no longer considered it their duty to help the poorest.

Speaking on iTELE, a French TV channel, on 19 September 2014, Jacques Attali, polymath, author of countless books and one of François Mitterand's spin doctors in the 1980s, talked about the referendum as a sign of the nature of our ideological times, that is as a sign of two reinforcing trends: the fragmentation that is wreaking so much havoc within our societies and the neo-liberal mantra ('every man for himself'). Most interestingly, the former chairwoman of the MEDEF (France's CBI), Laurence Parisot, a staunch supporter of competition and public spending cuts, who was also on the programme, agreed; although she said she was aware Paris, as a financial hub, could have benefitted from a Yes vote (e.g. with the City of London being destabilised by the ensuing constitutional crisis), she nevertheless emphasised the fact that it would have been bad for Europe, and warned against its fragmentation.

My own take on the foregoing is that these were essentially ideologically motivated responses to a problem which none of the people mentioned saw with fresh eyes. The reactions more or less all came down to either excitement at the prospect of seeing the UK state collapse, or downright impatience due to banal nationalism, that is the belief that only existing nation states – as opposed to separatist movements – are legitimate. One way or the other, these reactions were certainly not an objective assessment of a complex situation as they stemmed from the impossibility of envisaging a different international political landscape, that is to say one which is more plural (in the name of democracy) and more strongly interconnected (to address global challenges) at the same time.

It will be seen that, despite the publicity, the talking, watching and listening, the 'Scottish conversation' on the French side of the Channel happened almost entirely as if nearly all of us still lived in a world where interconnectedness (whatever the form) had not yet materialised. Although we tend to bask in the glory of our great thinkers, from Michel Foucault to Jacques Derrida, and pride ourselves on our contribution to the expansion of the social sciences and the study of politics, there remain many doubts as to the impact all of this has had on the way we, collectively, approach current affairs.

If anything, French people's understanding of the Scottish referendum debate never truly reached the stage where actual principles of political and socio-economic organisation, not technicalities or 'potential repercussions for us', were discussed. Naturally, I realise that, however disappointing, it apparently chimes in with a vision of the present and the future informed by little more than the notion that principles are fine but cool-headed realism is a whole lot better. I also realise that, as an academic, I am, unlike many, in a privileged position to raise these issues. However, the truth of the matter may well be that far from being a debate too far, laying down principles is a necessary prerequisite for any subsequent practical decisions to make utter and complete democratic sense as they are then not context-dependent, but partake of values which define the framework for discussions to come.

Notes

1. See last chapter of the May 2013 issue (no. 411).
2. See 'L'Ecosse face aux défis de l'indépendance', by Marie Charrel (25 November 2013), and 'Les indépendantistes écossais cherchent à rassurer la population', by London-based reporter Eric Albert (27 November 2013).
3. See Claire Gatinois, 'Comment la Grande-Bretagne veut appliquer une pression monétaire sur l'Ecosse'.
4. See 'L'avertissement de Barroso à l'Ecosse'.
5. Available at <https://fr-fr.facebook.com/pages/Les-Fran%C3%A7ais-pour-lind%C3%A9pendance-de-l%C3%89cosse/455598757900955> (last accessed 13 September 2015).
6. See François Gorin, 'La touche écossaise' – Télérama (no. 3372), 27 August 2014, pp. 38–41.
7. Edwige Camp-Pietrain, author of 'Le référendum d'autodétermination en Ecosse – Origines et enjeux des revendications indépendantistes', Presses Universitaires du Septentrion, April 2014; and Nathalie Duclos, author of 'L'Ecosse en quête d'indépendance: Le référendum de 2014', PU Paris-Sorbonne, July 2014.

8. See '*L'Ecosse qui dit non*' – M (*Le Monde*'s magazine).
9. See '*Que reste-t-il du Royaume-Uni?*'.
10. See '*Indépendance: les Basques, Bretons et Corses envient le référendum écossais*'.
11. Matthieu Courtecuisse, '*L'indépendance de l'Ecosse serait un séisme pour l'Europe*' – *LesEchos.fr*, 17 September 2014.
12. EELV *Communiqués*, 10 September 2014, <http://eelv.fr/2014/09/10/eelv-dit-oui-a-lindependance-de-lecosse-pour-une-ecosse-plus-democratique-et-plus-verte/> (last accessed 16 September 2015)
13. 'Hollande – *Le référendum écossais peut décider de l'avenir de l'UE*' – *Zonebourse.com*, 18 September 2014.
14. '*Référendum: et si la France s'inspirait de l'exemple écossais?*' – *lefigaro.fr*, 18 September 2014.

16

The Scottish Referendum in Austrian, German and Swiss Media

Klaus Peter Müller

'Story' is a term often used in journalism, but here it is employed in the context of narratology, where story-telling is a cognitive schema, that is, the most basic human ability of making sense of life, giving meaning to it, and passing this understanding intelligibly on to others. This is a fundamental faculty of the human mind.[1] In this context, the stories told about Scotland and the referendum in different media in three important European countries where German is spoken have been investigated: Austria, Germany, and Switzerland. A fairly comprehensive and representative number of newspapers, illustrated magazines, TV, and radio stations have been scrutinised and have provided an impressive amount of material (see Tables 16.1 and 16.2 at the end of the chapter).[2] The topics dealt with in this article have evolved out of this material, rather than been forced on to it, as it quickly became evident that there is a great deal of similarity in what is presented in texts on Scotland, discussed in the first part of the chapter. The chapter will then discuss the differences in these stories and their causes, and then present the conclusions drawn in the media themselves and those developing out of this investigation.

The Basic Story and Other Key Story Elements

The simplest way of telling a story is to speak about what happened and use the structure E. M. Forster employed for his definition of 'story' in *Aspects of the Novel*:[3] 'and then, and then'. This creates a chronology of events, which in connection with the referendum and the media investigated has roughly this shape: (1) the September referendum, (2) a fairly certain majority for No, (3) the possibility of a Yes victory, (4) (producing) an increase of political threats, economic warnings, and eventually the Prime Minister's, Labour's and Liberals' 'Vow', (5) the referendum result, (6) the first impression that the independence question is settled for at least one generation, (7) Salmond (therefore) stepping down, (8) Cameron's demand for English votes for English laws, (9) (producing) huge new problems and consequences, (10) (so that eventually) nothing has been settled.

These key events in the Scottish referendum story found in the media investigated create a storyline and also contain elements that surfaced in all of the stages mentioned, such as the warnings of an economic disaster in the case of independence. There are also plot elements, which add causality to chronology and, of course, one finds an endless number of variations of these events in the individual media stories, variations connected with the other key story elements.

One of the media's general claims is that they provide basic information, facts about the people involved, their actions, the settings, but also about possible consequences of independence. Thus many texts appeared in all media about 'what Scottish independence would mean'.[4] It has been clear for quite some time, though, that one never has basic information or facts as such and that one fact does not have only one meaning. Ludwig Wittgenstein[5] pointed out that the meaning of a word or text depends on how people use it, and Hayden White emphasised that the particular form in which historical facts are presented significantly shapes their meaning, which is why he highlighted *The Content of the Form*.[6] The way in which the referendum story is narrated, its form, thus also defines its meaning.

Another decisive factor determining the content and form of referendum stories is whether the journalist is in favour of Scottish independence or not (assuming a stance is taken). Ideology is often directly revealed in the words used: independence versus disruption, and so on. But it is not always so easily detected and needs to be analysed in connection with how language as a whole is used.[7] Language can camouflage ideology, but it is also employed in the media by journalists simply repeating what they have found in other sources. The German illustrated magazine *Spiegel* thus had two different articles on the same day (10 September 2014) about what Cameron had said to Scotland: one telling its readers that Cameron had warned Scots not to vote for independence, the other saying Cameron implored the Scots to stay in the union. The reason for this was not ideology, but simply the fact that *Der Spiegel* used two different press agencies, AFP for the first, then dho/Reuters. This is a widespread phenomenon in the media: they like to repeat themselves, and in this way produce something that sometimes looks like variety, but is in fact often simply an example of their enormous redundancy. Quality papers such as the *Süddeutsche Zeitung* (SZ) offer real variety and creativity, in this case: 'Schottland, vernimm mein Flehen' (10 September 2014), 'Scotland, heed my supplication'.

The section into which a story is put also influences its shape. Scotland usually appears (though not often) in the travel, sports and arts sections. Accidents such as the Glasgow Art School fire are mentioned in the news of the day. In the politics, finance or business sections, Scotland is generally presented in connection with the UK. Here the old blunders of saying England when one means Britain, or of disregarding Scotland completely, were still happening in the lead-up to the referendum, but hardly at all in September.

In the business reports on the referendum most texts express concern about or clear opposition to independence. Typically in these contexts, negative terms like '*Abspaltung*' (secession) are used, rather than 'independence'. The Austrian quality paper *Standard* speaks in this way and is generally clearly against independence. But all media use business experts expressing their warnings and thus reiterating the statements of politicians in opposition to independence. This is part of the ideological jargon used, trying to give readers the impression that these people know what they are talking about. One could refer to the 2008 financial crisis in order to demonstrate instantly that economic experts lost their credibility a long time ago, but it is actually enough to point out that in the case of Scottish independence they simply do not know because they, too, cannot predict the future. Everything would depend on long and serious negotiations between Scotland and the rest of Britain, the EU and NATO. The often repeated statements by Manuel Barroso, President of the EU Commission, and many others that Scotland would have to leave these international organisations are not based on any single fact or law, but only on the opinions and wishes of those who made them. This is almost completely ignored in most of the business and political texts expressing such opinions. One intriguing exception will be discussed later in the chapter.

Threats and warnings abounded in all media and increased in number when survey results suggested that the independence movement was ahead.[8] Reports of the increased possibility of a Yes vote began on 2 September, and the projected independence majority was reported by most media on 7 September. All these reports used the official YouGov polls, and then on 10 September the media began speaking of 'top Brits' going on a promotional tour to Scotland, also often described as a 'panic reaction', culminating first in 'Cameron's final appeal', and then in the 'vow and many gifts for a Scottish No' (Deutsche Welle, 15, 16 September 2014). One sees clearly that the media followed the events and shaped them only in their wording. But they soon and emphatically pointed out that whatever the result, Britain would have to change dramatically (see for example *Wiener*, 8 September 2014; *FAZ*, 18 September 2014; Deutsche Welle, 19 September 2014; *Handelsblatt*, 20 September 2014).

The problem of a divided Scotland familiar from the eighteenth century was still topical in 2014. That Scotland faced an historic decision was mentioned with equal frequency.[9] Celebrities were used in all media in connection with the referendum, with texts speaking of the *Royal-Faktor*, or wondering how 'Kate's second child might help to unite the kingdom' (ORF, 8 September 2014; *Stern*, 9 September 2014). On the other hand, 'James Bond (Sean Connery) wants to leave, too' (*Ö24*, 10 September 2014), and Vivienne Westwood or Andy Murray were among the persons mentioned as being in support of independence (*FAZ*, 30 August 2014; *WZ*, 15 September 2014). J. K. Rowling's upholding of the union was covered by most media (*Handelsblatt*, 11 June 2014, and *Heute*, 11 June 2014, are just two examples), but the most analytical text on her was presented by *NZZ* (18 June 2014), explaining Rowling's reasons, even though she does not like the Tories, and comparing her with the different position taken by Mairi McFadyen (a social scientist aligned with the National Collective, in online commentary on Rowling). Opposition to Rowling was also mentioned in the papers, but only *Die Welt* described it as an 'army of trolls' (12 June 2014).

Other key story elements are historic events and stereotypes, such as Bannockburn (DLF, 1 March, 10 March, 13 September 2014) and 'Braveheart' (DLF, 13 September, 16 September 2014). Alex Salmond was repeatedly called 'Braveheart' (WZ, 7 September 2014; *taz*, 19 September 2014), but *Die Welt* (18 September 2014) typically, and not favourably, called him 'tribune of the plebs', whereas the *NZZ* (18 October 2014) did not use stereotypes, but simply spoke of the 'highly brilliant Salmond'. When Nicola Sturgeon took over from Salmond, she was a representative of 'Frauenpower' (*Standard*, 21 September 2014; *NZZ*, 'Powerfrau', 19 November 2014), but also a 'romantic politician' ('Politikromantikerin', *Standard*, 16 November 2014), because for *Der Standard*, Scottish independence generally was romantically unrealistic. But the same text also described her as very pragmatic, with clear ideas for the general election in 2015, and it emphasised the key result of the referendum process: it has had a dynamic and refreshing effect, significantly and favourably increasing the people's interest in politics.

This was indeed the general opinion in the media, connected with the understanding that the Scotland question has not been solved at all, that the England question and a great number of serious new problems have been added, and that change and more autonomy are now absolutely necessary (*Standard*, 19 September (three times), 21, 23 September, 27 November 2014; *FAZ*, 24 September 2014, etc.).

Differences in the Media Presentations and their Causes

Two simple reasons explain the differences in the media texts: (1) how the story is narrated and (2) what is mentioned and what is left out. Basic and typical examples from the media investigated will be presented now, with a comparison of the two biggest German TV stations, ARD and ZDF, both public service broadcasters. They usually appeared to be very similar in their presentations of the referendum campaign, but ZDF was generally more sceptical about independence and also wondered, 'are the Scots really serious?' (11 August, 15 August 2014). ZDF began speaking of 'possible independence' fairly late (25 August 2014), while ARD adopted a different perspective and investigated reasons that might contradict independence (16, 17 September 2014). According to ZDF, Cameron sent an 'emotional plea to Scotland' (10 September 2014); the word 'separatists' was often used; they declared that a Yes would be a No to federalism (17 September 2014); blamed the 'lousy style' and manners of independent cybernats (17 September 2014), and thus adopted the evaluations of the *Daily Telegraph* and the *Daily Mail*.[10] For ZDF, Scotland even belonged to a group of 'rebels', regions bringing about 'Kleinstaaterei in Europe' (18, 19 September 2014), that is, sectionalism with no element of independence or democracy, only full of egoism. These characteristics of ZDF's reporting could not be found on ARD, which spoke of Scotland fighting for independence, saw this as a serious historical question, and usually adopted an optimistic point of view, even directly after the result, which it called 'stimulating' and 'encouraging', as it promised and demanded improvements for Scotland (7, 10, 19 September 2014).

The sometimes strongly negative language of ZDF was even hiked up by a notch by *Die Welt*, which called supporters of independence 'defectors', 'deserters' or 'secessionists'.[11] The 'narrow-minded Scots' could bring about the collapse of the pound (8 September 2014) and produce a 'heavy storm over Britain', London was making 'panicky offers to renegade Scots' (9 September 2014), and there was no irony in their report about the 'Three musketeers on their way to Scotland' (11 September 2014). They typically used war imagery, the 'last battle of Scotland' (11 September 2014), also employed by *Stern* ('Showdown', 7 September 2014) and *Handelsblatt* (19 September 2014), detecting similarities to 'D-Day summer 1944'.

The absolute climax of how *Die Welt* spoke about Scotland and how the paper has seen the idea of Scottish independence was bluntly expressed by the deputy editor-in-chief, Andrea Seibel, in her op ed piece on 13 September: 'Schotten, ihr nervt – und zwar beträchtlich!', 'Scots, you are a serious pain in the neck!'. She continues with 'nobody understands what the Scots want, all Europeans think, we've got better things to do'; so why this kind of nonsense that we are currently also being offered in Catalonia? What all separatists want would be the 'utmost collateral damage. Please don't do this mischief to us.' This last sentence, like the entire text, is concerned only with the speaker, nowhere with Scotland and what the Scots might want. The paper repeats the negative business predictions, and even has the Queen warn the Scots against independence (15 September 2014, twice).

A very different language from that used by *Die Welt* is to be found in the *FAZ*, even though both are fairly conservative papers. But in contrast to Seibel's comments, the deputy head of the *FAZ* (17 September 2014) arts section claims 'they are not at all crazy, these Scots', and concludes that the Scots are much more sensible Europeans than the English. The danger of Britain disintegrating, another piece says (16 September 2014), was caused by Cameron himself, and whatever the result of the referendum, 'Cameron has already lost'. But, the text continues, we have all lost by presenting Scots as atavistic nationalists and claiming that the EU is seriously endangered because of them. We should rather acknowledge that by doing so we are simply repeating the weak arguments of the opponents of independence and understand that the extent of social and economic chaos depends on us all. In order to be successful, it goes on, two things are necessary: (1) Scots will have to stop blaming others for their problems, and (2) the rest of Britain and Europe must be interested in Scotland's success. And while admitting that neither of these were likely to become reality, it saw Scottish nationalism as characterised by a social-liberal, Europhile attitude, representing no threat to Europe and, therefore, worthy of support, even when we personally think national identity is not really relevant.

It is a sign of the quality of the *FAZ* that well considered opinions like this one get published there. The text was not by a journalist but by Thomas Weber, chair of history and international affairs at Aberdeen University, currently at Harvard. In general, the *FAZ* was against independence, had 'experts' speak against it, also used the word 'secession', and thought that a No result would definitely produce faster, safer, and better changes. Changes were what people wanted, the *FAZ* emphasised, and, like the other media, they repeatedly pointed out that the promises made to Scotland must now be kept.

The Swiss quality paper *NZZ* had a similar view of Scotland to the *FAZ*, but with a stronger focus on economics, and is particularly interesting because of its point of view from outside the EU. Its London correspondent Peter Rásonyi praised the Yes movement as full of 'wit, charm, and cheerfulness', though in the end it was unable to convince the silent majority (19 September 2014). He, too, speaks highly of the amount of democracy revealed in the process, criticises London's attitude to Scotland, but is perhaps too quickly and naively convinced that the promises made will be kept. On 18 October, however, he notes that new problems abound, Cameron's time schedule is totally unrealistic, narrow-minded party politics dominate, and that the idea of finding solutions through a Westminster-established commission that excludes the public is simply the breeding ground for the next independence movement.

The referendum was 'a success even in defeat', showing that Britain would never be the same again, because the No majority did not support the status quo either. Britain's 'reform deadlock' had been revealed and must now be dealt with (another text on 19 September 2014). The *NZZ* (12, 14 September 2014) also points out that Scotland has a much more egalitarian idea of society which it starkly contrasts with the dominant conservative and neo-liberal thinking in England, and that the EU cannot continue simply ignoring or suppressing independence in Scotland or Catalonia (13 September 2014). Rásonyi is also one of a few journalists who emphasise that politicians and investors usually adopt a dangerous short-term perspective, whereas the Scottish nationalists see things in larger contexts, stress their close links with the community, and expect greater productivity, more fairness, and a much more sustainable economy in this way. Independence would, therefore, he maintained, have both 'costs and opportunities' (9 September 2014).

The negativism of the No campaign is also pointed out by the *NZZ* far more often and critically than in most other media (e.g. 7 September 2014), as well as the fact that London ignored the referendum for too long, because it generally tends to neglect Scotland (5 September 2014). It is not really surprising that the quality papers *FAZ*, *NZZ* and *SZ*, offer the best information and the greatest variety of opinions, include long-term perspectives with regard to the past and the future, and present the deepest analysis of Scotland. The *SZ* is even more open to changes in society, more critical of politicians than the other two, and it delivers the best investigative journalism of the countries studied. The diversity of information, opinions, and background analyses offered by these three papers is a very pleasant marvel in contemporary media.

Differences can always be expected in the *tageszeitung* (*taz*) with its strong social democratic left-wing tendency, where the use of lower case already signals its desire to be different. With regard to the referendum, its journalists indeed had different opinions, openly presented on 17 September 2014, when Ralf Sotschek, foreign correspondent for Britain and Ireland, and Dominic Johnson, head of the Foreign Desk section, expressed their views. Johnson said he wanted to remain British, saw not a single advantage in secession, repeated Westminster's position, but also pointed out the negative effects of the Tory government on the British public in another piece the same day, which, however, again spoke of the 'Scottish blighters' and their 'stupid, little referendum'. He even put Alex Salmond and Nigel Farage on the same level, and thought that with independence English national pride would soar. How wrong he was has been made evident by the fact that Britain today is very close to where he thought it could be only with a Yes vote.

Sotschek was clearly in support of independence and pointed out that one should consider the advantages for Scotland more than the disadvantages for the UK or the EU. Keeping the pound as well as Scotland in the EU would be in everybody's interest. Later (23 September 2014), Sotschek said that Cameron had cunningly fooled the Scots once again: the vow of devo max had been turned into a general election topic, thus made unacceptable to Labour, and had in this way been emptied of meaning. But, the piece finishes, Scottish independence is only a question of time.

Key Conclusions in the Media

Old Britain is dead, Scotland is a new country and Europe must change too

A remarkable number of texts expressed what *Der Stern* (19 September 2014) turned into a headline: 'Die alte Union ist tot'. Even after the No vote, Scotland is clearly a new country (DLF, 20 September 2014). The whole 'island has definitely been changed' (DLF, 19 September 2014), and in fact the whole of Europe has got a 'Wake-Up-Call' (DLF, 19 September 2014). Changes thus are necessary everywhere.

The general public has become political, democracy has come alive and regional diversity in Europe has been enhanced

Scotland is giving everybody an 'object-lesson in democracy and rule of law', the *NZZ* had already said on 16 August. Others saw a 'model democracy in practice' (SRF 4, 19 September 2014; ZDF, 19 September 2014; FAZ, 19 September 2014), found that 'we have all learned much about politics' (DRK, 19 September 2014), and that the neglected idea of subsidiarity is now relevant again everywhere in Europe (*Handelsblatt*, 12 September 2014).

Europe must learn from Scotland (*FAZ*, 20 September 2014), in particular learn to accept the importance of diversity. Scotland has shown the benefit of independence movements for European regions, and Brussels must make sure that its enormous bureaucratic apparatus does not disregard regional needs and desires.[12]

Federalism – the best solution?

The *WZ* (17 September 2014) stated that the United Kingdom must change completely, expressing the general opinion in the media, which often suggested federalism as the best solution (*Bayernkurier*, 27 September 2014). 'The debate about federalism is now beginning' (*FAZ*, 19 September 2014). The problems are also evident: 'the referendum has triggered an avalanche' (Deutsche Welle, 25 September 2014), because it is totally unclear how British federalism, giving England the same powers as Scotland, Wales and Northern Ireland, could work. But nineteenth-century nationalistic concepts as well as a centralistic idea of the EU are evidently not what most people want, who today favour both more regionalism and more powers to local authorities. Federalism is also the best 'answer to separatism', as it keeps the awareness of being connected with larger units alive all the time and thus avoids sectionalism. Democracy will be enhanced in this way, plurality and diversity supported.[13] Such democracy was not found in Brussels, whose evident lack of any helpful ideas, apart from rejecting independence, was often pointed out, and even described as the 'deafening silence in Brussels' (ARD, 18 September 2014; similarly *Zeit*, 3 June 2014; *NZZ*, 8 September 2014; *Welt*, 21 September 2014, etc.).

'Federalism is a modern way of organising the state' and much more, and better, than a 'rag rug' (*NZZ*, 15 October 2014). This awareness is an evident result of the referendum, thus contradicting repeated claims that an independent Scotland would lead to the balkanisation of Europe, already strongly refuted by the *SZ* on 17 February.

Gerald Hosp (*NZZ*, 16 August 2014) makes some further important statements about federalism in the current economic system. He is actually one of the very few commentators who clearly says that all economic studies presented by business people and politicians in favour or against independence are extremely unreliable, mainly hypotheses, and completely depend on the eventual results of negotiations. He is an economist and, therefore, concludes that a right to secede is good, because it increases the competition between states and regions. Extreme solutions, he says, are not necessary whenever the public is involved, not excluded, and more federalism is, therefore, an excellent solution.

The nation state today is actually a 'battle zone' for reasons other than those of the nineteenth and twentieth centuries. Today's reasons are connected with the question 'do we still need frontiers?' (ZDF, 23 May 2014). This programme described the current problems in Russia and the Ukraine as being dealt with in the old militaristic way, whereas Britain was handling frontier problems in a much more civilised democratic form (also in WZ, 6 March, 14 March 2014). Contemporary sociologists describe nationalism as producing new unnecessary forms of violence and dangers. Historically – and, in connection with the Scottish referendum, ironically – we are indeed at a stage where the dissolution of nation states makes much sense and is clearly possible, attractive, and challenging in a free, democratic Europe.[14] Federalism is a supreme idea in this context, too.

Two further consequences are that 'Business and politics as usual is not accepted by the public', but in many respects 'Business as usual is back'. All Scots, whether Yes or No voters, expect the promises made to them to be fulfilled, and the media support this. But at the same time, Scotland is no longer in the headlines. Old topics are back in the press account studied here, connected with tourism, whisky, or sports, and the old party-political opposition between Tories and Labour.

Conclusions concerning the Media

All media present the story described above. The same elements often appear at the same time. There are many repetitions, and variety is created by the way in which stories are narrated and which content or perspective is highlighted or left out. The different media do not produce any significant differences through their inherent characteristics as media. The main differences arise from different concepts of the world, divergent value systems, thinking, etc., which then also influence the media text's language.

The media in Austria, Germany, and Switzerland have presented a fairly comprehensive picture and given their readers a new understanding of Scotland within a federal Europe. Not a single important difference based on a national perspective is visible. They also do not adopt just one European position, but quite generally in the majority the attitudes of business 'experts', politicians and others in opposition to independence. Texts in support of independence are in the minority and also never based on national reasoning. Only one minor national difference becomes evident that people in Austria and Germany are usually not aware of: the Swiss way of writing Edinburgh is without the 'h'! Consumers of these media will have gained a favourable understanding of Scotland, wherever its impressive democratic process has been described as such. How all this will now change people's attitudes and behaviour and Scotland's as well as Europe's political future remains to be seen and depends on everybody's future actions.

The Media Investigated

Table 16.1 The media investigated (incl. their abbreviations, number of texts on Scotland*).

	March–August and October	September and October
Austria		
Heute (www.heute.at) (daily tabloid)	1	5
Krone (www.krone.at) (daily tabloid)	2	17
Ö24 (www.oe24.at) (daily tabloid)	0	8
Standard (www.derstandard.at) (daily broadsheet)	19	52
Wiener Zeitung (WZ) (www.wienerzeitung.at) (daily broadsheet)	3	43
Österreich 1 ORF (http://oe1.orf.at/) (radio)	11	24
ORF (http://tv.orf.at/) (TV)	1	10
Germany		
Bild (www.bild.de) (daily tabloid)	2	14
Handelsblatt (http://www.handelsblatt.com/) (daily business broadsheet)	17	127
Frankfurter Allgemeine Zeitung (FAZ) (http://www.faz.net/) (daily broadsheet)	15	78
Frankfurter Rundschau (http://www.fr-online.de/home/1472778,1472778.html) (daily broadsheet)	15	107
Junge Freiheit (www.jungefreiheit.de/) (weekly)	1	6
Neues Deutschland (http://www.neues-deutschland.de/) (daily quality)	20	40
Süddeutsche Zeitung (SZ) (http://www.sueddeutsche.de/) (daily quality)	13	71
tageszeitung (*taz*) (http://www.taz.de/) (daily broadsheet)	6	29
Welt (http://www.welt.de/) (daily broadsheet)	23	117
Zeit (www.zeit.de) (weekly quality)	18	52
Focus (http://www.focus.de/) (weekly magazine)	3	75
Spiegel (http://www.spiegel.de/) (weekly magazine)	7	74
Stern (http://www.stern.de/) (weekly magazine)	3	57
Deutschland Radio Kultur (DRK) (http://www.deutschlandradiokultur.de/) (radio)	46	132
SWR 1 & SWR 2 (http://www.swr.de/swr1/-/id=266634/1kqaztk/, http://www.swr.de/swr2/-/id=7576/otnbb1/) (radio)	0	7
WDR 5 (http://www.wdr5.de/) (radio)	1	8
ARD (www.ard.de) (TV and radio)	29	166
ZDF (http://www.zdf.de/) (TV)	14	84

Table 16.1 (continued)

	March–August and October	September
Switzerland		
Basler Zeitung (http://bazonline.ch/) (daily)	9	37
Berner Zeitung (http://www.bernerzeitung.ch/) (daily)	18	56
Blick (http://www.blick.ch/) (daily tabloid)	2	21
BZ Basel (http://www.bzbasel.ch/) (daily)	4	33
Handelszeitung (http://www.handelszeitung.ch/) (daily)	13	100
Neue Zürcher Zeitung (NZZ) (http://www.nzz.ch/) (daily broadsheet)	32	71
20 Minuten (http://www.20min.ch/) (daily tabloid)	3	32
'SRF' Schweizer Rundfunk (http://www.srf.ch/) (radio &TV)	35	143

* Averages given in Table 16.2.
Media with an insignificant amount of reporting (less than 6 texts in the whole period):
Germany:
Bayerische Staatszeitung (http://www.bayerische-staatszeitung.de/staatszeitung.html) (weekly): September (1), October (2)
Bayernkurier (http://www.bayernkurier.de/zeitung/startseite.html) (quality weekly): July (1), SEP (4)
Bayern 2 (http://www.br.de/radio/bayern2/index.html) (radio): May (1), September (3)
BR 3 Bayerisches Fernsehen (http://www.br.de/fernsehen/bayerisches-fernsehen/index.html) (TV): May (1), September (3)
Switzerland:
Weltwoche (http://www.weltwoche.ch/) (weekly): August (1), September (2)
Wochenzeitung (http://www.woz.ch/) (weekly): May (1), September (2)

Table 16.2 Averages for each country.*

	March–August and October	September
Total	55.2 t/m (386 t in total)	474 t/w (1896 t in total)
Austria	5.3 t/m (37)	39.8 t/w (159)
Germany	33.3 t/m (233)	311 t/w (1244)
Switzerland	16.6 t/m (116)	123.3 t/w (493)

* Without the media with insignificant numbers of texts listed under Table 16.1.
t = texts, m = month, w = week

Notes

1. See Frith, *Making Up the Mind*; Herman, *The Cambridge Companion to Narrative*; Herman, 'Cognitive narratology'.
2. The online and print sources examined can be found at the end of the chapter, in Tables 16.1 and 16.2, with the abbreviations used here. This extensive work would have been impossible without the support of Sherry Ishak Abadeer, Stefanie Brenneisen, Heide Cech, Katharina Leible, Miriam Schröder, Ilka Schwittlinsky and Melanie Sommer, to whom I owe special thanks.
3. E. M. Forster employed his definition of 'story' in *Aspects of the Novel* (1927).
4. 'Was die schottische Unabhängigkeit bedeuten würde', *Stern* (12 September 2014). A single quote sign indicates my translation of a source text. Similar texts appeared in *FAZ* (12 September 2014); *taz* (17 September 2014); *Heute* (19 September 2014); *Krone* (18 September 2014); *Standard* (18 September 2014); *NZZ* (17 September 2014), etc., in fact in all media. 'Text' is used here in the broad sense of the term, referring to print products as well as to TV, radio programmes, etc.
5. Wittgenstein, *Philosophical Investigations*.
6. White, *The Content of the Form*.
7. See, for example, Pinker, *The Stuff of Thought*.
8. See, for example, the warnings and threats in *NZZ* (8 March, 16 April, 7 September 2014); *Krone* (10 September 2014); *Standard* (10 September, 14 September 2014). Here and everywhere else, only typical examples are mentioned, not all media expressing the same.
9. *Stern* (13 April 2014); ARD (5 August 2014); DFL (6 August 2014); *Krone* (12 September 2014); *Standard* (13 September 2014); Deutsche Welle (16 September 2014); *WZ* (17 September 2014); *Handelsblatt* (18 September 2014); NZZ (18 September 2014); *FAZ* (19 September 2014), etc.
10. See *Telegraph* (7 March 2012), available at <http://www.telegraph.co.uk/com ment/9129998/Welcome-to-planet-Cybernat-where-the-air-is-toxic.html>; *Daily Mail* (25 November 2014), available at <http://www.dailymail.co.uk/ news/article-2545901/Cybernats-unmasked-Meet-footsoldiers-pro-Scottish-independence-army-online-poison-shames-Nationalists.html>. The term was among the words of the year in 2013 (see <http://www.scotsman.com/lifestyle/geek-twerking-cybernat-among-words-of-the-year-1-3234374>) and its use is, of course, not limited to these papers, but the ZDF did take over their point of view. (All articles last accessed 29 December 2014.)
11. For example on 5 March, 31 August, 3 September, 11 September and so on. *Handelsblatt* often cooperates with *Welt* and uses the same language and ideology, even speaking of 'splitters', 'Siegen die Spalter?' (7 September 2014), a very negative term in German.
12. Deutsche Welle, 21 September 2014. Similar ideas were expressed, for example, by *Krone* (13 September 2014); *Standard* (12 September, 19 September, 14 October 2014); *WZ* (19 September 2014); DRK (20 September 2014); *FAZ* (21 September 2014); *Bayernkurier* (4 October 2014).
13. *Standard* (12 September 2014), referring to Jósika, *Ein Europa der Regionen: Was die Schweiz kann, kann auch Europa.*
14. Compare the articles on Scotland in *taz* on 12 and 17 September, which state that the 'principle of national frontiers is out-of-date' and 'no longer in keeping with the times', and Müller, 'Scotland 2014 and beyond'.

Bibliography

Frith, Chris, *Making Up the Mind. How the Brain Creates Our Mental World* (Oxford: Blackwell, 2007).

Herman, David (ed.) (2007), *The Cambridge Companion to Narrative* (Cambridge: Cambridge University Press, 2007).

Herman, David, 'Cognitive narratology', in Peter Hühn, John Pier, Wolf Schmid and Jörg Schönert (eds), *Handbook of Narratology* (Berlin: de Gruyter, 2009), pp. 30–43; updated 2013 version available at <http://www.lhn.uni-hamburg.de/article/cognitive-narratology-revised-version-uploaded-22-september-2013> (last accessed 29 December 2014).

Jósika, Peter, *Ein Europa der Regionen: Was die Schweiz kann, kann auch Europa* (Basel: IL-Verlag, 2014).

Müller, Klaus Peter, 'Scotland 2014 and beyond – key contexts of innocence and maturity: Scotland, the UK, the EU, the global & digital worlds', in Müller (ed.), *Scotland 2014 and Beyond – Coming of Age and Loss of Innocence?* (Frankfurt am Main: Peter Lang, 2015), pp. 11–42.

Pinker, Steven, *The Stuff of Thought: Language as a Window into Human Nature* (London: Allen Lane, 2007).

White, Hayden, *The Content of the Form: Narrative Discourse and Historical Representation* (Baltimore: Johns Hopkins University Press, 1987).

Wittgenstein, Ludwig [1953], *Philosophical Investigations* (Hoboken: Blackwell 2001).

17

The Scottish Referendum: the View from Quebec

Catherine Côté

For Quebecers, the holding of the Scottish referendum was of great significance. For various reasons, Quebec felt challenged by this referendum. First, it has in common with Scotland its past of being a nation which became part of the British Empire, in Quebec's case as a result of conquest, in Scotland's by agreement between the parliaments of the two countries. Second, Quebec also shares with Scotland a sense of national identity which distinguishes it from the state to which it belongs. Finally, like Scotland, it is a 'small nation' seeking to acquire more sovereignty in a very different global context from the one usually associated with independence of peoples, such as decolonisation, war, or the collapse of empire. In addition, for many Quebecers, a vote in favour of Scottish independence could revive the Quebec sovereignty movement which, even if it is still present in the Quebec political landscape, does not have the same vigour any more, especially after the defeat of the Parti Québécois in provincial elections in April 2014. Therefore, the past of Quebec, and its future, are associated with the Scottish referendum. As a result, the media coverage of this event could not be anything other than a distinctive one.

The Political Context in Quebec

'Referendum' is not a neutral word in Quebec. Associated with divisive issues in recent history, it was a device notably used by the federal government in 1898 to allow the prohibition of alcohol.[1] The majority of provinces voted Yes, except Quebec which voted against at 81.5 per cent. However, since the overall majority in favour was not high (51.3 per cent), the federal government left to the provinces the decision to prohibit the sale of alcohol on their territory. The federal government also held a plebiscite[2] in 1942 in order to be released from its promise of not imposing compulsory military conscription, as it had done in 1917.[3] In fact, the country was deeply divided, since for French Canadians,[4] who bitterly recalled their forced involvement in the Boer War and in the First World War, compulsory conscription for a war being held in Europe was a symbol of British domination.[5] For English Canadians, it was a question of loyalty to the motherland. Quebec voted against (72 per cent), while the rest of the country voted in favour (66 per cent). Therefore, conscription became compulsory and, once again significant differences between Quebec and the other Canadian provinces were highlighted.

By the early 1960s, with the Quiet Revolution, French-Canadian nationalism turned into Quebec nationalism, that is to say, a nationalism of emancipation stemming from the position of inferiority in which French Canadians were living,[6] some authors even suggesting the Quebecois were the 'white niggers of America'.[7] In the wake of the various world decolonisation movements, several parties advocating the independence of Quebec were created. The Parti Québécois, headed by René Lévesque, was elected in the province in 1976 on the basis of promising Quebec sovereignty. However, once in power, the government started by implementing various progressive measures before holding a referendum in 1980 which sought a mandate to negotiate 'sovereignty-association' with the federal government.[8] Meanwhile, pan-Canadian nationalism, thanks to strong nation-building efforts, replaced British patriotism. A crucial figure in this development was Pierre Elliot Trudeau, Liberal minister and then Prime Minister of Canada. During the Quebec referendum campaign, Trudeau promised to make constitutional changes in order to accommodate Quebec. After Quebec voted No (59.56 per cent), Trudeau triggered the process of the repatriation of the constitution, thus enabling Canada to modify its constitution itself, without having to seek the approval of the British Parliament. The subsequent constitutional accord was signed by all Canadian provinces in 1982, except, however, Quebec, which felt betrayed and never signed but had to abide by the decision of the Supreme Court legitimising the repatriation.[9]

The referendum defeat, followed by the constitutional *coup d'état*[10] produced great gloom among Quebec nationalists. To address the constitutional impasse, the Conservative Prime Minister Brian Mulroney began a round of negotiations out of which came the Meech Lake Accord, which had to be ratified by each province. At the deadline of ratification, two provinces, Manitoba and Newfoundland, still refused to ratify, the second actually denying its signature. The following day, 24 June 1990, which was Quebec national day, a parade in Montreal featuring 200,000 Quebec flags chanted independence slogans. A federal minister, Lucien Bouchard, and seven other Members of Parliament subsequently resigned to create a new sovereignist party at the federal level: the Bloc Québécois. The sovereignty movement then experienced a second wind, all the more so as this period coincided with the socio-economic emancipation of Quebecers. In order to find a solution, Robert Bourassa, then Liberal Premier of Quebec, created the *Commission on the political and constitutional future of Quebec*. However, this Commission concluded that it was necessary to hold a new referendum on sovereignty-association. The federal government then tried to find a constitutional solution through a series of meetings between the federal, provincial and territorial governments, as well as indigenous representatives, out of which came the Charlottetown Accord. The latter was submitted to a public referendum in 1992.[11] But the agreement was rejected by Canadians (54.3 per cent), English Canadians maintaining that it involved too many concessions to Quebec, and Quebecers taking the view that it offered far too little. In the 1993 federal election, the Bloc Québécois won fifty-four seats and became the official opposition in Canada. In Quebec, the Parti Québécois returned to power in 1994. Jacques Parizeau, its leader, promised a new referendum on sovereignty. Despite the disappointing polls, he launched a campaign[12] in 1995, with Lucien Bouchard designated the future 'chief negotiator' between Quebec and Canada. The No side won by a very small majority (50.6 per cent), and Parizeau left politics. Lucien Bouchard then replaced him at the head of the Parti Québécois. Bouchard concentrated on improving the Quebec economy, notably through the pursuit of a 'zero deficit', and on encouraging solidarity, particularly during the Saguenay flood of 1996 and the Ice Storm Crisis of 1998.

For the sovereignty movement, the second referendum defeat was a tough one and the movement still struggles to recover. The subsequent leaders of the Bloc Québécois and of the Parti Québécois continued to profess their faith in sovereignty, but did not propose concrete actions other than promising to hold another referendum if the conditions were right. With the collapse of the *Bloc Québécois* at the federal level in 2011 and the challenges faced by the *Parti Québécois* on regaining power as a minority government in 2012, the word 'referendum' became a drag on the sovereignists. In fact, they now continue to wish for a referendum, but do not agree on the right schedule. And since the word was associated with divisive debates in Quebec society, the Quebec Liberal Party, headed by Philippe Couillard, campaigned in 2014 saying that the PQ sought only to divide the population with a referendum instead of dealing with 'real business'. Couillard won the majority of seats in April of that year while the incumbent premier was defeated in her own riding. It was a real blow for the *Parti Québécois*, which had not only to rebuild itself, but also to find a new leader. The Scottish referendum was a very timely demonstration that other nations were also facing similar issues. Thus, some of the aspiring leaders of the *Parti Québécois* took the opportunity to visit Scotland as observers in order to be inspired and to undergo renewal.

The Importance of the Scottish Referendum

The media, constantly looking for audiences, have a predilection for events which can upset the established order and create emotional drama. For the Quebec media it was not surprising that the interest was so high in a referendum taking place elsewhere in the world, especially in a 'small nation' sharing similar characteristics with Quebec. According to *Influence Communication*, the Scottish referendum was the thirteenth most covered news item by the Quebec media overall in 2014.[13] It was ranked higher than several other important matters for Quebecers, such as the budget of the new Minister of Finance. Actually, the Scottish referendum was the second most covered international news item after the Olympic Games in Sochi. The interest had been more tenuous during previous years. For instance, in 2011, the Scottish issue garnered only 70 references in Quebec. In contrast, in 2014, the interest increased dramatically: there were 3000 references in the Quebec media, including 526 between September and 15 October, and 275 the following month.[14]

However, even if the interest in the Scottish issue was huge, the media coverage was filtered largely through the Quebec experience. Thus, whereas the usual journalistic practice with international news is to rely on experts from the specific region, this time, we saw very few specialists on Scotland. Actually, the media chose to give voice to MPs from the Parti Québécois who were present in Scotland, and also to Quebec observers and committed nationalists based there who wanted to revisit their own referendum experience. For instance, on 20 September, more than 50 per cent of the media coverage specifically referred to the Quebec referendums.[15] And Quebec was not alone in this regard. Indeed, in the rest of Canada, from 2011, about a third of the media coverage of the Scottish referendum also used this comparison. In fact, the international press as a whole looked back at the Quebec experience in order to understand the issues and consequences of the Scottish vote. Between 2011 and 2013, there were around 2000 reports per year worldwide which treated both Quebec and Scotland at the same time. In 2014, there were nearly 5500 reports comparing the two nations.[16]

Nevertheless, if the comparison with the Quebec case seems so natural for most countries, for Quebec, the comparison is at a different level. The Scottish referendum campaign was seen through the prism of the Quebec experience, as if Quebecers were performing their own psychoanalysis using this external experience as both a justification and an outlet. For instance, the coverage would seek to discuss whether this quest for Scottish independence is justified or not; how Scottish nationalism differs, and how Quebecers could be inspired; or how the agreement on the referendum process and the respect for the results are stronger in Scotland than Quebec. The close result of 1995 remains traumatic for the supporters of both Yes and No, a wound that has not yet healed. The Scottish referendum induced Quebecers to remember their own experience and one can even argue that the fact that No has prevailed in Scotland, as in the two Quebec referendums, probably allowed reporters and columnists to continue their coverage long after the vote, and to make further connections between these events.[17]

The Quebec Media Coverage

We focused our analysis on six weeks, from 1 September to 15 October 2014, which was the most concentrated period of articles, features and blogs on the Scottish referendum.[18] Using the software *Eureka.cc* that identifies French media in America, we found nearly 1200 entries containing the keywords *'référendum'* and *'Écosse'*. However, after removing the entries that were not published in Quebec (for example in Acadia), but mostly by eliminating all duplicates, that is to say, the items which appeared on more than one media platform (for example, in different newspapers owned by the same company), we ended with a corpus of 181 unique units from all types of media: radio, television, newspapers, magazines, blogs. Taking into account all platforms, half of our corpus was in the form of articles (54 per cent), then columns (14.9 per cent) and interviews (13.3 per cent), but also open letters (5 per cent), editorials (4.4 per cent), expert letters (2.8 per cent), *reportages* (2.2 per cent), short news items (1.7 per cent) and blogs (1.7 per cent).

Since the Scottish referendum is a subject so inextricably linked to Quebec political life, it was not surprising that, unlike other international news covered by foreign news agencies, the majority of our corpus came from Quebec sources. And less than a quarter came from news agencies (AFP, Reuters, Associated Press: 24.3 per cent) or the BBC (0.6 per cent), and it mainly consisted of articles with technical information, such as the voting results. As is the case in many other parts of the world, the Quebec media landscape is dominated by a few large groups which own several media platforms. Some 26.5 per cent of our material came from the Gesca Group, a subsidiary of Power Corporation (*La Presse, Le Soleil, Le Droit, La Tribune, Le Nouvelliste* and *Le Quotidien*); 14.4 per cent from the independent newspaper *Le Devoir*; 11.6 per cent from the *Québecor* Group (the TV channels *TVA* and *LCN*, the dailies *Le Journal de Montréal, Le Journal de Québec* and *24 heures*, the Internet portal *Canoe.ca* and the news agency QMI); 10.3 per cent from the public broadcaster ICI Radio-Canada (the TV Channels ICI and RDI, the group of radio stations ICI Première and the Internet portal ICI *Radio-Canada.ca*); and 6.1 per cent from the Transcontinental Group (the magazines *Les Affaires, Finance et Investissement* and the *Métro* daily). Other items came from the Canadian Press (2.8 per cent), Rogers Telecommunications Group (the magazine *L'Actualité*: 1.7 per cent), *Le Huffington Post Québec* (1.1 per cent) and the radio stations of the Cogeco Group (0.6 per cent).

Most of this coverage was derived from Quebec sources, but even more significantly, the majority of the authors of articles and reports published by Quebec media (thus excluding foreign news agencies) were based in Quebec (52.2 per cent), while only a quarter of the authors were located in Scotland (25.4 per cent), or in the rest of the UK (6.4 per cent), Europe (3.8 per cent) or the rest of Canada (3.3 per cent), the remainder coming from a non-identified location (8.9 per cent). When the media coverage came from Scotland, it gave voice to few foreign correspondents, but rather to Quebec observers who went there to follow the campaign. Therefore, the Scottish referendum campaign was often covered with the Quebec issue clearly in the background. In over half of the material (55.8 per cent), open comparisons were made between the two referendum campaigns; Catalonia, which faces a similar situation, was only mentioned in a quarter of the cases (24.9 per cent).

The issues at the forefront

Despite what one might expect, the media coverage of referendum campaigns is very similar to that of election campaigns.[19] Coverage of the 1995 Quebec referendum was no exception and consequently put much more emphasis on the personalities of the leaders and the various events of the campaign than on real issues and contextualisation.[20] In order to compare the Scottish referendum coverage, we took some elements from the analysis grid of Jenkins and Mendelsohn who studied media coverage of the referendum campaign of 1995. We noted that the coverage of the Scottish referendum campaign differed fundamentally in one important respect from the coverage of the Quebec referendum campaign of 1995. Because of the constant comparison with Quebec, authors had to constantly explain the issues and the context. As a result, discussion about the referendum issues (60.8 per cent) was greater than the coverage of the campaign itself (39.2 per cent).

The main topics covered were related to the division of powers between Scotland and the UK (87 references), as well as to the issues related to the independence of Scotland (61). Also addressed were the costs of sovereignty (54) and the shock wave that could affect other nations (53) following the result (51). The most important concerns were related to exchange rates and currency (40 references), management of natural resources (36), international treaties (32) and social programs (21) which Scotland shares with the UK. The shadow of the 1995 Quebec referendum was still present though, in references to the clarity of the question (31 references), the referendum process itself (30) and the impact on the unity of Great Britain (30). As in 1995, economic issues were also one of the main concerns, for example, those related to banks and finance (30 references). Finally, several articles focused specifically on issues related to Scottish nationalism (26 references), the history of Scotland (24) and Scottish culture (18). Also addressed were the differences between Scottish nationalism and Quebec nationalism, some reports taking the opportunity to say that the two nationalisms are different in many ways.

The importance of testimony

Although we noticed that the referendum issues were given much more attention than the referendum campaign itself, some aspects were very similar to the coverage of the Quebec referendum of 1995. For example, when items referred to events of the campaign, they concerned mainly strategic issues (32.8 per cent) and the activities of politicians (23.1 per cent). One difference though was the high number of citizen testimonies (25.4 per cent) while opinion polls, although quite important when the trend turned in favour of Yes, were little covered (10.4 per cent), as was also the case for other campaign events (8.3 per cent). The coverage also adopted a more human face, including the presence of observers from Quebec in Scotland who related their experiences, and also in Scottish testimonies collected by journalists, including testimonies from 33 people associated with the Yes side and 19 associated with the No side. Thus, in addition to the authors who were observers, there were eight references to observers being interviewed by journalists. In the 181 news items, there were also 72 references to politicians from Quebec who observed the conduct of the referendum campaign in Scotland. Canadian and Quebec politicians who were not associated with the sovereignty movement were mainly cited in relation to their reactions to the results of the vote, including the federal Prime Minister Stephen Harper (8 references), the Quebec Premier Philippe Couillard (13) and other politicians (9). It is interesting to see that Jean Chrétien, the former Canadian Prime Minister associated with the No camp in 1995, and Stéphane Dion, former federal minister associated with the 2000 Clarity Act, which seeks to define the terms of a possible future referendum in Quebec, received respectively 15 and 10 mentions, even though they are no longer in office,[21] indicating the importance of the historical approach Quebec has followed in seeking to explain the Scottish referendum. In addition, the constant reference to the past was also shown by the high number of references to experts (46), although none are specialists on Scotland.

Scottish and British protagonists were also present. This coverage was marked by the presence of Alex Salmond (86 references) and other politicians or groups supporting the Yes side (18), by David Cameron (71), Alistair Darling (27), Gordon Brown (21) and other politicians or groups associated with the No side (39 references). Thus, despite the high stakes, the referendum was not in any way disembodied, coverage focusing mainly on the roles of protagonists who defended their positions. Many references were made to well-known personalities, such as Sean Connery (7 references), Andy Murray (6) and other 'stars' associated with Yes (21); and J. K. Rowling (7), and 22 other personalities supporting the No side. This coverage thus tried to provide 'faces' to the Scottish referendum campaign.

A balanced media coverage

The general tone of journalistic commentaries was factual (85.6 per cent), a few times negative (6.6 per cent) – especially in the newspapers from Gesca and those from Quebecor – occasionally humorous (3.3 per cent), or sarcastic (1.7 per cent) and even dramatic (0.6 per cent), but very little was positive (2.2 per cent). With respect to the tone of coverage of the Yes side, it was rather nuanced (79 per cent), but 18.8 per cent of the coverage was favourable, especially in Le Devoir, Le Huffington Post Québec and Gesca, while only 2.2 per cent was not favourable. As for the tone of the coverage of the No side, the majority of articles were nuanced too (86.7 per cent), while 10 per cent were unfavourable (especially in Le Devoir and Gesca) and only 3.3 per cent were favourable. Journalism was thus quite nuanced; most pieces came mainly from the pens of editorialists, columnists or bloggers. Presumably the editorial positions of the different newspapers explains the greater prominence of pro-Yes material in the case of Le Devoir, the only newspaper to support Quebec sovereignty, while the pro-No bias of Gesca can be explained by its editorial policy in favour of Canadian unity. There were also many columnists and bloggers linked to this group. In the case of Québecor, even if the owner has now made the leap into politics under the banner of the Parti Québécois, the company's newspapers never had a defined editorial line. Sun Media, a subsidiary or Québecor published in the rest of Canada, has often been accused of 'Quebec bashing', despite the political position of the owner. Thus, the overall comparison with Quebec was rather nuanced (82.3 per cent); it was nevertheless positive in 10 per cent of cases and negative in 7.7 per cent, *Le Devoir* and *Le Huffington Post Québec* providing much of the most positive coverage (in relation to the Yes side), while Quebecor and Gesca were once again more negative than others.

Conclusion

The Scottish referendum campaign came after a Quebec election campaign where the Parti Québécois (the sovereignist party) lost power in favour of a party which had held up throughout the campaign the spectre of a new referendum on the national question as the ultimate diversion for voters. As was noted earlier, the word 'referendum' has a deep significance for Quebecers, being linked to several difficult historical episodes in the province's relationship with the rest of Canada. The sovereignty movement is still present, in a latent mode, but no longer has the strength of the early 1990s. However, the Scottish referendum was for many Quebecers a good opportunity to recharge their ideas and motivation, hence the significant presence of Quebec observers in Scotland. There is a great curiosity about this small nation which has had a somewhat similar past to that of Quebec. Even though international news is usually not at the front of the media scene in Quebec, the Scottish referendum broke all media coverage records. Quebecers felt challenged by what was happening there. The Scottish referendum was an opportunity for various editors, columnists and bloggers to make a comparison between the two situations, particularly with respect to the type of nationalism, but also between the two referendum processes. And as was the case with much of the international press, Quebec media coverage could not escape the comparison. However, in the case of Quebec, there was more. Indeed, it was a way to revisit its past, its dreams and aspirations. Consequently, media coverage did analyse and dissect all aspects and issues of the campaign, much more than it did during its own referendum in 1995. At the same time, it gave a human face to this campaign, offering much room to the testimony of observers, citizens and politicians. It thus presented a reality rooted in the aspirations, hopes and concerns of its protagonists. The Scottish referendum was actually covered as if it were a domestic Quebec issue.

Notes

1. The exact wording of the question was: 'Are you in favour of the passing of an Act prohibiting the importation, manufacture or sale of spirits, wine, ale, beer, cider and all other alcoholic liquors for use as beverage?'.
2. The word 'plebiscite' was used instead of the word referendum, but it means the same concept. Chief Electoral Officer of Quebec, *La consultation populaire au Canada et au Québec*, 3rd edn, 2011.
3. The exact wording of the question was: 'Are you in favour of releasing the Government from any obligations arising out of any past commitments restricting the methods of raising men for military service?'
4. André Laurendeau, *La crise de la conscription* (Ottawa: Éditions du Jour, 1962), p. 40.
5. On 1 April 1918 riots took place in Quebec City against compulsory military service

and the army, sent by Ottawa, dispersed the crowd with machine guns, killing four people and injuring seventy others.

6. According to the report published by the *Royal Commission on Bilingualism and Biculturalism* (1963–9), Francophones were under-represented in the public service and the country's business community. Statistics dating from 1961 about the average salary of Quebec men classified by ethnicity also revealed that all ethnic groups were better paid than Francophones with the exception of Natives.

7. Pierre Vallières, *Nègres Blancs d'Amérique* (Montreal: Parti Pris, 1968).

8. The exact wording of the question was: 'The Government of Quebec has made public its proposal to negotiate a new agreement with the rest of Canada, based on the equality of nations; this agreement would enable Quebec to acquire the exclusive power to make its laws, levy its taxes and establish relations abroad – in other words, sovereignty – and at the same time to maintain with Canada an economic association including a common currency; any change in political status resulting from these negotiations will only be implemented with popular approval through another referendum; on these terms, do you give the Government of Quebec the mandate to negotiate the proposed agreement between Quebec and Canada?'

9. Even before its ratification, six provinces challenged the legality of the unilateral repatriation of the constitution and three of them, Quebec, Manitoba and Newfoundland, appealed to the Supreme Court of Canada. On 28 September 1981, the Court held that even if one could question the legitimacy of the process, the repatriation was legal if it was approved by a number of provinces, but without specifying the number.

10. Frédéric Bastien, *The Battle of London: Trudeau, Thatcher, and the Fight for Canada's Constitution* (Toronto: Dundurn, 2014).

11. The question was: 'Do you agree that the Constitution of Canada should be renewed on the basis of the agreement reached on August 28, 1992?'

12. The question was: 'Do you agree that Quebec should become sovereign after having made a formal offer to Canada for a new economic and political partnership within the scope of the bill respecting the future of Quebec and of the agreement signed on June 12, 1995?'

13. Influence Communication, *État de la nouvelle: Bilan 2014 Québec* <http://www.influencecommunication.com/sites/default/files/bilan-2014-qc.pdf>, December 2014, p. 25.

14. Ibid., p. 24.

15. Ibid., p. 25.

16. Ibid., p. 25.

17. Ibid., p. 24.

18. I would like to thank Bernard Beausoleil-Chartrand, Master student at Université de Sherbrooke, who participated in the codification of the corpus for the content analysis.

19. Stephen Tierney, *Constitutional Referendums: The Theory and Practice of Republican Deliberation* (Oxford: Oxford University Press, 2012), pp. 123–4.

20. R. W. Jenkins and M. Mendelsohn, 'The news media and referendums', in M. Mendelsohn and A. Parkin (eds), *Referendum Democracy: Citizens, Elites and Deliberation in Referendum Campaigns* (Houndsmill: Palgrave, 2001), pp. 211–30.

21. Stéphane Dion is still Member of Parliament in Ottawa.

18

The Scotland Referendum in the English-language Canadian Media

Christopher Waddell

Coverage of Scotland's referendum in Canada's English-language media highlights all the shortcomings that have come to dominate the performance of the Canadian media in the last decade as a result of the online revolution, the dramatic decline in advertising revenue and massive layoffs and cost-cutting across reporting and editing ranks in all the country's mainstream print, broadcast and online media.

Canadian news organisations reported on the referendum campaign in a largely episodic fashion that reflected the cutbacks in foreign correspondents employed by the Canadian media. Much of the time the story was simply ignored. When it appeared possible that Scots would vote for independence, there was a rush of last-minute coverage with all the contextual shortcomings that are integral parts of parachute journalism by foreign correspondents.

At least, however, in the last days before the vote, major Canadian news organisations sent their own reporters to Scotland from Canada so Canadian audiences would get the story through Canadian eyes. For almost all the preceding year that simply did not happen, largely due to the decline in the number of foreign correspondents. Even the remaining few Canadian correspondents based in London rarely ventured north during the year before the vote, as they were often preoccupied by whatever major international stories were underway in Europe or the Middle East at the time. That meant for much of the year before the referendum, any knowledge of the campaign Canadians received from their media came from reporters working for international news wire services such as Bloomberg and Associated Press or the syndicated service of Britain's *Daily Telegraph* or the *Washington Post* in the United States. Canadians were not told most of the story through Canadian eyes.

There were two other common features of coverage during the year before 18 September 2014. Much of the material published and broadcast did not emanate from Scotland but instead came from Toronto, London, Montreal and Ottawa. There is rarely, if ever, a situation where either reporting or commenting is better done from a distance than from on the ground where events are taking place. But in an era of squeezed financial resources and cutbacks, that long-distance reporting is now commonplace, frequently to the detriment of audiences' understanding of the stories presented to them. Issues and context integral to understanding the significance of stories are often blurred. Few journalists would advocate reporting from afar but newsroom managers increasingly rely on it as a way of creating the illusion of 'covering' stories. It should be noted here that this critique is only partly applicable to stories filed from London. It was an important place line for half the story – how the British government addressed economic concerns and details of how London promised to change the status quo if Scots voted no. Frequently though, in the Canadian media, it was the place line of choice for covering the broader campaign itself.

Linked to the place lines far removed from Scottish voters was the degree to which coverage of the campaign in the Canadian media relied on columnists rather than news reporting. Instead of facts, Canadian audiences frequently received opinions and interpretations from afar about elements of the campaign, issues and the potential outcome. This, too, is consistent with the blurring of lines between news and opinion in the Canadian mainstream media as it tries to maintain its relevance in the face of the onslaught of online competition and widespread criticism of the media's deteriorating performance and credibility.

Finally, much of the coverage tended towards parochialism. Scotland's campaign, decision and post-referendum future and options were regularly framed for Canadian audiences through the prism of Quebec and the long struggle for independence by the Parti Québécois (PQ) that lost referendums in 1980 and 1995 (the latter by the narrowest of margins, 50.58 per cent voting no and 49.42 per cent voting yes). Some of the Quebec tinge to coverage of Scotland reflected the communication in the years leading up to Scotland's vote between the Scottish National Party and the PQ. Additionally, many of the issues in the Scottish campaign, such as use of the United Kingdom's currency, post-independence economic prospects, the specifics of how to break up a country and even the clarity of the question facing Scottish voters (as compared to the convoluted questions asked in Quebec) were echoes of what had happened and was happening in Quebec.

Framing foreign stories and coverage in a context with local references that are familiar to a domestic audience is nothing new. In this instance, to some degree, that was hard to avoid and might have helped Canadians understand the arguments of the Yes and No forces in Scotland. But there are important reasons to believe there was inherent interest among Canadians in Scotland's fate, independent of the Quebec context. Yet that rarely seemed to enter the minds of Canada's media managers in determining how much attention to devote to the referendum. The limited coverage of the campaign seemed to ignore the fact that Scots have been prominent leaders in Canada's cultural, social, business and economic development:

> The Scots have immigrated to Canada in steady and substantial numbers for
> over 200 years, with the connection between Scotland and Canada stretching

farther – to the 17th century. Scots have been involved in every aspect of Canada's development as explorers, educators, businessmen, politicians, writers and artists.

The Scots are among the first Europeans to establish themselves in Canada and are the third largest ethnic group in the country. In the 2011 National Household Survey, a total of 4,714,970 Canadians, or 14.1 per cent of the population, listed themselves as being of Scottish origin (single and multiple responses).[1]

Despite that, English-language Canadian media had at best limited interest in Scotland's referendum until the campaign's final two weeks when it suddenly appeared that the Yes side might win. That Canadian media ambivalence to the referendum likely had a domestic cause that can be traced directly to the events of 7 April 2014. That night the federalist Liberal Party of Quebec scored a stunning provincial election victory, easily winning a majority government defeating the twenty-month-old separatist Parti Québécois minority government that had called the vote in the certain expectation it could win a majority and move Quebec closer to independence from Canada.

It was not so much the defeat itself, but the comprehensive nature of the PQ's collapse and the demonstration of the shrinking support for independence that was so breathtaking. The party won only 25.4 per cent of the vote. That was its worst result since its first election campaign in 1970 when the party took 23.1 per cent. Pauline Marois, the PQ premier, lost her own seat and the party struggled throughout the remainder of 2014 without a leader, with no replacement to be selected until the first quarter of 2015. Adding to the sense of defeat around the independence movement, support for the PQ began to collapse not long after the Parti Québécois' star candidate recruit Pierre Karl Péladeau, who controls Quebecor, the province's dominant media player, proclaimed early in the campaign that he wanted Quebec to be a country. It was quickly clear in response that many voters had no interest in another round of brinksmanship with the federal government that would be the prelude to a third independence referendum. Quebeckers were more concerned about practical issues such as the state of the economy.

A mid-campaign statement by Liberal leader, soon to become premier, Philippe Couillard highlighted the degree to which the independence movement's world, based largely on the argument on the need for a separate country to preserve the French language and culture, had turned upside down.

'There's not a single parent in Quebec that doesn't hope their child will be bilingual. Not a single one,' Couilliard bluntly commented. 'It's a tremendous advantage in life and it's been portrayed as a threat. I cannot accept that.'[2]

The collapse of the Parti Québécois changed the dynamic completely in terms of Canadian interest in Scotland's future. Instead of a spring and summer heading to 18 September, in which the Quebec government would be regularly trying to turn media attention and the national political focus to events in the

United Kingdom, there was suddenly nothing. There was no PQ using the regular media platform of Quebec's National Assembly and the levers of government to ask why won't Ottawa match whatever Westminster might offer to Edinburgh to vote no. Even when PQ members tried to raise such comparisons, the media paid no attention. Independence had just been shown to be a fading dream of a shrinking segment of Quebec society, so why should the media pay attention to what they said about Scotland?

If independence had evaporated as an immediate threat in Canada, there was no domestic angle to Scotland's decision which could be covered. Combine that with what seemed at the time little chance of Scotland voting Yes, and the English-language media in Canada concluded there were more important stories to cover with their diminishing resources. That changed suddenly in early September. A No victory was no story but a Yes win would be news. The Canadian media responded with print, online and broadcast coverage in the campaign's final ten days, dispatching Canadian reporters to Scotland and giving their stories some prominence. That lasted until about 22 September. By the end of September it was back to normal, with no consistent attention paid to the longer-term future of Scotland and of the United Kingdom.

The Structure of the English-language Media in Canada

The structure and financial struggles of the Canadian media played a major role in how Canadians learned about the referendum campaign. Few countries can match the degree of media concentration of ownership in Canada. Postmedia owns the daily newspapers and news websites in virtually all of Canada's major cities and also operates the *National Post*, the country's second national newspaper behind the *Globe and Mail*, the longstanding leader, owned by the Thomson family, and BCE, a major telecom, wireless and Internet service provider. The *Toronto Star*, in addition to being Canada's largest newspaper by circulation in the country's biggest city, owns a handful of other daily papers in Ontario, Canada's largest province, and many community and weekly newspapers across the country. Its main competitor in community newspaper ownership is a subsidiary of Quebecor, which also owns many dailies in smaller Ontario cities. Quebecor also owns the *Sun* tabloid chain of dailies in Ottawa, Calgary, Winnipeg and Toronto. There are three national television networks: CTV, Global and the Canadian Broadcasting Corporation (CBC), the public broadcaster. All three have local stations across the country as well as producing daily national newscasts. CTV and the CBC also have all-news specialty channels but their content was not included in this study.

The Canadian media faces the same economic challenges as media in other countries, with sharply declining advertising revenue and shrinking audiences. That means publications within a chain all tend to run the same story from the same reporter at the same time. This study's tabulation of the number of stories published and broadcast about the referendum captures the range of publications reporting on the issue, but there is frequently considerable duplication across news organisations, with the same story or column by the same journalist appearing in several publications almost concurrently.

Methodology

The study collected all stories written and produced about the Scottish referendum or Scottish independence found in the Canadian Newsstand Compete database[3] between 1 September 2013 and 15 October 2014. This includes newspaper and online stories and broadcast scripts. A searchable database built to include all the stories identified the date and name of publication or broadcast, the place line, the headline and reporter and categorised each as news, opinion, feature, editorials or letters to the editor. Each story was also categorised according to the main topic or issues covered in the story, with many listed as covering multiple topics.

Overall Coverage

The review found 691 stories in the mainstream Canadian media database over the 13 months. Of that total, 549 were published, broadcast or posted in September 2014, highlighting the degree to which the referendum was a less than a one-month event for most of the Canadian media. By two weeks after voting day, coverage had fallen to 12 stories during the first half of October. There were only three other months where the total number of stories in the Canadian media topped single digits. In November 2013, 10 stories ran, primarily concurrent with the Scottish government's release of *Scotland's Future* – its vision of how Scotland would progress to independence after a Yes vote. There were 16 stories in February 2014 and 30 in March 2014, before the total fell back down to 9 in April. That burst of Canadian media interest was linked to the Quebec provincial election campaign running from late February throughout March, leading to the 7 April vote. The Parti Québécois's desire for independence was a dominant theme of that campaign, drawing inevitable media comparisons to what was happening or going to happen in Scotland. When the election revealed limited interest in independence among Quebeckers, Scotland dropped off the Canadian media map.

The extent to which the attention of the Canadian media centred around referendum day itself can be seen in Figure 18.1, which charts on a daily basis the number of referendum-related stories that appeared during September 2014.

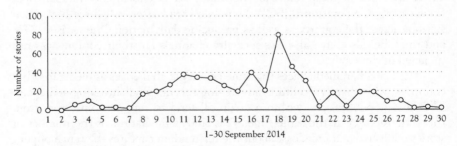

Figure 18.1 Number of stories in September 2014.

Coverage peaked around voting day. The earlier spike around 10–12 September reflected the publication of polls that suggested the Yes side just might win. From that point Canadian television networks assigned reporters to cover events on the ground in Scotland until referendum day.

Two caveats are worth noting. There are relatively few Sunday newspapers in Canada, which is reflected in the minimal number of stories on Sundays in September (7, 14, 21 and 28). Additionally, Canada's five and a half time zones can create confusion about when campaign issues and results appeared in which day's publications or broadcasts. As an example, voting results from Glasgow (although narrowly in favour of independence but not enough to offset the number of No votes elsewhere) sealed the fate of the Yes side when announced just prior to midnight on 18 September in North America's Eastern time zone (Toronto, Ottawa and Montreal), which is 9:00 p.m. in Vancouver. So some newscasts had definitive results the night of 18 September while other media outlets, caught by deadlines, did not publish results until 20 September as the evening press deadlines for 19 September morning newspapers passed before the final outcome was known. After 20 September there is a relatively sharp drop-off in the volume of stories published about 'what happens next', after Scots rejected independence.

Types of Stories

Figure 18.2 classifies the stories between September 2013 and 15 October 2014 by type. It is no surprise that news dominated coverage of the referendum and its aftermath. However, for much of the campaign, until its last couple of weeks, there were almost as many columns as news stories appearing in the Canadian

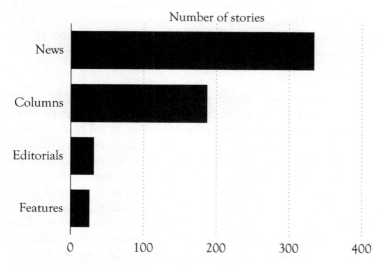

Figure 18.2 Stories by type, September 2013 to 15 October 2014.

media about the referendum. Many were written from Canada or from London but the extent of column and opinion writing compared to news reporting reflects a broader media trend as commenting replaces reporting as a staple of media coverage of many events. There are fewer journalists dedicated to finding out and reporting the news while more and more coverage devolves to commenting on the news, news events or personalities in the news.

During the thirteen months covered by this review, there were almost twice as many news stories as column and opinion pieces written about the campaign and the issues surrounding it. There were very few features written on the referendum and the campaign, which also reflects two growing trends in the Canadian media. The decline of advertising has meant newspapers are thinner with fewer pages and less space for longer feature-length treatment and presentation of stories. Space constraints do not exist online but few Canadian news organisations commission material only for their online sites. It is much more common to take print material and put it online. As well, cutbacks in reporting staff in the face of falling revenue have left few feature writers at most publications so there is both little space and no one to fill it even if it existed. That is also true in television where current affairs programmes have been abandoned by many broadcasters and even newscast stories are getting shorter. Assigning their own reporters to Scotland only for the campaign's final days was a clear sign that the interests of Canadian news organisations did not extend to any substantive degree beyond straight news coverage. Independent of the tally of columns and opinion pieces, Canadian news organisations did run editorials about the referendum that reached a unanimous conclusion – Scotland should remain in the United Kingdom. There were no editorials advocating independence for Scotland but several noted that Scotland's many legitimate concerns could be best addressed by the United Kingdom introducing a form of federalism, as in Canada. There were also almost four dozen letters to editors about the referendum, some advocating a Yes vote and many coming from those with a link to Scotland.

Sources of the Coverage

An analysis of place lines for the stories in September 2014 (Figure 18.3) is consistent with the financial problems facing the media. The largest single place line for Canadian media stories about the referendum was Toronto – not surprising, since it is the epicentre of the country's media and many columnists are based in Toronto. London was second. This reflects actual campaign conditions in which the pronouncements of the Conservative–Liberal Democrat coalition government, particularly in the frantic final week when it appeared the Yes side might win, were an integral part of the campaign. London is also the home of all Canadian foreign correspondents based in the UK. Coverage from Edinburgh came predominantly in the final days of the campaign as Canadian journalists reported from Scotland, covering the results and the immediate day or so after the referendum. News organisations in Canada also used wire service stories in

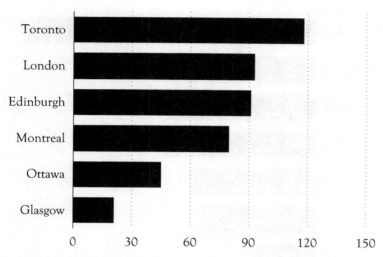

Figure 18.3 Place lines, September 2014.

September that came mostly from Edinburgh. Glasgow was the location of significantly fewer stories. There were also stories from Aberdeen, the Isle of Skye, the Isle of Arran (about whisky), Inverness, Gleneagles and Aviemore. There was an individual story from each of these communities but that story was often published concurrently by several members of a newspaper chain.

Montreal featured fairly prominently as a source of coverage as this often centred on views of the Parti Québécois about the Scottish campaign, including the fact that some PQ members of the National Assembly travelled to Scotland for 18 September. Stories from Ottawa came from the parliamentary press gallery, usually linking Scottish developments to Canadian national politics.

News Organisations

Figures for the number of stories in English-language media in September are presented in Figure 18.4.

The broader the reach of a news organisation across Canada, the more likely it was to cover the referendum in depth. However, as the overall figures demonstrate, most of this coverage came in September 2014. Canada's self-proclaimed national newspaper, the *Globe and Mail*, published 70 stories in September, more than a third more stories than any other Canadian news organisation. Over the full thirteen months the *Globe* ran 96 stories. The *Montreal Gazette* had the second highest with 39 (61 during the thirteen months leading up to the vote). The *Gazette* spread its coverage more widely, focusing on the last weeks of the campaign but also making more regular references to Scotland often in columns in April during the Quebec provincial election campaign.

This is consistent with expected approaches to coverage. The *Globe* has more

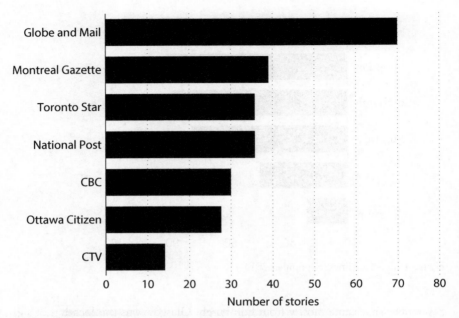

Figure 18.4 Stories by news organisation, September 2014.

foreign correspondents than any other Canadian media outlet and prides itself on its international news. The *Toronto Star* and *National Post* also covered the issue more extensively than other Canadian media, with the *Star* sending one of its Ottawa parliamentary reporters to Scotland for the last ten days of the campaign. The *Gazette* also used a former member of its staff to report from Scotland on a freelance basis in the campaign's final days. That supplemented *Gazette* coverage provided by Postmedia's roving international reporter Matthew Fisher, while the *Globe* sent its London-based correspondent Mark MacKinnon to Scotland fairly regularly in September both for news and feature stories.

Television broadcasters CBC and CTV followed the referendum campaign, sending London-based reporters during the last ten days before 18 September. With the benefit of an hour-long combined national newscast and current affairs program nightly, CBC also took one longer eight-minute look at the Yes campaign with a mini-documentary two days before the vote. CTV supplemented its newscast reporting with a second reporter from its Ottawa bureau who tended to do feature news stories rather than hard news.

Although the statistics suggest a wide range of Canadian media covered the referendum, in fact the coverage came from relatively few journalists. Stories by Postmedia's Fisher appeared in about a dozen separate publications, while the work of London-based freelance columnist Gwynne Dyer is syndicated to many smaller daily and community papers across the country. Each of his columns that dealt with Scotland tended to appear concurrently in more than half a dozen publications across the country.

Finally, Canadian media often used wire services to follow developments in the months leading up to September, with Associated Press stories from both Edinburgh and London appearing 39 times. There were 30 Bloomberg stories published across Canada and a further 21 came from Canadian Press.

Content of the Coverage

Figure 18.5 lists the issues raised in the coverage of the referendum. With coverage centred on the final days of the campaign, it is not surprising that the Canadian media concentrated its attention on the question of who would win and what a Yes vote would mean for Scotland and the United Kingdom. Whether it was stories previewing voter intention, predicting the outcome or even news organisations asking Scots in Canadian communities what they thought should happen, the outcome dominated media coverage. Surprisingly there was not much attention paid to a phenomenon in Quebec that was replicated in Scotland. The Yes side

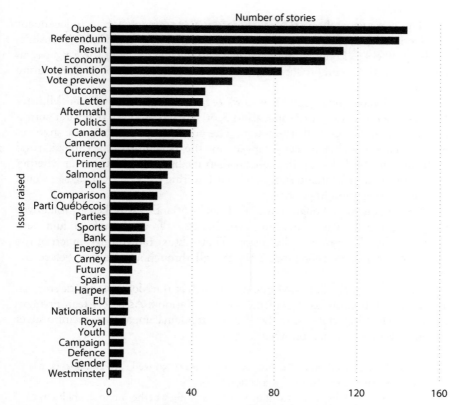

Figure 18.5 Content of coverage, September 2013 to 15 October 2014.

in Quebec tends to poll higher than it actually achieves at the ballot box, which is attributed to the fact that publicly supporting the status quo is usually not a socially acceptable thing to do. It is much easier to at least say you are voting Yes even if you actually vote No. That has happened in Quebec and seemed to have occurred in Scotland as well.

Beyond concentrating on the outcome in the campaign's final couple of weeks, Canadian media organisations had earlier paid some attention to economic issues, principally the currency question, for several reasons. As Governor of the Bank of England, Mark Carney's comments about the limitations of an independent Scotland using the pound attracted Canadian media attention. This was a result of Carney's previous position as the high profile Governor of the Bank of Canada. At the same time the same currency issue has always swirled around the PQ's independence plans – could an independent Quebec use the Canadian dollar? That issue in fact arose again during the spring 2014 Quebec election where the PQ leader Pauline Marois asserted that an independent Quebec could continue to use the Canadian dollar and would like a seat on the board of the Bank of Canada.[4] That comment was ridiculed in other parts of Canada.[5]

The more general question of the economic prospects for an independent Scotland also received some media attention as did corporate threats about shifting head offices to London after a Yes win and the debate about the longer-term future of North Sea oil production and what Scotland could count on for future revenue.

Beyond economics, Canadian news organisations covered Prime Minister David Cameron's last minute appeals to Scotland and promises of greater autonomy if Scotland stuck with the union. The possible link between the involvement of sixteen- and seventeen-year-olds and the dynamism of the campaign and high turnout also led some in the Canadian media to speculate about whether what happened in Scotland suggested that lowering Canada's voting age would increase participation in politics.

Most frequently though, coverage from Scotland was linked in some way to Quebec and the Parti Québécois, whether issues from past referendum campaigns or the 2014 provincial election. That subtext ran through much of the coverage not just in September 2014 but all throughout the year before the vote.

In some cases the link was quite direct, such as the *Montreal Gazette* story on 18 September that quoted PQ member of the National Assembly Jean-Francois Lisée, a leading PQ strategist in the 1995 referendum campaign, as seeing a silver lining for his party no matter what happened.

> He said if Scotland votes Yes and the negotiations go well, 'it's going to be a shining example for the next generation in Quebec.'
>
> If Scotland votes no, it will be worth watching whether London abides by its promise of devolution because that, too, can help Quebec's status, he added.

Contrary to that bravado, there was no evidence as 2014 ended that anyone in Quebec was paying attention to what happened in post-referendum Scotland.

The *Globe and Mail* seemed much closer to capturing the spirit of what was now happening in Quebec in its 13 September editorial, written as a 'Dear Scotland' letter calling for a No vote. The *Globe* noted:

> Once upon a time in Quebec, the independence option was the choice of the young as it is in Scotland. That time has passed; most young Quebeckers today do not imagine that their very real economic and social challenges will be addressed by drawing a new border. But it took us half a century to get to this point. The same can happen for you too.
>
> So dear cousins from beyond the seas, here is our advice and our plea. Stay in the United Kingdom. Let time pass and passions subside. Make changes happen, but within the U.K. And meet us back here in, say 2040. You can take the U.K. apart then if you want to. We think you will not. And we know this: if you take it apart now, you can never, ever put it back together again.

The companion post-referendum editorial from the *Globe* was a 'Dear Great Britain' letter on 20 September stating bluntly:

> Federalism makes sense for Britain now . . . federalism works when the various constituencies making up the federation feel they are treated equally. There can and will be arguments about what 'equal' means. But any constitutional set-up that gives one province or state extra powers or guarantees denied its peer governments, and the voters of those other constituencies, is liable to turn into a source of festering resentment.

The editorial concluded by reviewing the historic links between Canada and the United Kingdom:

> You can learn something from our experience because we have so much in common. We used to be close family and now we're more like ever more distant relatives, which means that your history and your points of tension are not exactly the same as ours, and neither will be your solutions. Based on our experience, our advice comes down to this: prudence. Exercise extreme caution. Change as much of your constitution as you must – and as little as you can. Good luck.

After the Vote

In the days and weeks following the vote, a few Canadian news organisations ran stories that cast their eyes to Spain, asking whether the Scottish results would have an impact in Catalonia. There was also Canadian media discussion about whether a No vote really means no, or is it the start of what some pundits called a 'Neverendum' – as in Quebec, pressure for endless votes unwilling to accept No for an answer until the independence side finally wins, which in their view would require no further votes. There was, though, no sustained journalistic interest in

Canada in what Westminster might do and how Prime Minister Cameron was meeting his pre-vote commitments to devolve more power to Edinburgh.

Conclusion

The English-language Canadian media provided competent yet far from memorable coverage of Scotland's referendum, with little focus on the campaign and an emphasis on the immediate run-up to voting day all framed by the question will it be a Yes or No. There was no sustained coverage leading to the vote that explained the issues at play or any effort in the coverage to chart why the tables seemed to turn so dramatically in the campaign's final couple of weeks. Despite the long history of linkages between Canada and Scotland, the media covered the referendum as it does most other events – a bit of a prelude before the main event, rising interest when the unexpected occurs, then a quick summary of what happened. For the Canadian media, once the result was known, the story was over and it was time to move on.

The frequent comparisons with Quebec meant Canadian audiences might have related more clearly to some aspects of the Scottish vote. At the same time the regular use of that comparison throughout the coverage may leave Canadians thinking that the issue in Scotland is now settled, as it finally appears to be in Quebec. To the extent that English-language Canadian media coverage left Canadians with that impression, it has done them a disservice.

Notes

1. Available at <http://www.thecanadianencyclopedia.ca/en/article/scots/> (last accessed 13 September 2015).
2. Available at <http://globalnews.ca/news/1200430/liberal-leader-speaks-out-on-bilingualism-in-quebec/> (last accessed 13 September 2015).
3. Available at <http://www.proquest.com/products-services/canadian_newsstand.html> (last accessed 13 September 2015).
4. Available at <http://news.nationalpost.com/2014/03/12/an-independent-quebec-wants-to-keep-canadian-dollar-have-seat-at-bank-of-canada-pauline-marois-says/> (last accessed 13 September 2015).
5. Available at <http://www.theglobeandmail.com/globe-debate/editorials/pauline-marois-loonie-delusions/article17472910/> (last accessed 13 September 2015).

19

Australia and the Scottish Independence Referendum

Brian McNair

Introduction

Australia is one of the countries where the Scottish independence campaign had the greatest resonance. Scots, or the descendants of Scots, comprise more than 1.9 million of the Australian population, or 8.9 per cent of the total. This author currently lives and works in Brisbane, where there is a suburb called Kelvin Grove, and streets with obviously Scottish names such as Dunsmore, Clyde and Moy. Across the country, from Perth on the west coast to Mackay in tropical northern Queensland, the evidence of Scottish influence abounds. Famous Australian Scots include Angus and Malcolm Young of iconic rock band AC/DC, the opera singer Joan Sutherland, and a successful newspaper proprietor by the name of Rupert Murdoch.

Having been colonised and shaped by Scots among other nationalities who migrated there from the United Kingdom in the late eighteenth century, whether voluntarily or on penal ships, on 1 January 1901 Australia, with a population of around 4 million, gained its independence from the mother country and was established as a federation – the Commonwealth of Australia – with six states (and later, two territories: the sparsely populated Northern Territory, and the Australian Capital Territory, where Canberra and the seat of government are located). The British monarch remained as Australia's head of state (and still holds that position), but henceforth the country would run its own affairs without the interference of a colonial power. The ousting of Prime Minister Gough Whitlam by the Governor General in 1975 on a constitutional technical-ity cast some doubt on that status, and the issue of Australia's relationship to the UK remains contentious, though dormant for the time being. A referendum on whether Australia should ditch the British monarch and become a republic was held in 1999 (the vote went against), and from time to time calls for a further plebiscite arise in the Australian media.

Those Australians who oppose a republic tend to be the descendants of British immigrants, still a majority of the 22 million population, who feel a cultural connection with the UK and wish to retain it. Supporters of a republic draw on the increasingly multicultural, non-Anglo Saxon make-up of the population, who care little for the rituals of British or any other monarchy. Those in Australia who advocate for a republic, or who do not much care one way or the other as long as the economy is healthy, tend to be from later waves of migration – from Southeast Asia, southern Europe and the Asia-Pacific region. Whether for or against a royal head of state, however, Australians prize their independence and national identity, and for that reason too, looked upon Scotland's recent debate with great interest.

In Scotland, on the other hand, the pro-independence lobby often cited Australia as an example of what independence could achieve. If Australia could do it, sitting down there on the other side of the earth, the SNP and others argued, why not Scotland, with its strategic position at the edge of Europe, its oil reserves, and its global profile to build on?

This essay does not seek to evaluate the merits of that comparison, or of the pro-independence case overall, but to examine how, given the close historical and cultural ties which exist between Australia and the United Kingdom (including Scotland), the Scottish independence referendum was reported, analysed and made sense of in the Australian media. The analysis is based on mainstream news coverage (online and print media) produced in Australia and accessed from the Internet between January 2012 and the end of September 2014 (two weeks after the referendum on 18 September). A total of 95 items were included in the sample, which does not include broadcast news coverage or specialist current affairs periodicals. The online sites of broadcasters such as the ABC and SBS were included in the sample. The great majority of these items were published in the run-up to polling day, in August and September 2014, with spikes in the frequency of items around particular events such as the Commonwealth Games in Glasgow.

Some Background

Since achieving its own independence in 1901, Australia's population has expanded to its current 22 million. Australians enjoy a prosperous economy, with a strong liberal democracy modelled closely on the UK's parliamentary system. Australia successfully avoided the worst effects of the global financial crisis of 2008, benefiting not just from a more tightly regulated banking system than was the case in the US and the UK, but a practically insatiable demand in nearby Asia for its raw materials, minerals and energy resources, and agriculture. As of this writing, Australia enjoyed one of the highest standards of living in the OECD, with unemployment and public debt comparatively low.

Australia's media system is sophisticated and well-resourced, though smaller than that of the UK. The main Australian public service broadcasting organisation, the ABC, has only a sixth of the budget of the BBC, with around a third of the population to service. The Australian market supports only five national press titles compared to the UK's twenty-two. As in comparable countries Australia's traditional media in print and broadcast are under pressure from online and digital platforms, and the industry is in transitional turmoil, shedding jobs and infrastructure as ratings and circulations fall. On the other hand, the decline of the 'old' Australian news media has been slower and less steep than in the US or the UK, and big corporations such as News Corp and Fairfax still make substantial profits.

The main Australian national press outlets are *The Australian*, the *Sydney Morning Herald*, *The Age*, the *Herald Sun* and the *Daily Telegraph* (the latter, unlike its namesake in the UK, a red-top tabloid owned by News Corp which functions as a propaganda outlet for the right wing of Australian politics).

Apart from News Corp, the main providers of news in Australia are Fairfax, which publishes the Melbourne *Age* and the *Herald Sun* amongst other titles, and the public service broadcasters – the Australian Broadcasting Corporation (ABC) and the Special Broadcasting Service (SBS). Commercial free-to-air channels operate local news services, and News Corp runs a twenty-four-hour news service on its Foxtel network.

In short, the Australian news media environment is similar in many ways to that of the UK: a small number of big providers dominate the market, with high concentration of ownership; there is a relatively well-funded public service media sector, bound by the same rules of impartiality as in the UK; and a burgeoning online sector comprising titles such as *Crikey*, bloggers and social networkers on Twitter, Facebook, and other platforms, and online editions of established providers.

Overview of Australia's Referendum Coverage

As a general statement, Australian news coverage of the Scottish independence debate can be divided into two categories: reportage of and commentary on the Scottish debate itself, including opinion polls, key moments in the campaign, and analysis of the consequences of a Yes vote for the UK and elsewhere. Second, coverage using the Scottish referendum debate as a hook to explore relevant issues in Australia, such as the ongoing campaign for republicanism, and the implications of independence for Australian banks with assets in Scotland (such as National Australia Bank, owner of the Scottish-based Clydesdale).

Australian media coverage of the Scottish independence referendum was, as one would expect, sparse in the years and months leading up to polling day on 18 September 2014. Despite the relative cultural proximity of Scotland and Australia, a referendum involving a small country of around 5 million people was not going to be very newsworthy to a nation 12,000 miles away until the official campaign began. Between 2011 and mid-2014, therefore, there were only a hand-ful of items on the issue, many of them reprinted from overseas publications such as *The Times* of London (sister title to *The Australian* and *Daily Telegraph*).

In that early phase of the campaign coverage tended to light-hearted, human interest stories such as a piece in *The Australian* of 21 February 2012, which reported that nationalists in the Basque region of Spain were jealous of the

Scottish referendum, and that if the latter were successful, nationalists in the Basque country would seek annexation by an independent Scotland.[1] The president of the Basque Nationalist Party was quoted as saying that 'we should annex the Basque country to Scotland because they are going to be able to choose their future whereas we cannot'. The statement was intended to be read as satirical humour, while hinting at the broader European significance of the Scottish debate.

In April 2012 the Melbourne-based *Herald Sun* ran a piece by legal correspondent David Denton linking the Scottish debate to the domestic debate on the merits of an Australian republic. Would independence have any impact, he asked, 'for Australia and its people who by our own Constitution agreed to unite in one indissoluble Federal Commonwealth under the Crown?'[2] The piece went on to explore the nuances of constitutional law, and Australia's relationship to the UK, with or without Scotland in it. This aspect of the question appeared again in coverage towards the end of the campaign. In early September 2014 the ABC's website quoted another legal expert on the possibility that an independent Scotland would lead to a republican Australia with no British monarch as head of state.

At the end of August 2012, two years before polling day, ABC radio broadcast a live debate on independence from the Edinburgh Festival, hosted by senior arts journalist and overtly republican Phillip Adams. The festival is a regular item on the ABC news calendar, and on this occasion the coincidence of the referendum campaign was judged to justify a dedicated hour of debate. Adams introduced the programme with facts and figures on Scotland's and the UK's economy, and his guests, former first minister Henry McLeish and Paul Henderson Scott, veteran Scottish nationalist.

The Australian media were silent on the issue from then until October 2012, when UK Prime Minister David Cameron formally authorised the referendum. This was the beginning of a 'two-year countdown', at the start of which only 28 per cent of Scots were reported as supporting independence. One article noted that Alex Salmond had achieved a victory in timing the referendum to coincide with the 2014 Commonwealth Games and the 700th anniversary of the Battle of Bannockburn, both events seen by commentators as being likely to boost nationalist fervour in Scotland.

In this case, as for most of the period under examination, Australian coverage reflected spikes in UK press interest. Australia's media do not have extensive networks of foreign correspondents in the UK, and tend to be reliant on stringers, feeds from news agencies, and partner titles such as *The Times*. Until close to polling day there were virtually no locally generated stories about the Scottish referendum in the Australian press. The Australian reader received the same news, if less substantively, on themes such as: would Scotland be able to keep the pound sterling after independence? Would it have to reapply for EU membership? Would the Queen remain head of state of an independent Scotland? Would Scotland remain in NATO, and if so, would it be able to get rid of nuclear weapons on its soil, as promised by the nationalists? As of early 2013, these were the questions emerging in Australian coverage. Articles in this period also reflected opinion polls showing a clear majority against independence.

In October 2013 *The Australian* published a commentary piece by sociologist Stuart Waiton of the University of Abertay, reflecting on the merits of the SNP's decision to give the vote to sixteen-year-olds. Waiton noted the inconsistency in a situation where sixteen-year-olds were deemed mature enough to vote for the future of their country (and by extension of the UK as a whole, which would be fundamentally transformed by a Yes vote) but too immature to be permitted to buy alcohol or tobacco in a corner shop. 'This is a patronizing form of inclusion', wrote Waiton, 'indeed an infantilisation of the importance of voting itself: something given to a section of society who are largely still at school, or dependent on their parents, and have not had to make any truly independent decisions in their lives'.[3]

In November 2013 the Australian Associated Press (AAP) reported the publication of the SNP's 'blueprint' for independence, and on the 27th of that month John McTernan, former media adviser to the Australian Labor Party Prime Minister Julia Gillard, commented on the issues raised by the referendum. McTernan, who has worked extensively for the Scottish and British Labour parties, pointed to the SNP's difficulty in reconciling future membership of the EU (a policy plank post-independence) with the population's dislike of the Euro and free immigration (both EU conditions of membership). 'Whatever else', he noted, 'the next ten months won't be dull.'.[4]

We note at this point the predominance of *The Australian* in coverage of the story. This reflects a general lack of foreign news in the Australian press as a whole. *The Australian* had the advantage of accessing not only agency copy but material produced by News Corp sister titles in the UK. One can also argue that it is in the main, as the only truly national press title, more committed to a decent foreign news coverage than most of the more locally focused outlets. News Corp's main rival in Australia, Fairfax, is widely recognised to be failing as a competitive news provider, sacrificing quality to profit in recent times. Apart from the public service ABC and SBS news services, both required to be impartial in their political coverage, only *The Australian* reported the Scottish referendum in any detail. An editorial on 30 November, for example, presented the arguments of the Yes and No camps in some depth, and provided historical context going back to the Battle of Bannockburn in 1314. A commentary by Gary Johns ('a proud Glasgow man') on 3 December reflected with some derision on the leftist ambitions of the Yes camp – 'a workers' paradise indeed!'.[5] Here we see an example of how *The Australian* often endeavours to encapsulate stories from overseas within a conservative (in Australian terms) framework consistent with the views of its proprietor, Rupert Murdoch. Johns, clearly, was no friend of the welfare state, trade unions, or fair wages, but a staunch advocate of what he called 'bourgeois virtues', and fearful of what would become of them in a post-referendum Scotland. It is perhaps ironic that the Murdoch-owned *Scottish Sun* adopted a less hostile approach to the pro-independence camp, many of whose members were of course *Sun* readers.

In January 2013 News Corp's online outlet *news.com.au* reported an aspect of the referendum story of relevance to Scots in Australia (such as this author). Alex Salmond, it was reported, while denouncing the undemocratic nature of the Westminster Parliament, had announced that only those resident in Scotland on the relevant census date would be entitled to vote. Scots living overseas, temporarily or permanently, would not be allowed to vote. 'This may come as a blow', noted the report, 'to some who may have hoped to support the convivial and polite revolution from the safety of their Aussie homes'.[6]

Australia's second public service broadcaster, SBS, commented in a blog by Scottish-born reporter Brian Thomson on 18 September 2013 (with links to video and audio reports), exactly one year before the referendum, that 'only one third of Scots are currently planning to vote for complete independence. In the eyes of many the Union is not broken and therefore does not need to be fixed'.[7] Throughout the campaign SBS produced or reproduced occasional coverage on the referendum, avoiding opinion in the main. Its coverage tended to adhere to verifiable facts, secondary sources and other corroborated information.

The Australian, on the other hand, published several commentaries and editorials on the subject over the two-year campaign, including a piece in July 2014 by historian Michael Sexton which interpreted the referendum as evidence of England's (elsewhere the article referred to Britain) further decline since the Great War of 1914–18. Sexton noted the irony that in the anniversary of that conflict the United Kingdom should have entered into a political campaign which might end it in its current form. 'What self-respecting nation would not only allow but actually facilitate the possible dismemberment of a centuries-old bond in such a cavalier fashion?'[8]

One of the biggest referendum stories in Australia concerned remarks made by Prime Minister Tony Abbott in August 2014 indicating that he was not a supporter of the Yes camp. Campaigners for independence were not 'friends of freedom' or 'friends of justice', he declared in an interview with *The Times* and 'as a friend of Britain, as an observer from afar, it's hard to see how the world would be helped by an independent Scotland'. Abbott is a strongly pro-UK, pro-monarchy politician in the Australian context, and such a comment is not inconsistent with his broader beliefs, including the controversial award of a knighthood to Prince Philip on Australia Day, 2015. But from a sitting prime minister, they were unusual in their directness. The remarks provoked a response from Alex Salmond, whose spokesperson noted:

> Tony Abbott has a reputation for gaffes, but his bewildering comments have all the hallmarks of one of the Westminster government's international briefings against Scotland. Many Australians, including the great number with close Scottish connections, will look on in bafflement at these remarks – Australia

is a country that has gained its independence from Westminster and has never looked back.[9]

By August 2014, boosted by Glasgow's hosting of the Commonwealth Games and the consequent presence of many more media personnel than usual in the country, the Scottish referendum had become a global news story. Coverage in Australia had become much more frequent, and was featured in more or less all news outlets with any remit to cover foreign affairs. Events such as the Abbott interview, and the implications of British constitutional change for Australia, in addition to the fact noted earlier that nearly 2 million Australians are Scottish or of Scottish descent, gave the story increasing news value as polling day approached.

The newsworthiness of the story further increased as opinion polls indicated a narrowing of the gap between Yes and No, and the increasing likelihood that indeed, one outcome of the process could be the end of the United Kingdom as it had existed for 307 years. As students of journalism know, the presence of drama and uncertainty heighten the news value which accrues to a given story. Just as coverage intensified in the UK itself, so too in the rest of the world, and in Australia, although it remained intermittent and sketchy, usually dependent on overseas sources.

There is no evidence, I will note at this point, of clear pro- or anti-independence bias in the Australian coverage as a whole. Some commentators in the right of centre press, as we have seen, read the campaign in overtly reactionary terms as an unwelcome defeat for 'Great Britishness' and evidence of a rapidly fading empire. Another commentator feared what would be for him an equally unwelcome victory for the advocates of welfare dependence and socialism – Scotland's global reputation as a bastion of publicly funded welfarism had grown steadily in recent years, and especially since the election of the Conservative-led Coalition government in 2010. As Britain moved to the right, Scotland remained on the left, and the SNP – not a traditionally left-of-centre party, but whose leadership had skilfully acquired Scottish Labour's clothes by pursuing social democratic left-of-centre policies such as free NHS prescriptions, free bus travel for the over-seventies and no student fees – were seen by conservatives in Australia as encouraging dependency culture. But these were individual viewpoints and not sustained editorial stances by the titles in which they appeared. No newspaper editorial took the interventionist stance of Tony Abbott, for example.

The Run-up to Referendum Day

Only in the final month of campaigning did the issue become more than one of passing curiosity to the Australian media and the majority of the people. As the possibility of Scottish independence began to look like a probability, with Yes support approaching that of the No campaign, and on the evidence of some polls surpassing it, the issue rose up the news agenda on all platforms.

Specific themes of coverage in the final month of campaigning included analysis of the constitutional implications of a Yes vote for Australia. If the

Australian constitution looked to the monarch of the United Kingdom to provide its head of state, what would happen if there was no UK as conventionally
understood anymore?[10] The *Sydney Morning Herald* asked if the Australian flag
would have to be changed since, in the event of a Yes vote, the UK flag, on which
the Australian flag is based, would no longer incorporate a saltire.[11] A piece in
news.com.au noted the irony that an independent Scotland would face its own
secessionist movement in the Shetland Islands, around whose waters a substantial proportion of Scottish oil reserves were located. The piece also explored the
implications for Scotland's currency and EU membership. The following typifies
the tone of this and other items which set out to explain the issues to Australian
audiences:

> The issue of currency is a crucial one. Mr Salmond wants to keep the UK pound
> and the Bank of England as a central bank, which would make things easy for
> businesses and markets. But the British government has ruled it out, saying they
> can't have it both ways.
>
> The other option is to create a new Scottish currency backed by a central
> bank, which would allow the Scots to maintain control over their own mon-
> etary policy – rather than having interest rates set by the Bank of England, for
> instance. It's thought a Scottish currency could be pegged to the pound to help
> reduce volatility.[12]

At the end of August the *Sydney Morning Herald* reported on the second
live TV debate between Alex Salmond and Alistair Darling. Where Darling had
won the first debate, noted the author, Salmond had 'easily won' the rematch.
'In a snap *Guardian*/ICM poll, 71 per cent of more than 500 respondents judged
that Mr Salmond had won, against 29 per cent who said they thought Labour's
Mr Darling had triumphed.'[13] The *Australian* reported a YouGov poll showing
that the No:Yes gap in the polls had shrunk to 6 per cent, from a 14 per cent
No lead in August.[14] On 7 September SBS reported that for the first time the
Yes camp had taken the lead in a YouGov poll, with 51 per cent to the No campaign's 49. Ten days before polling the SNP now appeared to be in the lead, and
for the first time in the entire campaign. This indicator of the mood in Scotland
prompted a good deal of coverage exploring the consequences of independence,
most of them negative.

On 8 September the *Sydney Morning Herald* reported that the National
Australia Bank, because of its ownership of the Clydesdale, stood to lose
A$100 million in the event of independence.[15] Other outlets reported the fall in
bank share prices overall as a result of the poll showing Yes in the lead, and analysed the risks and vulnerabilities associated with independence for the financial
sector. By 10 September the ABC was reporting 'banks alarmed about increasing
prospect of Scottish independence'.[16]

On a lighter, if still serious note, the announcement of a royal pregnancy on
9 September produced speculation as to which side would gain from Kate and Will's
glad tidings. A mischievous piece in *Morning Herald* reported that 25 per cent of

Scots believed MI5 was working in cahoots with the UK government to sabotage the Yes campaign. Could this announcement be part of a grand conspiracy?

Australian news media reported the heightened campaigning by UK politicians in Scotland in the final days, noting that polls showing a Yes majority had stimulated a new level of urgency in the No camp. As the pound sterling tumbled in the financial markets, and senior Westminster politicians headed north, Australian media reported many of the stories which appeared in the UK media at this time, concerning such issues as Scotland's rights of EU membership, the future of Scotland's financial industry, and other matters. By the end of the final week before polling it was reported that the supporters of a No vote had regained the lead in opinion polls, as what the *Morning Herald* claimed to be 'the grim economic reality of leaving the United Kingdom rose to the top of the referendum agenda'.[17] From here until polling day on 18 September coverage tracked the opinion polls, which again showed a consistent No majority, while reporting high profile interventions such as that of the Queen on 15 September, who had urged Scots to 'think carefully' about their vote.

It is fair to say that interest in the story was maintained by the construction of an intensifying sense of drama around the outcome. Despite the longstanding consistency of the No lead in polls (albeit a declining lead over time), the media in Australia, like elsewhere, highlighted polls showing a Yes lead, and several more showing a very close result. The *Morning Herald* declared on 15 September that Scotland was 'on a knife edge'.[18]

As polling day neared the same paper published a long and thoughtful piece exploring the complexities of the independence debate with a depth rarely equalled elsewhere in the Australian media. Author Ben Wellings of Monash University placed the current campaign in the context of Scottish nationalism's history, and the more recent history of Scottish Labour's collapse. He observed:

> New Labour's growing unpopularity provided an opportunity for the Scottish National Party. No longer derided as the 'Tartan Tories' on the lunatic right of Scottish politics, nor as 'ninety-minute nationalists' prepared to support the Scotland football team (and anyone playing England) but otherwise politically quiescent, the SNP positioned themselves left of New Labour.[19]

This level of background was rare in the Australian coverage, and restricted to broadsheet titles such as the *Morning Herald* and *The Australian*. Elsewhere the focus remained on matters such as the future of the Australian flag, Andy Murray's opinion on the independence issue – the Brisbane-based tabloid *Courier-Mail* reported Murray's pro-independence tweet of 18 September, noting that in the event of a Yes vote, 'the Poms will yet again be waiting decades for a Wimbledon winner after Fred Perry's victory in 1936. At the very least there will be a large asterisk next to Murray's breakthrough in 2013'[20] – and folksy material such as an item on Scotland's many inventions (including the toaster, whisky and the bicycle). On the eve of polling the *7 News* website speculated on what an independent Scotland would look like,[21] leading with 'implications for Australia'.

The Aftermath

Following the result of the referendum, Australian coverage duly reported the competing claims and counterclaims of the contenders: a resounding victory for the No camp (according to its leaders); a narrow defeat for Yes, according to SNP deputy leader Nicola Sturgeon. There was coverage of the clashes in Glasgow city centre which followed the result, between unionists (described in one report as 'British nationalists'[22]) and pro-independence supporters. Alex Salmond's resignation was widely reported, and coverage noted the beginnings of a post-referendum debate about the future of devolution. There were no editorials or attempts to make sense of the outcome from an Australian perspective, and the story quickly receded from the forefront of the news agenda. One story, on 19 September, introduced a note of humour by reproducing referendum-related jokes and memes about the campaign from social media. One had a photograph captioned 'Meanwhile in Scotland', of two toddlers in a Scottish housing estate somewhere, swigging from (empty) beer bottles. Whatever else the Australian media communicated about the referendum campaign, Scotland's reputation for hard-drinking delinquency had survived.

Notes

1. Available at <http://www.theaustralian.com.au/news/world/basques-keen-to-follow-scottish-lead/story-e6frg6so-1226277086727> (last accessed 15 September 2015).
2. Available at <http://blogs.news.com.au/heraldsun/law/index.php/heraldsun/comments/scottish_independence_and_the_path_to_an_australian_republic/> (last accessed 15 September 2015).
3. Available at <http://www.theaustralian.com.au/national-affairs/opinion/tapping-kids-for-votes-is-a-shame/story-e6frgd0x-1226762074423>.
4. Available at <http://www.theaustralian.com.au/national-affairs/opinion/breaking-up-not-so-hard-to-do/story-e6frgd0x-1226769042062#>.
5. Available at <http://www.theaustralian.com.au/opinion/columnists/scotland-the-brave-requires-innovation-and-dignity-too/story-fn8v83qk-1226773724177#>.
6. Available at <http://www.news.com.au/world/australian-scots-will-miss-out-on-independence-vote/story-fndir2ev-1226555628049> (last accessed 15 September 2015).
7. Available at <http://www.sbs.com.au/news/article/2013/09/18/scottish-independence-referendum-braveheart-not> (last accessed 15 September 2015).
8. Available at <http://www.theaustralian.com.au/national-affairs/opinion/scotland-chips-away-at-the-english-empire/story-e6frgd0x-1227004828768>).
9. Available at <http://www.abc.net.au/news/2014-08-16/prime-minister-tony-abbott-criticised-over-opposition-to-scotti/5676148> (last accessed 15 September 2015).
10. Available at <http://www.abc.net.au/news/2014-08-26/scotland-referendum-could-leave-australia-without-head-of-state/5696770> (last accessed 15 September 2015).
11. Available at <http://www.smh.com.au/national/scottish-referendum-could-change-fabric-of-aussie-flag-20130608-2nx7t.html> (last accessed 15 September 2015).
12. Available at <http://www.news.com.au/world/europe/scottish-independence-referendum-shetland-islands-and-north-sea-oil-crucial-to-the-debate/story-fnh81p7g-1227039755054> (last accessed 15 September 2015).

13. Available at <http://www.smh.com.au/world/scotlands-independence-leader-wins-fi nal-tv-debate-before-historic-referendum-20140826-108q2t.html> (last accessed 15 September 2015).
14. Available at <http://www.theaustralian.com.au/news/world/jump-in-support-for-scot tish-independence/story-e6frg6so-1227045459611?nk=43330d149919f2b5123b1885 e16a4247>.
15. Available at <http://www.smh.com.au/business/banking-and-finance/scottish-indep endence-could-be-costly-for-nab-20140908-10duan.html> (last accessed 15 September 2015).
16. Available at <https://au.news.yahoo.com/a/24948727/banks-alarmed-about-increas ing-prospect-of-scottish-independence/>.
17. Available at <http://www.smh.com.au/world/england-oils-economic-fears-as-scottish -independence-bandwagon-slows-20140911-10fafj.html?skin=text-only> (last acces sed 15 September 2015).
18. Available at <http://www.smh.com.au/world/scottish-independence-on-a-knife-edge -as-referendum-looms-20140915-10gx8t.html> (last accessed 15 September 2015).
19. Available at <http://www.smh.com.au/comment/scottish-referendum-not-just-a-ques tion-of-yes-or-no-20140916-10hhem.html> (last accessed 15 September 2015).
20. Available at <http://www.couriermail.com.au/sport/more-sports/andy-murrays-scot tish-referendum-tweet-stuns-fans-after-weeks-of-silence/story-fnii0hmo-12270614 92926?nk=43330d149919f2b5123b1885e16a4247> (last accessed 15 September 2015).
21. Available at <https://au.news.yahoo.com/world/a/25039897/scottish-referendum-wh at-would-an-independent-scotland-look-like/> (last accessed 15 September 2015).
22. Available at <https://au.news.yahoo.com/world/a/25053017/stay-or-go-scotland-vot es-on-independence-from-britain/>.

20

Afterword:
Reimagining Scotland in a
New Political Landscape

Neil Blain

As matters turned out, the independence referendum proved as much a beginning as an end; or perhaps just another stage in the constitutional re-imagining of Scotland. As the months passed after September 2014, its impact on public and media alike became continuous with what seemed to be the entry of the Scottish constitutional question into the heart of British politics.

This chapter has two main purposes. First, it extends discussion of significant trends in general media coverage of the Scottish constitutional issue, reconsidering some continuities from 2012 until the day when the new Westminster Parliament convened on 18 May 2015. This aspect of the discussion also further addresses, in a broad context, some questions of media influence and of partisanship and impartiality.

The chapter additionally summarises the findings of a number of the volume's contributors, who took the opportunity to gauge reactions in their own nations to the electoral events of May 2015, and communicated their thoughts to us by email.

Looking first at developments in the UK media, a direct result of the SNP poll surge in the wake of the referendum was that traditional London-produced accounts of elections on television, which in previous elections had spoken of 'the three main parties' as Labour, Conservative and Liberal Democrat, started to take account of the SNP. That is to say, some UK news broadcasts on the BBC, Sky, ITV and Channel 4 began to include the SNP in their general consideration of British/Westminster politics; although, and right up until the election, other news editions on all of these channels often produced more traditional accounts too, with the 'big three' parties, as formerly defined, to the fore.

Such episodes of inclusiveness did not invariably indicate that London-based reporters or editors were beginning to understand Scottish politics any better than previously. This could be seen in responses to the report of the Smith Commission in late November 2014, the establishment of which was announced by David Cameron the morning after the referendum vote. The Commission was charged with producing proposals for the further devolution to which the main

Westminster parties had committed after fears of a Yes win. In a *Guardian* piece titled 'The SNP's negative response to Smith could set it adrift from Scottish people', Martin Kettle speculated that the Scottish Labour leadership contest would have to be decided 'before the devolution parties can be confident they have begun to wrest the agenda back from the SNP'. 'The SNP will breathe a sigh of relief if Jim Murphy loses', Kettle concludes.[1] This prediction could hardly have been more wrong, since the Smith proposals were widely seen as a gambit, Murphy was regarded by many in Scotland as a gift to the SNP, and by April the following year the SNP had seized the agenda entirely.

The Smith Commission was the consequence of front page coverage in Scotland's *Daily Record* (15 September 2014) of 'The Vow', presented as a copy of an actual (in reality non-existent) document in which David Cameron, Nick Clegg and Ed Miliband had signed a pledge, three days before the referendum vote, to deliver both safeguards and new powers for the Scottish Parliament in the event of a No vote. The degree to which the newspaper had fabricated the document 'reprinted' on its front page was the subject of much debate (Greenslade, 31 October 2014, *Guardian*, '"The Vow" and the Daily Record – creative journalism or political spin') but it was undoubtedly an extreme example of press intervention in electoral process.

The Smith Commission proposals quickly became overtaken in the media by the May election coverage, and had by the time of the SNP landslide been widely understood as a starting point for a discussion of more powers. Kettle's misreading of the Scottish political situation was only one of many offered, in the view of a number of Scottish commentators, in what was sometimes a misinformed or scattershot approach by London-based commentators to the detail of Scottish politics.

The pattern of coverage in the London-based media was, as noted, uneven, but the inclusive tendency became very emphatic when the results of the May 2015 Westminster election were known, and the Scottish National Party took fifty-six of the fifty-nine Scottish seats in the UK Parliament. By the time a whole series of later polls had foretold a massive SNP victory and, albeit wrongly, predicted a minority Labour government with the SNP holding the balance of power, the Scottish Nationalists and their leader, Nicola Sturgeon, were playing a new role in British media coverage.

Irregularities in the pattern aside, there was by April 2015 really something of a quantum shift in the amount of coverage of the SNP and its recently elected leader in London-based media accounts of Westminster politics, when compared to all previous general elections. Both the SNP and its leader were propelled from near invisibility in general election coverage from London in 2010, to what struck some English commentators as undue prominence in the London media in 2015. In turn this led a newly strengthened focus on Scottish politics generally, including the decline of Scottish Labour; though neither the Conservative nor Liberal Democrat parties north of the border received proportionate attention, especially given the latter's eleven Scottish seats prior to the election.

No doubt Nicola Sturgeon's succession to the leadership played a large part in this, since she appeared not to divide popular opinion in the manner of her predecessor, Alex Salmond, which in turn meant that journalists and editors had more space to consider her positively should they wish. Salmond had been recognised (and indeed honoured more than once) by the British journalistic profession as the most effective politician in the UK, but that had impacted little on often hostile accounts of his political personality from both London-based and Scottish commentators.

The shift which takes place, and whether temporary or not, within the London journalistic account in Sturgeon's case is very remarkable:

> If the Scottish Labour leader, Jim Murphy, were to walk along a balance beam in his stockinged feet, it would look like the desperate act of a man wobbling to obliteration. When Sturgeon does it, she's walking the line, she's holding her nerve, she's acing the highwire. When you're hot, you're hot.[2]

Marina Hyde's *Guardian* account above is a far from unusual response to Sturgeon's eruption into the consciousness of the London media after strong performances in party leader TV debates. Even the *Telegraph*, in general wholly damning of the SNP if more guarded about its new leader, printed an ironical tribute to Sturgeon's astuteness by Fraser Nelson, subheaded 'Fraser Nelson is baffled by the SNP leader's bizarre decision to mix with members of the public', in which he satirises the campaigns of the other parties by listing Sturgeon's contrary campaigning tactics, such as recruiting party members and holding 'genuine rallies and meetings'.[3]

With what prior tendencies, it might be asked, is this new tone in contrast? Generalisations about any dominant position on the part of the media in Scotland on the subjects of devolution and independence, and its professional political advocates, would be unsatisfactory. A popular perception has existed since the late 1970s of a traditional media whose Scottish voice generally sounds resistant to constitutional change. There have been important exceptions, however, as noted earlier in this volume, in both press and broadcasting.

It has been possible to discern some consistent lines of approach in the press to SNP/independence debate stories, as well as some which broke new ground, not least in London coverage. After United Kingdom Independence Party (UKIP) leader Nigel Farage had accused the SNP of anti-English racism (during a campaign visit to Hartlepool in late April 2015), many newspapers, not least London newspapers such as the *Telegraph*, hostile to the SNP, reported the story prominently. On BBC News 24's nightly press review ('The Papers', 28 April 2015), Farage's accusation was discussed by *Independent* newspaper editor Amol Rajan and TV presenter/press columnist Richard Madeley, Rajan beginning sceptically by characterising Farage's claim as a deflection tactic to offset racist allegations against UKIP. Madeley acknowledges this, then says there may be a factual basis for the accusation in the trolling behaviour of 'cybernats', though he admits that their connection with the SNP is not proven. At this point programme presenter Chris Rodgers breaks in to encourage Madeley further with the 'cybernat' theme, noting that Madeley 'has had experience of this himself', and Madeley then recounts 'cybernat' abuse directed at him after a TV discussion. Rajan now reinforces this emphasis, observing that 'this is the future, the battle of the nationalisms, Nicola vs Nigel'. Discussion of the item ends on this note, with no suggestion from any of the three that the SNP and UKIP are ideologically as far apart as UK mainstream politics gets.

In this respect, the discussion was very typical of an SNP = nationalism = UKIP theme common in London media coverage before the 2015 election, and in which Sturgeon as the object of analysis is at times indistinguishable from her party, while at other times appears to be judged quite separately from it. There are elements of both ideology and an assumption of moral distaste in such equations, UKIP and the SNP bracketed together as extreme and beyond the 'reason' of mainstream politics.

In one strand of the pre-referendum coverage characterised as 'Project Fear' (referred to elsewhere in this volume), there had already been a forceful narrative linking the SNP with negative characteristics of 'nationalism' (operating in abstract dissociation from the SNP's centre left agenda), ending in accusations of threat and thuggery, such as this *Daily Mail* headline from just before the September referendum: '"Vote yes or else": Police out in force at the polls as Salmond's bullies are accused of intimidating voters – and even punching a blind man in the face for just saying "no"' (*Daily Mail*, 17/18 September 2014). The attached report declines to offer evidence for the assertion, but is typical of a persistent narrative, especially visible in the *Mail*, the *Express* and sometimes the *Telegraph*, from 2014 on, of a nationalist movement apparently taking on the traditional accoutrements of European fascism.

In an adjacent *Mail* account by Quentin Letts, Alex Salmond's security detail become 'skinheads' and 'goons', also 'thuggish', and 'beefy morons' who 'narrow their eyes' at a BBC reporter. Letts contrives to see Salmond's security detail as 'men in black suits and black shirts with skinhead haircuts and skinhead attitudes'. (A neutral reader might wonder with which long-haired, good-humoured, compassionate security details Letts was comparing Salmond's 'goons'.) He concludes 'Good luck, Scotland. You may be needing it'.[4] This account of a quasi-fascistic form of nationalism persists as a trope in the media account right up until the 2015 election. 'Scuffles' between 'hardline nationalists' (two SNP members were indeed suspended thereafter) and Labour supporters during a Scottish Labour event in Glasgow on 6 May were given great prominence by the *Herald* newspaper and some London titles, as well as Channel 4 News and BBC News, whose Scottish news site landing page still contained a mention of 'scuffles' from this incident some way into the morning of the election.

Another major theme of London media coverage in the emotional sphere focuses on supposed anti-English sentiment in Scotland. Indeed, a journalistic trope visible from 2012 onward links the entire independence/devo max enterprise with dislike for, and ingratitude toward, England and the English:

The Scots know they stand to lose big time if they divorce themselves from Westminster. For its part, however, England is fed up to the back teeth with the Scots pocketing a whacking subsidy from Westminster while constantly – and offensively – whingeing about England.[5]

Many Scots don't much like the English and appear ungrateful for every-thing that England does for them in showering them with money.[6]

Some amidst Scotland's journalistic diaspora in London, and even some indig-enous commentators, become emotional too, on the pro-union side, about the SNP's rise in the polls during 2015, compromising ideals of impartiality in the fourth estate to a sometimes extreme degree. When we read:

The stinking hypocrisy on the part of Nicola Sturgeon in telling a foreign dip-lomat something that she dare not tell the Scottish people – namely that she'd prefer David Cameron to win the election – is typical of the wholly duplicitous campaign the SNP is running[7]

then we might reasonably infer some loss of professional self-control, as well as edi-torial judgement. This pre-election phase was marked by many other similar out-bursts from Scottish journalists and commentators. In a contribution reminiscent of that by Simon Heffer noted above, Iain Martin refers to the 'repeated provoca-tion' of English observers by Scottish SNP supporters, the former characterised as 'patient', 'reasonable' and 'friendly', and 'sad' and 'baffled' at the phenomenon of SNP support, while Scotland is gripped by 'a wave of hysteria', expressed by 'sinis-ter nationalist demonstrators', who 'genuinely scare many of their quieter and less demonstrative countrymen [sic]'. He invokes G. K. Chesterton to describe the English as long-suffering and patient, slow to ire and undemonstrative, and frets that 'the risk is that the division and ill-feeling that predominates in Scotland will spread rapidly to England'.[8] Martin's approach to journalistic balance – he is a former editor of *The Scotsman* and *Scotland on Sunday* – is well-illustrated by another *Telegraph* piece of his headed 'Don't believe the SNP's lies about wanting to help England'.[9]

In a recycling of Enoch Powell's apocalyptic 'rivers of blood' speech of 1968, Allan Massie, like Cochrane and Martin another Scot, had claimed (March 2015) to foresee 'the Thames foaming with much blood' if 'the Scottish Nationalists take control of English affairs'. Massie has seen around him in Scotland 'vile behaviour in the course of the Scottish referendum campaign', with 'insults flying and open hostility on the streets'. The mood in Scotland is 'tense and ugly'. Massie invokes 'the English bulldog', which apparently 'has woken from a long sleep, and is beginning to snarl'.[10] Like Martin, Massie seems to have missed some 'ill-feeling' and 'snarling' which had already taken root south of the border:

Look at the readers' comments left on any UK newspaper website and you will often see Scots derided as educationally subnormal scroungers, whingers, dupes, drunks, parasites and much worse. There is a patronising, scolding tone to much

UK newspaper commentary, which would be offensive were it applied to ethnic minorities[11]

and whose history is rather a lot older than either acknowledges.[12]

These examples, like the various crude caricatures of Labour leader Jim Murphy and other Scottish unionist politicians which populated the front pages of the independence-supporting *The National* (which, as noted above, appeared from the Newsquest stable in late 2014), make no obvious claim to impartiality. The *Telegraph* and *Mail* examples construct a narrative of Scottish politics difficult to reconcile either with the pre-September campaign, in which the most violent evidenced incident involved one egg (if an egg too many) aimed at Jim Murphy, or with the many images of Sturgeon's cheerful campaigning walkabouts, which motivated a number of London-based journalists in April 2015, as we have seen, to produce very positive accounts of her campaign, and often of her supporters too.

Andrew Tolson comments thus on the London-based broadcast news coverage of the election, and on the metrocentic nature of much British broadcasting:

In the lead up to an election of course, every news bulletin carries the day's 'election news', but the critical issue for British broadcasting (in the general election as for the Scottish independence referendum) is that this TV news coverage is London-based. TV news is invariably anchored in London (the only exception being the BBC news of 20 April, the day of the SNP manifesto launch, when Huw Edwards made another of his trips to Edinburgh's Calton Hill). For most of the campaign the 'day's events' began with the three main English party leaders on the 'campaign trail' in choreographed photo opportunities where they were accompanied by designated 'campaign correspondents'. Only following that did the reporting move north of the border (and very occasionally to Wales, never to Northern Ireland). Here, unlike the photo opportunities, Sturgeon was filmed amongst, and addressing crowds, occasionally delivering soundbites. The impression was of a spontaneous street politics, which might have contributed to a sense of authenticity.

On the other hand in these news bulletins Scotland seemed remote. This was most apparent in programmes that contained extended interviews where Scottish politicians, because they were not in London and therefore not available to visit studios, were routinely filmed in live two-ways. Alternatively a secondary presenter was sometimes used (such as Krishnan Guru-Murthy on Channel 4) to introduce the Scottish segment of a programme primarily anchored (by Jon Snow) in London. Guru-Murthy presented his reports from a bar in Glasgow's Merchant City. The remote and secondary status of these Scottish pieces was also apparent in the time given to political correspondents. The BBC of course has its 'Scotland political correspondent', Brian Taylor; but his two-way exchange with Huw Edwards on 6 May (eve of the poll) lasted 1 minute 25 seconds as opposed to the 2 minutes and 40 seconds commanded by the chief political correspondent, Nick Robinson, in the London studio.

The determining factor in all of this is not simply bias, or even geography – it is to do with the institutional organisation of British broadcasting. In particular, Scotland (and Wales, and Northern Ireland) are traditionally defined as regions, and in British broadcasting regional news follows, and is secondary to, national news. This means that even when Scottish politics is critical, as it was in May 2015, to the UK's political formation, in the news agenda it is usually a secondary matter. (Tolson, email to the editors)

A more difficult example to evaluate, and this time in the important context of the role of BBC Scotland, and one which illustrates the need for some fine judgements about impartiality, can be found in reporting of a series of polling predictions for the 2015 election which seemed to be represented with different emphases on the BBC News website by comparison with other online outlets. These were: a Scottish poll by former Conservative Party deputy chairman Lord Ashcroft (reported 17 April); a poll reported on 27 April predicting that the SNP would take fifty-seven out of fifty-nine seats in Scotland; and a poll reported on 29 April indicating that the SNP might take all Scottish seats.

The fact that the Ashcroft poll, predicting high profile casualties Douglas Alexander and Jim Murphy, was missing from BBC News websites despite being reported on numerous mainstream news outlets including the STV news website, was picked up by some online commentators; for example, a contributor to the *Wings Over Scotland* website who observed 'I was just looking at the BBC Scotland website, interested to see what they had to say about the Ashcroft poll. Not a mention so far . . . 17 April 2015, 11.07 p.m.'.

The poll on 27 April was prominently reported online by, among others, Reuters, *The Independent*, the *Telegraph*, *The Herald*, the *Daily Record*, *Courier*, *The Scotsman*, *Business Insider*, *Huffington Post*, *City A.M.*, and featured on many other publications and broadcast sites, in all cases as the headline of a separate news item. It was the lead item on the STV news site. Reporting of the poll on the BBC Scotland news site was (putting this carefully) under-emphasised, not an item in itself, appearing in no headline on the landing page, nor the 'Scottish Politics' section, nor the 'Scotland Live' section but in the fifth paragraph of an item titled 'Labour lays out differences with SNP'. This discretion was repeated on 29 April when a further poll by Ipsos MORI, commissioned by STV ('SNP on course to win EVERY Scottish seat at General Election') appeared as a discrete item on very numerous Scottish and UK news sites (e.g. *Huffington Post*, *Sky News*, *ITV News*, *Herald*, *Telegraph*, *Guardian*, *Spectator*), yet was obscurely located in the fourth paragraph of an item headed 'Fighting talk on Scottish campaign trail' on the BBC Scotland news website.

There is more than one possible explanation for this, for example the under-resourcing of BBC Scotland and a consequent difficulty in updating key political developments on its news site, though that explanation is less persuasive when considering that the low emphasis on these polls was true also of the main UK BBC news website. This, like its Scottish counterpart, seemed very alert to events such as the 'hardline nationalist' disruption of the Glasgow Labour event noted above, and the suspension of two SNP members thereafter, a story visible on the BBC Scotland news landing page until late morning of election day.

Was the BBC more concerned than commercial news providers that to headline the SNP surge would be interpreted as a form of support? Or on these occasions did it stay particularly true to its own guidelines on reporting polls during election campaigns? Such questions are unavoidable given visible public disquiet over the stance of Scottish broadcasters during the referendum period (including demonstrations outside BBC Scotland's headquarters), a disquiet difficult to attribute entirely to partisan sentiments. John Robertson continued his previous analysis of Scottish broadcast news, summarised in an earlier chapter in this volume, into the pre-election phase, finding some disparity between the approach of BBC Scotland and STV in their reporting of aspects of Scottish government activity relevant to the public perception of the SNP.[13]

It is true that there were signs of the BBC in London thinking, as it were aloud, about how to approach the Scottish factor before the May general election, and in the light of online criticism. For example, after selecting the political editor of the *Record*, David Clegg, as an interviewee in an outside broadcast from Glasgow, the day before the May election, on its likely results and consequences, the reporter very scrupulously noted that Clegg worked for a Labour-supporting newspaper. The BBC had previously been criticised during the referendum campaign, as had other news providers, in arguments stretching back to devolution coverage before 1979, for using elite sources liable to provide negative views of constitutional change. The Clegg interview was one of a number of instances in 2015 when it was possible to notice editorial habits as a process, rather than fixed.

Polling had not been the only evidence available before the general election. As another contributor to this volume, Margot Buchanan, observes:

> The results of the 2015 General Election raise questions which focus on political campaigning online. The first must be whether the unprecedented success of the Scottish National Party might have been predicted, given the extent of the reactions expressed online by Labour Party members and supporters to the Better Together campaign's final efforts. Posts to social media platforms revealed the dismay and annoyance by those who had supported the unionist cause until then at the pronouncement of 'The Vow' and its very public launch without Better Together recognition of the process the promises made would be subjected to. The response by those voters indicated they were abandoning their membership of the Labour Party, and in the weeks that followed SNP membership grew dramatically. While there is no way of knowing exactly how many party supporters left Labour, and the Conservatives and Liberal Democrats, it would be simplistic to attribute the massive swing to the SNP purely to the Scottish Referendum result. That would be to ignore the very effective General Election campaign run by the SNP and in particular its leader, Nicola Sturgeon, whose demeanour during the weeks of televised debates and interviews drew

supportive and admiring comments on social media from not only Scottish voters, but from people across the UK, who expressed dismay that they were unable to vote for her. The second question must be whether these General Election results will be mirrored in the 2016 Scottish Parliament election; less than one week after the General Election, the Labour Party, obviously looking ahead, began campaigning on its social media accounts for new members. (Buchanan, email to the editors)

Nothing can alter the conclusion that media coverage of the Scottish dimension of UK politics altered very markedly after the referendum period, when, as seen in other contributions to this volume, there was a short concentrated phase of reporting and opinion on the Scottish vote. In the approach to the May 2015 election, Scotland became improbably central to coverage, though as noted by one of our other contributors, Marina Dekavalla, the election also produced yet further divergences in the manner in which Scottish and London newspapers addressed their readers:

Perhaps the most significant impact of the referendum was that it precipitated a process which had slowly started earlier in the post-devolution period: the marginalization of Westminster parties in Scotland made the Scottish vote more distinctive this time than it was in previous general elections. In this election there was a greater difference in how Scottish newspapers addressed the electorate compared to the case south of the border – comparisons between English and Scottish editions of the same titles provide evidence of this. (Dekavalla, email to editors)

Contributors to this volume from beyond Scotland likewise noted high volumes of coverage in April and May 2015. Didier Revest noted extensive French reporting, in particular because a hung Parliament was expected, as well as a UKIP breakthrough and an SNP landslide, which some French commentators saw as the herald of a second referendum. As also noted in his chapter, the dynamic behind the French interest was always perceived parallels between France and the UK, as similar states in the EU whose interests were not served by European breakaway regions; nor, in French perceptions, by any electoral consequences threatening UK withdrawal from the EU.

As Peter Müller comments, a similar point can be made about the approach of the German media:

Before the election, media in German were almost unanimous in these respects: 1) no sympathy for Farage and Ukip, 2) the British electoral system is evidently unfair, even un-democratic, 3) GB can survive only with more federalism. 4) Media with sympathy for liberalism and left-wing tendencies did not present the British government favourably, whereas papers with opposite tendencies emphasised its economic achievements, as did those with a strong focus on business. They all wondered, however, how Cameron might be able to pay for his promises. 5) There were also many reports on both Cameron's and Miliband's failure to connect with people. The best example of this was Christian Zaschke, 'GB Bitte nicht anfassen' (= GB – Please don't touch), Süddeutsche Zeitung 5-5-15 (http://sz.de/1.2465806). He included all other candidates in his criticism, said that Farage had become a 'caricature of himself', and that Nick Clegg was always making promises nobody believed anyway. The only exception was the SNP and Nicola Sturgeon with their election campaign that evidently spoke to people and got them involved.

After the election, there was general surprise about the Tories' clear victory, amusement about the pollsters' evident failure, and first of all the question whether Britain will stay in the EU. This is clearly seen as the most important problem now, and all media say that GB will definitely lose, if they quit, but that it would also be negative for Europe. All of them exclude the possibility that the European treaty will be changed. Many also say that the public (in Austria and Germany) is more and more fed up with Britain demanding special arrangements again and again. All still agree that preserving the British Union will be very difficult. GB has clearly not become more stable. Many wonder whether Cameron will remain to be as susceptible to blackmail by right-wing backbenchers as he had been before the election. (Müller, email to editors)

Returning to the situation in the UK, no doubt the Scottish dimension was, so to speak, weaponised within pro-Labour or pro-Conservative rhetoric rather than really engaged with, at least in some parts of the media account of the Westminster election. But that is only a part of the story and perhaps not even the main part. The sequence of events in which SNP support surged after defeat for the Yes camp in September 2014 saw the London media debate, for the first time with seriousness over a prolonged period, the UK/Scottish constitutional question, and the ideological redispositions of Scottish politics more generally.

These shifts were well illustrated by the final Channel 4 News broadcast on the eve of the election. Jon Snow interviewed what appeared to be a notably English political line-up (Conservative, Labour, LibDem, UKIP) outside Westminster, but pressed them for almost the entire interview about Scotland, very insistently. The programme then switched to Krishnan Guru-Murthy who anchored the other half of the edition from Glasgow – something reflected on in Andrew Tolson's comments above, which note the continuing sense of distance from London as a base. Nonetheless, it is not only that the salience of a Scottish pre-election location ahead of a Westminster vote on a London news programme was unprecedented: the sequence which moved from Westminster to Scotland seemed in itself emblematic of the opening up of political space in UK politics.

This, as reported by volume contributors Enric Castelló and Fernando León Solís, was also the perception from Spain, the European country with a political movement most closely comparable with the SNP:

At the May 2015 general election Scotland took centre stage, particularly in *El País* (Madrid based and centre left) and *Ara* (Barcelona based Catalan language title, unaligned), which focused on the ascendancy of the SNP and its leader Nicola Sturgeon – 'Nicola Sturgeon eclipses out David Cameron and Ed Miliband', wrote *Ara*. If, just after the referendum, it was argued that 'the winner (doesn't) take it all', the general interpretation this time round was that 'The loser takes it all'. Indeed, the SNP was presented as having lost the September referendum but having had 'a victorious defeat' (*El País*, 26 April). The causal link between the referendum and the SNP pre-election position was a recurrent theme in all dailies. For *La Vanguardia* (Barcelona based Spanish language title, moderately conservative), the massive support for the SNP was the result of the 'seeds' sown by Alex Salmond (10 May). As a result of the referendum setback, as *El Pais* argued, the pro-independence party now had 'wings' (*El Pais*, 16 April); it had even 'resurrected' (*El País*, 7 May) and had become a rejuvenated and exciting key player that was wreaking havoc in the British political system; by wiping Labour off the Scottish political arena; by its assault on bi-partisan politics (Basternier, *El País*, 28 April); and for being the reason for the eventual change in the British constitutional set-up. Even *El Mundo* (Madrid based, right wing) conceded that the real winner was Nicola Sturgeon for having 'burst into the British political scene with the force of a hurricane' (6 May). The depiction of the might of the SNP as a natural phenomenon was echoed by *El País*, which called it the 'epicentre' of a political 'earthquake' (*El País*, 16 April).

Despite this recognition of the magnitude of the pro-independence movement its scale was qualified. *El País* noted that if the aim of the SNP during the campaign had been to 'evict the Tories' from Westminster, Sturgeon had failed (Sauquillo, *El País*, 8 May). It also warned that despite the gains in Scotland, the SNP would not declare independence (Sauquillo, *El País*, 8 May) – a direct reference to the pro-independence Catalan parties' decision to announce the independence of Catalonia in the event of overall majority in the next September regional elections. Again, as during the referendum campaign, lessons to be learned and transferred between different realities. (Castelló and León Solís, email to the editors)

Domestic concerns were also reflected in the English language Canadian coverage, as Christopher Waddell makes clear:

Coverage of the British election followed the same pattern as media attention to the referendum campaign and vote. There was little news coverage of the campaign, the emphasis was on the results on May 7–8 followed by some post-election speculation about the future of the United Kingdom. Scotland and the SNP really only figured in post-election analysis. News coverage prior to May 7 focused on the possibility of a hung Parliament, with the potential for coalitions or informal support for a governing party by a smaller one. In part that reflected the view there would be interest in the British result in Canada due to the potential for a similar hung result and post-election bargaining after the next federal election in October 2015.

Throughout the limited pre-election coverage, there was little attention devoted to the SNP, beyond noting it would likely do well. For example, the

CBC, the public broadcaster, did run a 12-minute British election documentary on its main newscast on the night of May 6. It looked at youth voting and highlighted Russell Brand, not mentioning Scotland at all. With David Cameron's majority, the attention of some columnists in Canada finally turned to the SNP and Scotland's future. Again parallels to the coverage of the referendum existed as columnists parsed the election results through domestic eyes, noting the possibility that the United Kingdom could ultimately opt for a federal system like that in Canada. (Waddell, email to the editors)

In Quebec by contrast, as Catherine Côté observes:

Coverage focused on the rise of the *Bloc écossais* and on its political consequences for the independence of Scotland. This time, there was no special observer in Scotland, but ICI Radio-Canada interviewed the former leader of the small sovereignist party, Option nationale, who lives in London, to seek his analysis of the situation. The general coverage of the event was once again closely linked to Quebec politics, but this time, it did not dwell on the past, but was more interested in the future. Indeed, in Quebec, the sovereigntist movement seems to have risen from the ashes through the race for the Parti Québécois leadership, which has ended with the powerful businessman Pierre-Karl Péladeau as the winner. Also, Federal elections must be held in October 2015 and the new leader of the Bloc Québécois, Mario Beaulieu, will play for all or nothing to increase its representation in Ottawa. In this context, the rise of the SNP, despite the failure of the Scottish referendum, has become a source of inspiration for Quebec sovereigntists. (Côté, email to the editors)

And finally, in this post-referendum survey, no sooner had the SNP contingent taken their seats in Westminster than the different threads of the media narrative were concentrated by that most bizarre symbol of demographic, ideological and aesthetic tensions in British society, fox hunting. This was perhaps a riposte to any expectations of modernisation in the new parliamentary disposition – indeed, SNP members were initially rebuked for various breaches of House of Commons etiquette, such as taking selfies and applauding SNP speeches (one does not clap in the Chamber). In both traditional and online media the possible intervention of SNP members to foil an anticipated attempt to repeal fox hunting legislation in England was variously: (1) energetically sought, in the SNP's embodiment of progressive politics; (2) strongly condemned, as the parliamentary eruption of an interfering nationalist grouping with no mandate in England, and who could not even behave properly in the Commons; and (3) also tactically disadvised, as a mistake which would legitimise unrepresentative legislation by Westminster in Scotland. It would turn out, in fact, that no intention to repeal the ban was included in the new legislative programme. But as scene-setting in May 2015, the fox hunting question well demonstrated both the new visibility of Scottish politics in the UK and the new diversity in its representation by the media. It illustrated, more widely, how the Scottish independence referendum would take on such extraordinary momentum for political life in Britain just a few months later.

Notes

1. Kettle, 'The SNP's negative response to Smith could set it adrift from Scottish people'.
2. Hyde, 'Nicola Sturgeon proves that when you're hot, you're hot'.
3. Nelson, 'Has no one bothered to explain the basic rules of politics to Nicola Sturgeon?'.
4. Letts, 'Barred by the goons in black suits with skinhead haircuts: Quentin Letts gets on the wrong side of the SNP's security boys'.
5. Phillips, 'The only way to save the Union is to stop throwing cash at the Scots – and treat them as equals'.
6. Heffer, 'Why the Scots MUST vote for independence! It'll save the rest of us a fortune, says a very provocative Simon Heffer'.
7. Cochrane, 'Nicola's appalling double standards exposed for all to see'.
8. Martin, 'Scots are in for a shock when the English run out of patience'.
9. Ibid.
10. Massie, 'To borrow the most incendiary saying of all: If Scotland rules England, I can foresee the Thames foaming with much blood'.
11. Macwhirter, 'After bullying and Bowie there will be nothing united about this Kingdom following the referendum'.
12. Blain, '"Project Fear" in a longitudinal context'.
13. Prof Robertson's further research, titled 'Propaganda or professionalism on Pacific Quay? How political issues were reported by BBC Scotland and STV News in the four months before the UK General Election 2015', can be found in detail at <https://thoughtcontrolscotland.wordpress.com/2015/04/29/propaganda-or-professionalism-on-pacific-quay/> (last accessed 30 May 2015). At the time of writing the editors of this volume had not yet encountered a response from broadcasters, or other responses to Prof Robertson's (then) very recently published additional research.

Bibliography

Blain, Neil, '"Project Fear" in a longitudinal context', in Klaus Peter Müller (ed.), *Scotland 2014 and Beyond: Coming of Age and Loss of Innocence?* (Frankfurt am Main: Peter Lang, 2015), pp. 95–155.

Cochrane, Alan, 'Nicola's appalling double standards exposed for all to see', *Daily Telegraph* (3 April 2015), <http://www.telegraph.co.uk/comment/11514682/Nicolas-appalling-double-standards-exposed-for-all-to-see.html> (last accessed 29 April 2015).

Heffer, Simon, 'Why the Scots MUST vote for independence! It'll save the rest of us a fortune, says a very provocative Simon Heffer', *Daily Mail* (18 September 2013).

Hyde, Marina, 'Nicola Sturgeon proves that when you're hot, you're hot', *Guardian* (28 April 2015).

Kettle, Martin, 'The SNP's negative response to Smith could set it adrift from Scottish people', *Guardian* (27 November 2014).

Letts, Quentin, 'Barred by the goons in black suits with skinhead haircuts: Quentin Letts gets on the wrong side of the SNP's security boys', *Daily Mail* (17/18 September 2014), <http://www.dailymail.co.uk/news/article-2760039/Salmond-s-bullies-hit-blind-man-face-just-supporting-No-campaign.html> (last accessed 4 May 2015).

Macwhirter, Iain, 'After bullying and Bowie there will be nothing united about this Kingdom following the referendum', *Sunday Herald* (23 February 2014).

Martin, Iain, 'Scots are in for a shock when the English run out of patience', *Telegraph* (3 May 2015), <http://www.telegraph.co.uk/news/general-election-2015/11578416/Scots-are-in-for-a-shock-when-the-English-run-out-of-patience.html> (last accessed 15 September 2015).

Massie, A., 'To borrow the most incendiary saying of all: if Scotland rules England, I can foresee the Thames foaming with much blood', *Mail on Sunday* (8 March 2015).

Nelson, Fraser, 'Has no one bothered to explain the basic rules of politics to Nicola Sturgeon?', *Telegraph* (21 April 2015).

Phillips, Melanie, 'The only way to save the Union is to stop throwing cash at the Scots – and treat them as equals', *Daily Mail* (16 January 2012).

Notes on the Contributors

Neil Blain is Professor Emeritus of Communications in the School of Arts and Humanities at the University of Stirling.

Margot Buchanan is a postdoctoral Teaching Fellow in the Division of Communications, Media and Culture at the University of Stirling.

Catherine Côté is *Professeure agrégée* in the School of Applied Politics at the Université de Sherbrooke, Québec.

Enric Castelló is Senior Lecturer in the Department of Communication at the Universitat Rovira I Virgili, Tarragona.

Marina Dekavalla is Lecturer in Journalism Studies in the Division of Communications, Media and Culture, University of Stirling.

Peter Golding is Pro Vice-Chancellor (Research and Innovation) at Northumbria University.

John Harris is Reader in International Sport and Event Management at Glasgow Caledonian University.

Gerry Hassan is a writer, researcher and commentator.

David Hutchison is Honorary Professor of Media Policy at Glasgow Caledonian University.

Anthea Irwin is Lecturer in the School of Communication in the University of Ulster.

Fernando Léon-Solís is Lecturer in Spanish at the University of the West of Scotland.

Brian McNair is Professor of Journalism, Media and Communication at Queensland University of Technology, Brisbane.

James Mitchell is Professor of Politics at the University of Edinburgh.

Klaus Peter Müller is Professor of British Studies at Johannes Gutenberg-Universität, Mainz.

Hugh O'Donnell is Professor of Language and Popular Culture at Glasgow Caledonian University.

Sian Powell is Lecturer in the Cardiff School of Journalism, Media and Cultural Studies.

Kevin Rafter is Associate Professor of Political Communication and Journalism, at Dublin City University.

Didier Revest is Senior Lecturer in British Civilization Studies at Université Nice Sophia Antipolis.

John Robertson is Professor in Media Politics at the University of the West of Scotland.

Fiona Skillen is Lecturer in Sports and Events at Glasgow Caledonian University.

Andrew Tolson is Honorary Visiting Fellow, Department of Media and Communication, University of Leicester.

Christopher Waddell is Director of the School of Journalism and Communication at Carleton University, Ottawa.

Karen Williamson is a graduate student at Northumbria University.

Index

Abbott, Tony, 222–3
Adams, Philip, 220
Age, The, 219
Agence France Presse (AFP), 173, 183
Albert, Eric, 177
Alexander, Douglas, 234
Anderson, Kenny (of Anderson
    Construction), 67
Andrew Marr Show, The, 97–107
Ara, 160–71
ARD, 185–6
Ascherson, Neal, 37
Ashcroft poll, 234
Aspects of the Novel, 182
Associated Press, 213
Atlantico.fr, 173, 174
Attali, Jacques, 179
Attwood, Alex, 141
Australia, 217–27
    flag, 224, 225
Australian, The, 219–26
Australian Associated Press (AAP),
    221
Australian Broadcasting Corporation
    (ABC), 218, 219–26
Austria
    interest on social media, 73
    media coverage, 182–94

Baker, Kenneth, 100
Barnett formula, 12, 53
Barroso, José Manuel, 73–4, 184
Basque Nationalist Party, 219–20
Basque region, 155, 177–8, 219–20
Bassas, Antoni, 162

Battle of Bannockburn 700th anniversary,
    220
Bayou, Julien, 178–9
BBC, 8, 24, 30–1, 59–68, 228
    coverage perceived as biased, 42–3,
        97–107
BBC Alba, 22
BBC News, 97–107
    website, 234–5
BBC News 24, 230–1
BBC Northern Ireland, 133–4, 140–3
BBC Radio Scotland, 22
    Good Morning Scotland, 64–7
BBC Scotland, 18, 21–2, 59–68, 234
    website, 234–5
BBC Wales, 122
Belfast Telegraph, 133–40
Bell, Ian, 30, 40
Better Together campaign, 4, 26–7
    as 'Project Fear', vii, 5
    as 'Tory money and Labour foot
        soldiers', 6
    vow on devolution, 46–7, 48
Bicker, Laura, 8
'Black Wednesday', 99
Blair, Tony, 39–42, 147
Bloc Québécois, 196–7, 239
blogs, 35–43, 155, 198–202, 219, 222
Bloomberg, 213
Bouchard, Lucien, 196–7
Bourassa, Robert, 196
Boyd, D., 73
Brewer, Gordon, 27
Britain
    broadcasting and the press, 26–32

differences between English and Scottish newspaper editions, 28–9, 31–2

establishment in state of 'panic', 99, 101, 126

metrocentric British broadcasting, 233–4

newspaper coverage of television coverage of White Paper, 28–9

newspaper coverage of television debates, 30–2

seen as England, viii, 183

television not just English, 98, 106–7

Brittany, 177–8

Broadcasting Commission, 22

Brown, Gordon, 6, 12, 32, 102, 113–14, 201

Buchanan, Margot, 235–6

business sector, 6–7, 11, 115–16, 179, 183–4

Butler, Rosemary, 123

Cameron, David, 4, 113–14, 127, 142, 167–70, 183, 201

  greater autonomy for Scotland, 214

  as 'the hero of the Catalans', 164–5

  Olympic Games, 84

  seen as stupid, 163

  sport, 92

  visited Shetland 2014, 11

  'vow', 50–1, 103

campaign, 3–13

  'designated lead campaigners', 4

  governing mindset and campaigning mindset, 7

  grassroots campaign, 8–9

  'Just Scotland', 11

  logos, 71–2, 75–6

  politicising civil service, 4–5

  position and valence issues, 9–10

  positive versus negative campaigning, 5–6, 102–3, 187

  purposeful opportunism, 11–12

  'rise of the town hall meeting', 8

  single-question referendum, 3–4

  sixteen- and seventeen-year-old voters, 3–4, 72, 163, 214, 221

Campbell, Alastair, 101

Campbell, Stuart ('Reverend'), 75–6, 79

Canada

  English language media, 204–16, 238–9

  French Canadian nationalism, 196–209

  interest on social media, 73

  media coverage, 204–16

  opinions and interpretations rather than facts, 205–6, 210

  see also Quebec

Canadian Broadcasting Corporation (CBC), 207–16

Canadian Newsstand Compete database, 208–16

Canadian Press, 199, 213–16

Canavan, Dennis, 4, 5

Carmichael, Alistair, 27

Carney, Mark, 10, 73–4, 99, 101, 214

Castelló, Enric, 161, 237–8

Castells, M., 72, 80–1

Catalan campaign for independence, 73, 155, 159–72, 186, 199, 215, 238

celebrities, 32, 151, 184, 201

  Connery, Sean, 184, 201

  Connolly, Billy, 151

  endorsement on social media, 74

  Geldof, Bob, 32

  Rowling, J. K., 32, 74, 184–5, 201

  Smith, Elaine C., 32

  Westwood, Vivienne, 184

  see also sportspeople

Channel 4 News, 26–7, 97–107, 228, 237

Charlottetown Accord, 196–7

Chrétien, Jean, 201

'civic memory', 36–7

Clegg, David, 235

Coburn, Jo, 102–3

Cochrane, Alan, 29, 30

Cochrane, Keith (of Weir Group), 67

coding, 60–7

Cogeco Group, 199

Cole, M., 123

'collective memories', 36–7

Collins, Gerry, 151

commentariat, 33–44

Common Weal, 80

Commonwealth Games 2014, 83, 85–8, 92, 220

'community of the communicators', 33–44

Confederation of British Industry (CBI), 6–7, 11

Connery, Sean, 184, 201

Connolly, Billy, 151

constitutional change, 7–9, 100, 125, 223, 237–8

  referenda (1979, 1997, 2014), 18–19, 46

Convention of Scottish Local Authorities, 11

Corsica, 155, 177–8
Corsica Libera, 178
Côté, Catherine, 239
Couillard, Philippe, 197, 206
Courier, The, 17, 20, 28
Courier Mail, 89, 225
Courtecuisse, Matthieu, 178
CTV, 207–16
curling, 85
currency, 10, 27, 99, 116, 174, 188, 200, 214, 224
Curtice, John, 31
'cybernats', 74, 185, 230–1

Daily Express, 19, 28
Daily Mail, 17, 20, 28–31, 101, 111–19, 185, 231, 233
Daily Mirror, 111–19
Daily Politics, The, 97–107
Daily Post, 122
Daily Record, 12, 18, 20, 28–32, 47–59, 110, 229, 235
Daily Telegraph, 17, 29–31, 78, 185, 219, 230, 233
Darling, Alastair, 4, 6, 26–9, 54, 201
television debates, 8, 30–2, 154, 160–1, 224
Davidson, Lorraine, 36–7
Davies, Geraint Talfan, 122
Dawson, Peter, 91
Dekavalla, Marina, 236
democratic renewal, 7–9, 13, 188–9
Denton, David, 220
Denver, David, 123
Devine, Tom, 40
Devlin, Martin, 153
Devoir, Le, 199, 201–2
devolution, 16, 18, 100, 228–9
referenda (1979, 1997, 2014), 18–19, 46
Dilema de Alba, El (documentary), 164
Dion, Stéphane, 201
Docherty, Brian, 7
Domingo, Florencio, 170
Donohoe, Paschal, 151–2
Dugdale, Kezia, 76
Dyer, Gwynne, 212–13

Echos, Les, 173
economic affairs, 10, 61, 63, 99, 115–16, 183, 187, 200
Irish Republic, 147–9
Edinburgh Agreement (October 2012), 3–4

Edinburgh Festival, 220
Edwards, Huw, 101, 233
Electoral Commission, 3–4
'elite narratives', 33–43
English coverage
commentary, 99–103
co-present journalists, 104–5
differences between English and Scottish newspaper editions, 28–9, 31–2
editorial practices, 99–103
evaluative coverage, 109–19
extent of coverage, 111–12
external locations of news reports, 98, 104–6
focus on leaders, 113–14
interpretitive coverage, 109–19
locations for 'roving reports', 98, 105–6
news agendas, 99–103
presentation and reporting, 104–6
press, 109–19
Scotland as foreign news/tourism location, 104–6, 118
television news coverage, 97–107
'tourist gaze', 105–6
English Votes for English Laws (EVEL), 79, 127–8; *see also* 'West Lothian' question
Espada, Arcadi, 163, 165–6
Eureka.cc, 198–9
Europe Ecologie Les Verts, 178–9
European Union, vii, 188, 236–7
Irish membership of, 149, 152
Scottish membership of, 10, 27, 100, 167–8, 174, 184–8, 220–1, 224
UK membership of, 236–7

Facebook, 70–81, 175
Fairclough, N., 134
Fairfax, 219, 221
Farage, Nigel, 113–14, 230–1
FAZ, 186–7
federalism, 189–90, 215
Femu a Corsica, 178
Figaro, Le, 173
lefigaro.fr, 174
Financial Times, The, 29
Fisher, Matthew, 212
Flanagan, Charlie, 156
Fleming, Adam, 106
Ford, David, 141

Forster, E. M., 182
fox hunting, 239–40
Frachon, Alain, 177
'Français pour l'indépendance de l'Ecosse, Le' Facebook page, 175
France, 173–80
    lack of interest in referendum, 175–6
    reporting of election, 236
France 2, 176
France Culture, 176
France Info, 174, 176
France Inter, 176
France Télévision, 174
French Canadian nationalism, 196–209
Furedi, Frank, 35

Gallacher, Stephen, 90
Galtung, J., 132
Geldof, Bob, 32
gender, 83–92
General Election (May 2015), 229, 235–6
    Canadian English language media coverage, 238–9
    French coverage, 236
    German coverage, 236–7
GEO, 173
Geoghegan, Peter, 153
Germany
    media coverage, 182–93
    reporting of election, 236–7
Gesca Group, 199, 201–2
Gillard, Julia, 221
Gillespie, Paul, 152
Gilmore, Inigo, 105–6
Global, 207
Globe and Mail, 207, 211–12, 215
Goldie, Annabel, 6
González, David, 165
Good Morning Scotland (BBC Radio Scotland), 64–7
Gourmelen, Herri, 178
Governor of the Bank of England, 10, 73–4, 99, 101, 214
Grainger, Katherine, 84
Grant, Helen, 91
Greimas' theory of semiotic analysis, 47–56
Guardian, The, 29, 111–19, 229, 230
Guardian/ICM poll, 224
Guru-Murthy, Krishnan, 237
Gutmann, Amy, 7

Harvie, Patrick, 5
Hassan, Gerry, 87
Heffer, Simon, 232
Henderson Scott, Paul, 220
Hennessy, Mark, 154
Herald, The, 17, 20, 28–31, 47–57, 86
Herald Group, 20–1
Herald Sun, 219–26
Hilton, Anthony, 39
Hobsbawm, Julia, 34
Hollande, François, 179
Homenatge a Escocia (documentary), 164
Hosp, Gerald, 189
Howlin, Gerard, 153
Hoy, Chris, 84
HSBC, 91
Huffington Post Québec, Le, 199, 201–2
Hutchison, D., 110
Hyde, Marina, 230

ICI Radio-Canada, 199, 239
ICM poll, 78, 224
independence of Scotland, 52–3, 183, 200
    as defence of traditional values, 40–3
    press hostile to, 4
Independent, The, 230
Influence Communication, 197–8
Institute of Directors (IoD), 6, 11
Institute of Welsh Affairs, 122
Ipsos MORI poll, 234
Ireland
    'Celtic Tiger', 147–8
    coverage as foreign, 149–50
    economic affairs, 147–9
    independence and referendum, 132–3, 151–3
    media coverage, 147–57
    membership of EU, 149, 152
    neutrality, 151, 155
Irish Examiner, 153
Irish Independent, 149–50, 153–6
Irish News, 133–40
Irish Times, 147, 149–56
iTELE, 179
ITV, 59–68, 228
ITV Wales, 122

Jenkins, Blair, 97, 98, 102–3, 104
Jenkins, R. W., 200
Johns, Gary, 221

Johnson, Dominic, 188
Jones, Carwyn, 125, 128

Kerevan, George, 30, 36
Kettle, Martin, 229
Kidd, Colin, 110
kilts, 105
King, Ian, 115
King Report, 127
Kuenssberg, Laura, 100
Kumar, K., 115

Labour Party in Scotland, 79, 101, 225, 229
Lal, 160–71
Lamont, Johann, 'something for nothing'
    speech, 39–40
language and ideology, 183–90
Lascia, J. D., 73
lefigaro.fr, 174
Leith, M. S., 75
LeMonde.fr, 174, 177
leparisien.fr, 177
Letts, Quentin, 231
Liberation, 173
    Liberation.fr, 178
Linklater, M., 117
Lisée, Jean-François, 214–15
Little, Alan, 103
Lloyd, John, 34
logos, 71–2, 75–6
Long, Jackie, 103, 105

McAllister, L., 123
McColl, Jim, 32
McConnell, Jack, 86–7
McFadyen, Mairi, 185
McGuinness, Martin, 151
McIlvanney, William, 36–7
MacInnes, J. M. Rosie, 111
McKay, Daithi, 141
Mackenzie, W. J. M., 33, 41–2
MacKinnon, Mark, 212
McLeish, Henry, 220
McMillan, Joyce, 40
McTernan, John, 29, 221
Macwhirter, Iain, 40
Madeley, Richard, 230–1
Mansergh, Martin, 153
Marois, Pauline, 206, 214
Martin, Iain, 232
Mas, Artur, 159, 165, 169–70
Massie, Alex, 29, 31

Massie, Allan, 29, 232–3
Matthew, Catriona, 91
MEDEF, 179
media, power of, 33–43
Mélenchon, Jean-Luc, 179
Mendelsohn, M., 200
Miliband, Ed, 32, 67, 113–15, 125
    'vow', 51, 229
Mirall Escocès, El, 161
Monde, Le, 173
    LeMonde.fr, 174, 177
Montgomery, Martin, 101
Montreal Gazette, 211–15
Morning Ireland, 154–5
Morris, Nick, 122
Muirhead, Eve, 85
Muller, Peter, 236–7
Mulroney, Brian, 196
Mundo, El, 160–72, 238
Munro, Bill (of Barrhead Travel), 74
Murdoch, Rupert, 55–6, 221–2
Murphy, Jim, 229, 233–4
Murray, Andy, 74, 84, 86, 88–9, 184, 201,
    225
Murray, Judy, 89

National, The, 18, 19, 21, 233
National Australia Bank, 224
National Collective, 80, 151
National Lottery Funding, 83
National Post, 207, 212
NATO, 66–7, 100, 184, 220–1
natural resources, 200
Naughtie, James, 66–7
Nelson, Fraser, 230
Nesbitt, Mike, 140
News Corp, 219–26
News Letter, 133–40
news.com.au, 222, 224
Newsnight, 97–107
Newsnight Scotland, 27
Newsweek Scotland, 64
Newyddion 9, 126–7
NHS, 10, 62, 123, 223
No Mean City, 139
Northern Ireland
    media coverage, 132–43
    press coverage, 133–40
    The Troubles, 137–8
Nouvel Observateur, Le, website, 174, 177
nuclear weapons, 10, 27, 100, 220–1
NZZ, 185–8

Obama, Barack, 73–4
Oborne, Peter, 35, 39
O'Donnell, Hugh, 85, 87–8
oil revenues, 27, 116, 167, 174, 214, 224
Olympic Games 2012, 84–5
Olympic Winter Games 2014, 84–5, 92
Oppenheimer, Walter, 164
Osborne, George, 27, 73–4
Our Islands Our Future, 11

Pais, El, 160–71, 238
Paisley, Ian Jnr, 138, 140
Parisien, Le, 173
    leparisien.fr, 177
Parisot, Laurence, 179
Parizeau, Jacques, 197
Parti Breton, 177–8
Parti de Gauche, 179
Parti Québécois, 195–8, 201–2, 206–8, 211, 214–15, 239
Partido Socialista Obrero Español (PSOE), 159
Péladeau, Pierre Karl, 206, 239
Pelle, Yves, 177–8
Peston, Robert, 106
Polat, R. K., 72
polls, 12–13, 17, 116–17, 234
    Ashcroft, 234
    Guardian/ICM, 224
    ICM, 78
    Ipsos MORI, 234
    Survation, 88
    YouGov, 99, 110, 115, 121, 125, 150, 184, 224
Postmedia, 207, 212
Press and Journal, 17, 20, 28
Prime Minister's Questions (PMQs)
    cancelled, 12, 101, 126
'Project Fear', vii, 5, 29, 231

Quebec
    balanced media coverage, 201–2
    Bloc Québécois, 196–7, 239
    coverage of election, 239
    media coverage, 198–202
    Meech Lake Accord, 196
    Parti Québécois, 195–8, 201–2, 206–8, 211, 214–15, 239
    political context in, 195–7
    Scottish campaign in local context, 197–8, 205–8, 213–15

Quebécor Group, 199, 201–2, 206, 207
Queen Elizabeth II, 77, 101, 186, 220, 225

Radio France, 176
Radio nan Gaidheal, 22
Rajan, Amol, 230–1
Rajoy, Mariano, 159, 164, 165, 167, 168, 169–70
Ramsay, Connie, 87
Rásonyi, Peter, 187
Redwood, John, 100
Reid, John, 76, 101
Reporting Scotland, 59–68
Revest, Didier, 236
Robertson, Gary, 66–7
Robertson, George, 66–7, 100
Robertson, John, 235
Robinson, Nick, 97, 100, 101–2, 233
Robison, Shona, 86
Rogers Telecommunications Group, 199
Rowling, J. K., 32, 74, 184–5, 201
Royal and Ancient Golf Club of St Andrews, vote over female membership, 90–1
Royal-Faktor, 184
Royo, Pérez, 168
RTBF, 173
RTE, 149–50, 153–5
RTL, 179
Ruge, M. H., 132
Ryder Cup 2014, 83, 85–6, 89–90

S4C, 122
Sagarra, Joan de, 171
Salmond, Alex, 28, 74, 138, 177, 201, 222–3, 230
    'Black Wednesday', 99
    as Braveheart, 185
    in cartoons, 28–9
    and 'Celtic Tiger', 147–8
    defeat of, 142, 168–9
    interviews with, 27
    and Nigel Farage, 188
    resignation, 47, 142, 226
    security seen as thugs, 231
    and sport, 85–7, 91
    television debates, 8, 154, 160–1, 224
    timing of referendum, 220
    unfurling of Scottish flag at Wimbledon, 86, 88, 92
Sampson, Anthony, 33–6, 38
'Scolympians', 86–7

Scotland
  anti-English sentiment, 231–3
  as anti-Tory, 39–42
  contract failure, 53–5
  decline of press in, 8
  difference between English and Scottish
    newspaper editions, 28–9, 31–2
  as example of democratic harmony,
    166–7
  independence repercussions on EU,
    176–80
  'indigenous' newspapers, 17–21, 20t,
    110
  journalists, 104–5, 107
  media landscape in, 16–26
  modal choice (between independence
    and increased devolution), 49–52
  national identity, 16–18, 75, 83–97,
    200, 225
  new political landscape, 228–40
  newspapers, regional orientation of, 19
  online media, 22–3
  press and national identity, 46–59
  press owned by non-Scots, 17, 21
  quest for change, 48–52
  television, 17–18, 59–68
  Westminster party leaders campaigning
    in, 100–1
'Scotland, Better Together' (television
  report), 164, 166–7
'Scotland analysis' series of reports, 4–5
Scotland on Sunday, 19, 47–59
Scotland's Future (White Paper November
  2013), 4, 10, 11, 22, 208
  television coverage, 26–9
  as 'work of fiction', 27, 28
Scots
  in Australia, 217–26
  in Canada, 205–6, 213
Scotsman, The, 18, 20, 28, 29, 30, 31,
  47–56
Scottish Labour Party, 225, 229
'Scottish mirror', 161–5, 169
Scottish National Party *see* SNP
Scottish Police Federation, 7
Scottish Refugee Council (SRC), 11
Scottish Social Attitudes (SSA) survey
  2013, 56
Scottish Sun, 18, 47–56, 221–2
  on Sunday, 47–56
Scottish Television (STV), 18, 21–2, 24,
  27, 30–1

Scottish Trade Union Congress (STUC),
  6–7
SDLP, 137
Seibel, Andrea, 186
Seligman, Martin, 5–6
7 News website, 225
Sexton, Michael, 222
Sheahan, Fionnan, 152
Shetland Islands, 11, 28, 224
Shortt, Robert, 155
Silk Commission, 125
Simmons, Stephen, 87
Sinn Fein, 137, 142–3, 151
sixteen- and seventeen-year-old voters,
  3–4, 72, 163, 214, 221
Sky, 228
Smith, Elaine C., 32
Smith, Owen, 100
Smith Commission, 79, 228–9
Smyth, Paddy, 152
Snow, Jon, 103, 105, 106, 107, 237
SNP
  behaviour in Parliament, 239
  blueprint for independence, 221
  election May 2011, 3, 5
  election of SNP May 2011, 12
  included with main parties, 228–9
  members suspended, 235
  membership growth, 79
  and Parti Québécois, 205
  as 'racist', 17, 230–1
social media, 42–3, 73, 226
  campaign on, 70–81
  continuance of campaign on, 80–1
  Facebook, 70–81, 175
  'flaming', 74
  post-referendum, 78–81
  pre-referendum, 73–8
  Twitter, 55, 70–83, 88–9, 225
Solano, Xavier, 161
Solís, Fernando León, 237–8
'something for nothing' speech (Johann
  Lamont), 39–40
Sotschek, Ralf, 188
Soule, D. P. J., 75
Spain
  Catalan campaign for independence,
    73, 155, 159–72, 186, 199, 215,
    238
  domesticating the news, 169–
    71
  interest on social media, 73

referendum as lesson for, 165–9
reporting of election, 237–8
Special Broadcasting Service (SBS), 219–26
Spiegel, Der, 183
sport, 83–92
'truce' over, 86–7
Sport for Yes vote campaign, 87
sportspeople
Grainger, Katherine, 84
Hoy, Chris, 84
Murray, Andy, 74, 84, 86, 88–9, 184, 201, 225
Murray, Judy, 89
Ramsay, Connie, 87
Simmons, Stephen, 87
Standard, Der, 184, 185
'Stands Scotland Where It Did?', 37
Stern, Der, 188
story, 182–92
STUC, 11
Sturgeon, Nicola, 17, 29, 156, 185, 229–30, 233, 235–8
STV, 8, 59–68, 234
as biased, 42
Süddeutsche Zeitung (SZ), 183, 187–8
Sun, The, 8, 20, 28–32, 207
Sunday Herald, 4, 18, 19, 21, 29, 47–56
'Power Map', 35
Sunday Mail, 47–56
Sunday Times, 176
Survation poll, 88
Switzerland, 182–92
Sydney Morning Herald, 219, 224

Taylor, Brian, 104
Team GB, 84–5, 86, 92
Team Scotland, 87, 92
Telegraph, The, 17, 29–31, 78, 185, 219, 230, 233
Télérama, 176
television debates, 26, 30–2, 114
newspaper coverage of, 30–2
party leader election debates, 230
tgeszeitung (taz), 188
Thatcher, Margaret, 140
Thatcherism, 36–42
Thompson, Alex, 105–6
Thompson, Dennis, 7
Thomson, Brian, 222
Times, The, 29, 30, 31, 111–19, 222–3
Tolson, Andrew, 233–4, 237

Toronto Star, 207, 212
trade unions, 6–7
Transcontinental Group, 199
Trident, 100; *see also* nuclear weapons
Trudeau, Pierre Elliot, 196
TV3, 160–71
TVC, 168
TVE (Television Española), 160–71
Twitter, 55, 70–83
Murray, Andy, 88–9, 225

UKIP, 75, 230–1, 236–7
UK's Changing Union project, 125
Union Démocratique Bretonne, 178
UTV (Ulster Television), 133–4, 140–3

Vanguardia, La, 160–71
'Vow, The', 12, 46–7, 48, 50–1, 79, 103, 229

Waddell, Christopher, 238–9
Waiton, Stuart, 221
Wales
coverage, 124–8
devolution and the Scottish independence debate, 121–9, 155
lack of engagement in, 123–4
media landscape in, 19, 121–2
politics, 128–9
Wales Today, 126
Wark, Kirsty, 103
Weber, Thomas, 187
welfare, 10, 223
Wellings, Ben, 225
Welt, Die, 185, 186
'West Lothian' question, 114–15; *see also* English Votes for English Laws (EVEL)
Western Mail, 121–2
Westwood, Vivienne, 184
What the Media are Doing to our Politics, 34
White, Jim, 83
White Paper, *Scotland's Future* (November 2013), 4, 10, 11, 22, 208
television coverage, 26–9
as 'work of fiction', 27, 28
Wilson, Sammy, 140–1
Wings Over Scotland, 75, 79, 80, 234

women, vote to be allowed to join
   Royal and Ancient Golf Club of St
   Andrews, 90–1
Women for Independence/Independence
   for Women, 75, 80
WZ, 189

Yes Scotland campaign, 4
   perceived as SNP campaign, 5
YouGov poll, 99, 110, 115, 121, 125, 150,
   184, 224

ZDF, 185–6